CALIFORNIA WINE LABEL ALBUM
By TERRY ROBARDS

Completely
Revised and Updated

WORKMAN PUBLISHING
NEW YORK

Library of Congress Cataloging-in-Publication Data

Robards, Terry.
  California wine label album.

  Bibliography: p.
  1. Wine and wine making—California.   2. Wine labels.
I. Title.
TP557.R58   1986   641.2'22'09794   85-40907
ISBN 0-89480-038-8

Maps on pages 24–33:
Copyright © 1986 Workman Publishing
Prepared by Allan Cartography, Medford, Oregon.

Art Directors: Paul Hanson and Kathleen Herlihy Paoli
Cover design by Tedd Arnold

Workman Publishing Company, Inc.
One West 39th Street
New York, New York 10018

Manufactured in the United States of America

"To Your Health"

All of the wines in this new edition of the CALIFORNIA WINE LABEL ALBUM have been reviewed since the original edition was published in 1981. With the exception of the Connoisseur Selections, which today can be found almost exclusively in restaurants or private cellars, the wines in this edition are widely available. The author has selected wines that tend to have national distribution and that should be available in every major market. The tiny, so-called "boutique" wineries of California, which rarely distribute outside the state, often produce excellent wines that are exciting to taste. But they can be difficult to find anywhere except at the winery itself. For the most part, these small wineries have been eliminated from the book. As a result, some wineries are represented a number of times, with as many as five or six different varietals and several vintages. This reflects their wide availability and the probability that stores will carry a complete line of products from such a winery. This edition also contains far more information on visiting wineries and touring the wine country, with each winery's visiting hours listed. These additions to the book will help the reader in his quest for taste experiences and should help make the drinking of wine a more pleasurable and stimulating experience.

Terry Robards

San Francisco
March 1986

Terry Robards is one of the nation's most esteemed wine writers. His writing has appeared regularly in *The New York Times*, the *New York Post*, *The Wine Spectator* and numerous other publications. He is the author of *The New York Times Book of Wine* and of *Terry Robard's New Book of Wine* as well as the original edition of the *California Wine Label Album*, published in 1981. He is an *Officier-Commandeur* in *La Confrérie des Chevaliers du Tastevin*, a *Gouverneur* of *La Commanderie de Bordeaux des Etats-Unis* and belongs to many other wine and food societies. He lives in Connecticut above a well-stocked wine cellar.

CONTENTS

Introduction

RED WINES

✪ Connoisseur Selection

Cabernet Sauvignon

Gamay and Gamay Beaujolais

Merlot

Pinot Noir

Zinfandel

WHITE WINES

Blush Wines

Chardonnay

Chenin Blanc

Gewürztraminer

Johannisberg Riesling (White Riesling)

Sauvignon Blanc (Fumé Blanc)

Sparkling Wines

RAISON d'ETRE

A wine lover is a collector of taste sensations. It matters not whether he drinks the most modest jug wines of America or the greatest wines of the world. The point is that he seeks a special flavor that is pleasing to his palate and, hopefully, challenging to his intellect. Moreover, if the wine pleases him, perhaps it will also please his friends and guests and help to create the kind of convivial atmosphere that only wine is capable of creating.

Upon entering a wine store or a cellar, the collector begins to recall the taste sensations that are familiar to him. If he is very sophisticated, these sensations will be many and varied. If he is inexperienced but knows what he likes, the taste sensations will be more narrowly defined. But in either case the collector will be seeking to recapture a special experience or to embark on a new one.

Even the most sophisticated collector needs help with his taste memory. The number and variety of wines produced in the world today are immense, and no person can recollect all of his taste experiences. The variations among California wines are especially wide, for California producers have been experimenting in their efforts to achieve the highest possible quality. The Cabernet Sauvignon grape is being vinified in many ways today—to yield supple and velvety red wines ready for immediate drinking or to create robust, intensely flavored reds that require years of bottle aging before they achieve the mellow quality that makes them ready for drinking. The Chardonnay grape is being vinified to produce fresh-tasting, zesty white wines that are immediately accessible and charming or to yield full-bodied, rich whites of great depth and complexity. The Johannisberg Riesling is vinified both sweet and dry, as it is in its native Germany. The style, quality level, and complexity are decided by each winery, depending on the goals that each winemaker wishes to achieve. Only by experiencing the various styles of wine himself can the consumer decide which he prefers. But in the United States, the consumer has an extremely broad range of styles to sample. California offers every style variation, every flavor nuance, usually at fair prices.

This album is a vehicle for the wine lover's taste memory. The label is the touchstone and emblem of the taste memory. It evokes thoughts of the occasions on which a wine was consumed. Sometimes the appearance of a label even creates a flavor sensation on the palate itself. By soaking off the labels from bottles and pasting them in the designated places, the oenophile amasses a recollection of his tasting experiences. Keeping the labels also enables him to return to the wines that he has found especially pleasing or to avoid the ones that he found too sweet, too dry, too tannic, or undesirable in some other way. Amassing a record also will enable the collector to follow the progress of individual wines as they mature in the bottle.

That is the raison d'être of this album: to aid the taste memory and to satisfy the collector's urge to record his taste experiences. No other wine book is capable of accomplishing this task.

Types of Wines

The best California wines are called varietals. These are wines that are named after the variety of grape used to produce them. The best California red wines generally are made from the Cabernet Sauvignon grape, which is also the basic grape of Bordeaux in France. Many different wineries produce wines made from the Cabernet Sauvignon, and the style of wine made from this variety can vary widely. The same is true of the other varietals. This album is organized alphabetically according to varietal and, within each varietal category, alphabetically by winery. To find Sutter Home Zinfandel, turn first to the Zinfandel section and then to the S section within Zinfandel.

Some wineries produce several different bottlings of the same varietal in each vintage. There may be late-harvested bottlings made from grapes of greater ripeness, for example, or there may be Napa Valley bottlings and Sonoma Valley bottlings from the same winery. When inserting a label into the album, be sure that it is the correct one.

The more modest California wines are the so-called generics—for example, California chablis, burgundy and claret. These are blended from a broad range of grapes and usually not from the better varietals. The reason is economics. The better varietals fetch a higher price, so they are not often used in making the generics. Why conceal the identity of a premium varietal such as Chardonnay by calling it chablis? Thus, the generics are not collector's wines, and they have no place in this album.

Connoisseur Selections

The majority of the wines selected are readily available to consumers all across the country. But there are some that are very special and of limited distribution. Intrepid collectors may be able to find them in stores or on the wine lists of certain restaurants that had the foresight to stock up on them when they were readily available. These are true collector's items, which merit a special place in an album such as this. Consumers fortunate enough to be able to sample any of them should make a special occasion of tasting them. These are the wines that often challenge the best wines of Europe in blind tastings, the wines that are the stuff of headlines. They merit a place even though they are difficult to obtain.

Collector's Notebook

Intrepid collectors often carry their own notebooks to jot down impressions when visiting wineries and tasting wines. Because this album obviously cannot include all California wines, you may want to keep your own supplementary notebook. It can be a journal that charts your great "finds." The joys of cherry picking the wine market, of discovering little known labels at better than average prices, can be recorded for enjoyment in future years and shared with fellow oenophiles.

Removing Labels

The best way to remove a label from a bottle of wine is to soak it off in hot water. The water dissolves the glue that attaches the label to the glass. Simply fill the kitchen sink with hot water and submerge the bottles. The labels should float free within about 15 minutes.

Some labels are more stubborn than others, reflecting the type of glue used to attach them or the type of paper, so longer periods of time may be required in the water. The most stubborn labels are those with metallic content in the paper, the ones with gold or silver borders or illustrations. The metallic content is resistant to water, sometimes preventing the glue from dissolving. Scraping carefully with a single-edged razor blade often will enable the collector to remove such labels. Some of the labels reproduced in this album show the marks of the author's efforts to remove them from the bottles.

Direct from the Winery

Most wineries keep supplies of labels and are willing to provide them to consumers as a means of maintaining good public relations. It is best to send a stamped, self-addressed envelope with your request for a specific label or set of labels. The address of each winery is printed with the reproduction of each label.

Tasting Notes

All of the wines listed in this album were tasted and evaluated by the noted wine critic and oenophile Terry Robards. His tasting notes accompany the reproduction of each label. An important function of the album is to enable each consumer to compare his or her own reaction with that of the author. Remember that wine is a living, changing thing. It evolves in the bottle as time passes, so your evaluation may be different from the author's. Remember also that taste is subjective. Follow your own instincts and use the impressions of Terry Robards as a reference point or guideline. You may agree or disagree with his evaluations, but it is important to develop your own ability to assess wines in your own terms. Eventually, with sophistication and experience, you will probably discover that your opinions will be similar to those of the experts. But this may not be the case initially, when you will be developing your own taste vocabulary.

How to Taste

There is a standard ritual in wine tasting that enables the taster to analyze the wine thoroughly. The experience is broken down into four elements: appearance, bouquet, taste and aftertaste.

Appearance. A great deal can be learned from the appearance of a wine. A red wine that is pale may have been made from unripe grapes. One that is very dark-colored is likely to be robust and intensely flavored. One that has a brownish tinge may be old and tired or may have been improperly stored, so that it has begun to deteriorate. As they age and begin to break down, all wines turn toward brown in the color spectrum. A tawny color in a white wine may be a sign of oxidation or the process known as maderization, by which the wine develops a sweetish, Madeira-like quality in both odor and flavor. So the expert taster always inspects a wine carefully before tasting. Holding the glass tipped slightly against a white background is the best way to perceive its appearance.

Bouquet. The smell of a wine also provides clues to its condition and state of development. Young, immature wines may emit little or no bouquet at all. Mature wines ready for drinking should display an aroma of fruit, suggesting the grapes from which they were made. Sometimes there are also suggestions of cedarwood or oak, from the barrels in which the wine was aged. Sometimes there are nuances of lilacs or honeysuckle. And if the bouquet is very pleasant and pronounced, the wine is said to have a nose. In the best wines the bouquet will be complex and challenging and will be an important contributor to the overall tasting experience. If it is awkward or contains rotten suggestions, the wine may have turned bad. The aroma of a great wine is always either very enticing or very subtle. Older bottles of wine, those from vintages a decade or more in age, may exude a bouquet for only a few moments after the uncorking, so it is wise not to let older wines breathe for too long before drinking them. The absence of a bouquet detracts from the tasting experience but is not necessarily a sign that the wine has turned bad. Only the flavor can confirm this.

Taste. This is the most subjective and varied part of the tasting experience, for everybody reacts in his or her own way to the flavor of wine. The experts tend to agree, but their accord is based on vast experience, and even when they agree, they often use different terms to describe their reactions. Should an individual react in a certain way to a wine? Is a wine supposed to have a certain flavor? Are the characteristics of a particular type of wine readily definable? The answers to these questions depend on the experience and sophistication of the taster.

Because of the degree of subjectivity involved, no one can tell another person how a wine is supposed to taste. There are many adjectives and metaphors used in describing wines, but their meaning to one person may be entirely different to another person, and nobody has the right to dictate how an individual should react to a tasting experience. Over time, as sophistication grows, the taster begins to develop a wine vocabulary and to recognize the signs of great wines.

The most important point for the taster to remember is to follow his own instincts, to decide for himself what he prefers. The Language of Wine section of this book, page 19, can be used to develop a taste vocabulary, but the taster will want to choose his own words as well.

The same standards applicable for evaluating the bouquet of a wine are useful in analyzing the taste. The flavor should be interesting and complex, and it should be challenging without being obvious. Some tasters prefer subtlety, others prefer flavor intensity. In evaluating a wine, it is best to taste it in comparison with another wine, to establish a frame of reference. Experience a Cabernet Sauvignon against a Zinfandel, a Pinot Noir against a Petite Sirah, a Chardonnay against a Sauvignon Blanc. Contrasts will be evident whenever one varietal is compared directly with another. More subtle comparisons occur when the same varietals from different producers are tasted. Buy six different Chardonnays, invite a group of friends to your home and have a tasting party. Your palate will benefit!

Aftertaste. The residue of taste left in your mouth after you have swallowed is the aftertaste or finish. Some wines leave a long, lingering flavor sensation behind. Others leave little or no aftertaste. Some wines high in acidity leave an acrid impression. Some leave a bitter impression. The best wines tend to have a full, long, pleasing aftertaste, indicative of ripe fruit, the grapes from which the wine was made.

Gargling. Professionals in the realm of wine inhale air with a mouthful of wine and gargle it to intensify the tasting experience. In so doing, both the positive and negative attributes of a wine become more evident. The wine is swished around in the mouth, is chewed upon and literally gargled on the back of the palate. Some observers are amused at the sight of such a process, others are appalled. But gargling has an important purpose, because it makes the flaws more obvious and the favorable qualities more identifiable.

Rating the Wines

Many systems exist for rating wines, but the most popular is the scale of 20—with 20 standing for the very best and 0 theoretically standing for the very worst, although in practice only a beverage not qualifying as a wine could receive a 0. Here is how the author brackets different quality levels on the scale of 20:

19–20 Best
16–18 Very Good
13–15 Good
10–12 Fair
0–9 Poor

The author has not included any mediocre wines. After all, this is a book for collecting favorable taste sensations, for recording memorable wines. So only wines meriting a rating of at least *good* have been included. Many of the wines are rated *very good,* and a few are rated *best.* Remember that ratings can change as wines evolve and that you will not necessarily agree with the author—partly because tasting is very subjective and partly because you will be tasting under different conditions. Heat and humidity have a negative impact on wine; cool conditions with high barometric pressures have a favorable impact. Even the ambiance and the congeniality of your fellow tasters may affect your reactions to a wine. But a rating system is useful as a ready reminder of your evaluation, so try to think in terms of a rating when subjecting a wine to your taste test.

When to Drink

Most of the red wines in this book are listed with an optimum time for drinking, the year or period of years when they should be at their peak. Because wine is a living, changing substance, it requires time to develop. White wines generally are ready for drinking virtually as soon as they are bottled, although some can develop additional qualities with a year or two or three of aging. Reds generally require longer to reach maturity. A well-made Cabernet Sauvignon may not reach its optimum stage for a decade, whereas a Zinfandel may reach the same point after five or six years.

Deciding when a wine will attain its peak is difficult. The years stipulated with the reds in this book represent the best judgment of the author. Does this mean the wines should not be sampled before or after these years? Of course not. Some tasters prefer their reds more intensely flavored and robust and tannic. Others may wish to wait for their reds to achieve the velvety quality of maturity. It is up to the individual to decide. Even when a wine is not tasted at its peak, it may still be very good, perhaps even better than another wine that has already reached its summit. Do not hesitate to try wines before or after they are mature. Sophistication in the taste experience comes from evaluating wines at all stages of their development.

Vintage

Vintage is the year in which a wine is made. Grapes are an agricultural product. The vines on which they grow send out tendrils and shoots in the spring, produce flowers around the month of June, and then develop fruit during the summer months. The grapes are harvested in the autumn and then are vinified—that is, turned into wine. Grapes made into wine in the autumn of 1986 yield the vintage of 1986.

Some wines are blended from more than one year. These are so-called nonvintage wines, which do not carry a year on their labels. Professionals identify them as "N.V." The best wines are vintage wines, made entirely from the grapes of one harvest. Sophisticated tasters often can identify a particular vintage by its flavor characteristics, the traits that resulted from the kind of weather that occurred during that year as the grapes ripened.

Alcohol Level

The level of alcohol in a wine, which usually is printed on the label, provides an indication of the wine's style. Most California wines are 12 to 12.5 percent alcohol. But wineries are permitted to vary 1.5 percentage points from the level stated on the label, so a wine that is ostensibly 12.5 percent alcohol could contain as much as 14 percent and still not violate any regulations.

Alcohol in wine is created through the process of fermentation. During the growing season, as the grapes develop and ripen, sugar is formed inside them. If the growing conditions are favorable, with plenty of sunshine and just enough rain or irrigation, the natural sugar content of the grapes builds up to a high level. In fact, the higher the sugar level, the higher the potential alcohol level.

Fermentation is the process whereby the grape sugar is converted to alcohol and carbon dioxide gas through the action of yeasts, which act as catalysts. Grapes of extreme ripeness and therefore of high sugar level may produce wines with as much as 17 percent natural alcohol. Such a level is very high and is not considered ideal for table wines. Some Zinfandels in the 14- to 17-percent range are best treated as Ports and consumed after the meal. Any wine of 13 percent or higher alcohol is likely to be aromatic in bouquet and full-bodied in texture, providing a mouth-filling sensation. Wines closer to 12 percent will tend to be somewhat more velvety, although not always. Wines with lower levels, in the 10- or 11-percent range, are likely to taste soft and sometimes lack character. It is possible, moreover, that they were made from unripe grapes, although certain Johannisberg Rieslings naturally achieve only about 10 percent alcohol and are very pleasant at that level.

The point to remember is that the alcohol level printed on the label may provide an early clue to the wine's style, so most wine lovers make note of it. It is one of the factors that becomes part of the tasting experience.

Touring the Wine Country

Visiting the wineries of California has become a popular pastime for thousands of tourists. In fact, the Napa Valley is now the state's second-largest tourist attraction, ranking behind Disneyland. Virtually all wineries now have facilities for visitors, and many offer free tastings. Some offer elaborate tours, others have their own restaurants, most have sales rooms where you can buy wines directly from the producers, either with cash or credit cards. Many are open seven days a week and are happy to receive visitors, because they consider it good public relations. With each individual writeup, the author has indicated the hours during which each winery is open to the public, whether or not an appointment is needed and whether or not credit cards are accepted.

It is possible to visit many of these facilities on a vacation trip—or even on a weekend. The key is advance planning. Use the maps in this book to locate the wineries that you may want to visit; then look up their business hours and policy on visitors. If in doubt, call them up and ask. Each winery's telephone number is listed with its writeup. Winery personnel may also be able to recommend local hotels or motels. A helpful guide is *The Wine Spectator*'s "Wine Maps—The Complete Guide to Wineries, Restaurants, Lodging in California Wine Country." It is a 110-page compendium that includes hotel and restaurant listings as well as winery information. It can be ordered by telephoning 1-800-443-0100, extension 560. (A credit card number will be necessary.) The cost of the 1985 edition was $3.95 plus $1.25 for postage and handling.

The Napa Valley is less than an hour's drive north of San Francisco. So is the Sonoma Valley. These two most famous of California's wine regions lie side by side, separated by the

Mayacamas Mountains. It is feasible to spend a day visiting each—or a week or a month, if you want to see dozens of wineries and taste hundreds of wines.

The Napa Valley is a long, north–south oval, some 40 miles in length (depending on where you start measuring), with mountains on either side. During the summer months the traffic can be heavy, because there are few roads and no superhighways. The Silverado Trail runs up the east side of the valley; the St. Helena Highway (Routes 128 and 29) runs up the west side. Various east–west roads (for example, Zinfandel Lane) link the two main north–south routes. Virtually every road has a winery; some have dozens.

Some Napa Valley wineries with extensive visitor facilities are Beringer Vineyards, Domaine Chandon, Robert Mondavi, Beaulieu Vineyard and Sterling Vineyards. The restaurant at Domaine Chandon in Yountville is one of the best in California. Many other good restaurants are clustered in Napa, Yountville, Calistoga and St. Helena. Motels and hotels abound, and their personnel will make recommendations about winery visits. Most will have winery brochures to hand out. Just ask. Wine country people are friendly and helpful.

The Sonoma Valley is not quite as well organized, geographically, as the Napa Valley. It has more nooks and crannies and sub-regions and sub-appellations. It is also more mountainous. Visit the town of Sonoma at the southern end of the valley. It has historic buildings and, among others, the Sebastiani Winery, probably the biggest tourist attraction in the Sonoma area, with well-organized tours. The collection of carved barrels there is worth the visit in itself. Farther up the valley, in Guerneville, is Korbel, the best known producer of California sparkling wine. An interesting museum can be visited there.

Napa and Sonoma are not the only regions to visit, of course, but they are good places to start. Mendocino and Lake counties, farther north, are much more sparsely populated and rural in character, with a rugged beauty all their own. The Sierra foothills, with Amador, Calaveras and El Dorado counties, are also ruggedly beautiful and peaceful. But you can drive almost all the way from the North Coast counties above San Francisco, southward past Los Angeles, to the San Diego area and find wineries all along the way. Most are delighted to receive visitors.

Where to Buy

Retail establishments with broad arrays of wine are cropping up all over the country. At one time, most stores selling alcoholic beverages dealt principally in whiskey and other spirits, but that has changed as America has become a wine-drinking country. Retailers have discovered that specializing in wine attracts a better clientele—customers willing to spend more, but who also demand more expertise from sales personnel and who want to browse through a big inventory. Now virtually every major metropolitan area has one or more wine retailers with a big inventory and knowledgeable salespeople.

The Language of Wine

The language of wine is entirely subjective and must develop with each taster. But over time the experts have created a taste vocabulary that consists mainly of metaphors. They taste cranberries or black currants or raspberries in some wines, detect violets or honeysuckle in the bouquet of others. The point is to be inventive in describing flavor impressions, to create your own vocabulary that will aid you in evaluating wines.

Nevertheless, here is a glossary that will aid in developing your taste vocabulary. Use it, but do not be restricted by it.

Acid, acidity: Most wines contain acids. Those with too much acidity tend to be bitter and harsh. But a certain amount of acidity is necessary to give a wine firmness on the palate. Excess acid often is detected in the aftertaste, on the back of the palate.

Aroma: The smell of a wine, the bouquet, but used only in a favorable context. Aroma also suggests alcohol level.

Balance: The harmony of all of a wine's components—its acidity, sugar, fruit, tannin, etc.—creating a pleasant taste.

Big: Intensely flavored, full-bodied, textured, chewy.

Body: Texture and flavor intensity. A full-bodied wine is intensely flavored and has a texture that can be sensed in the mouth.

Botrytis, botrytised: A fungus called *Botrytis cinerea*, also known as noble rot, sometimes attacks grapes, especially Rieslings, Sémillons and Sauvignon Blancs, imparting a special flavor and quality. The fungus makes microscopic holes in the grape skins, facilitating evaporation of water from the juice. Highly concentrated, intensely flavored juice is left behind. The phenomenon normally occurs late in the autumn and thus may be present in wines with a "late-harvested" designation on the label. The flavor and bouquet are identifiable and suggest honey. Such wines normally are quite sweet.

Bouquet: The smell or aroma of a wine. Some wines have a bouquet, others do not. Sometimes it is flowery, sometimes subtle.

Boutique: Term for a small winery with modest production, one that may specialize in only a few varieties of wine.

Bramble: Term used to describe the prickly, peppery texture and bouquet of some Zinfandels.

Buttery: Quality evident in some Chardonnays and other white wines, similar to the taste of rich creamery butter.

Candlewax: Aroma of some wines, similar to wax candles.

Cassis: Similar to cassis, the purple liqueur made from currants.

Cherry: Having the aroma or flavor of cherries, typical of some Pinot Noirs and Zinfandels.

Chewy: Having a texture that can be detected on the palate, usually accompanied by strong flavor intensity, creating the impression that flavor particles can actually be sensed on the palate.

Chocolaty: Conveying the flavor of chocolate, a characteristic evident in some Zinfandels and other red wines.

Coconutty: Quality in both reds and whites that combines texture and coconut flavor nuances. A favorable trait.

Coffee: Some wines, mostly Cabernet Sauvignons and some Zinfandels, are said to have a coffee-grinder bouquet, evocative of the aroma of coffee.

Complex: Quality of being challenging and interesting, of being many-faceted, in contrast to being simple or one-dimensional.

Cranberry: Some red wines with good texture and body are said to have a "berry" quality, suggesting that the flavor of berries can be detected in the wine. Sometimes this flavor is of cranberries.

Creamy: Quality typified in Chardonnay wines that have been aged in oak barrels, conveying an impression of rich cream, just short of buttery, which is more intensely flavored.

Dark: Red wines of a dark color often are rich in flavor and very intense. The darkness comes from very ripe grapes and long contact with the grape skins during fermentation.

Depth: Complexity, flavor intensity, texture.

Dry: The absence of residual sugar in a wine, the opposite of sweet. The term implies no positive or negative qualities.

Dusty: Textured, conveying an impression of solid flavor particles sensed on the palate. Similar to chewy.

Earthy: Conveying an impression of the soil in which the grapes were grown. Not a negative quality if it exists in moderation.

Elegant: Having refinement, finesse and balance. Not robust or intense, but complex.

Fat: Heavy, obvious, intense; rich but lacking in acidity and complexity.

Fined: Some wines are "fined," that is, egg whites or gelatin or some other substance is dropped into the aging barrels to cause the solids, the particulate matter, in the wine to sink to the bottom of the barrel. Fining thus is the process of clarifying. Unfined red wines tend to have greater texture and flavor intensity, but whether or not a wine has been fined is not an indication of quality.

Finesse: Having splendid character, harmony and balance, high quality.

Finish: Aftertaste. The way a wine's flavor ends in the mouth. The best wines have a lingering, pleasant finish.

Floral: Flowery. Conveying an impression of flowers.

Flowery: Having an intense bouquet suggesting various kinds of flowers, perhaps lilacs or honeysuckle or jasmine.

Forward: Early-maturing; velvety and charming at a young age. Unlikely to be long-lived.

Fruity: Conveying an impression of fruit, sometimes grapes but often other kinds of fruit, including raspberries, peaches, apricots, cherries or black currants. Erroneously used to mean sweet. A fruity wine can be completely dry, with no residual sugar.

Grapy: Similar to fruity, but suggesting immaturity and awkwardness.

Grassy: Having a vegetal or herbaceous quality, smelling of freshly mown grass or hay. Typical of some Sauvignon Blancs and many of the wines of Monterey County, California.

Green: Young, immature; implying unripe grapes.

Hard: Undeveloped, immature, unyielding, tannic, lacking fruit.

Herbaceous: Grassy, vegetal, slightly awkward.

Hot: Having excessive alcohol, above 13 or 14 percent, when the alcohol level is not balanced with a high level of fruit and complexity.

Hybrid: The best California wines are the so-called European varietals, but many American wines are made from European-American hybrids or crossbreeds. They are produced mostly in the eastern states and usually do not exhibit the high quality of the European varietals.

Leathery: Suggesting the odor of rawhide and the taste of wood from barrel aging.

Legs: The narrow rivulets of wine that run down the sides of a wine glass after the wine has been swirled around inside. Indicative of full body and texture. Wide legs are called sheets.

Licorice: Having a flavor suggesting licorice, occurring rarely in some red wines.

Light: Low in alcohol, lacking in body and texture, shallow.

Méthode champenoise: Literally, "champagne method," the method of making Champagne in France, whereby a second fermentation of the wine is encouraged to occur inside the bottle. As a result, the bubbles of carbon dioxide gas naturally given off during that fermentation are captured in the bottle.

Minty: Suggesting fresh green mint, typical of some Cabernet Sauvignons and Zinfandels, a favorable trait.

Muscular: Robust, full-bodied, assertive, having great texture.

Needles: Sharpness in a wine resulting from either spiciness or high acidity. Either a negative or a positive characteristic, depending on the degree and the preference of the taster.

Noble: Having great balance and character. Also a wine made from noble grapes—the best varietals, such as Cabernet Sauvignon or Chardonnay.

Nose: Intense aroma or bouquet. A purist would say that only a very big, strong bouquet should be called a nose, but nose is widely used today as a synonym for bouquet.

Oaky: Having the aroma and flavor of oak, from the barrels in which the wine was aged. Can be a negative characteristic if too intense, masking the fruit and other qualities.

Off: Having turned bad, possibly due to improper storage.

Oxidized: Having deteriorated through excessive exposure to the air. An oxidized wine will have turned brown and will emit an unpleasant odor.

Peppery: Spicy, evocative of herbs and spices, and slightly tannic or hard.

Pétillance, pétillant: Slightly sparkling as a result of a fermentation within the bottle, yet not as fully sparkling as a champagne. *Pétillance* is the noun, *pétillant* the adjective.

Rawhide: Leathery texture, tack-room aroma; found in some wines that have been aged in oak barrels.

Reedy: Woody, slightly herbaceous, short on fruit.

Residual sugar: Unfermented sugar left in the wine after fermentation, providing sweetness. An attribute in certain Johannisberg Rieslings, but a negative characteristic in most other table wines. A necessary quality in Ports and some Sherries.

Restaurant wine: Term used for early-maturing, subtle wines lacking in intense flavor, which need not have long bottle aging and thus can be offered for immediate drinking by restaurants.

Rim: The appearance of the rim or edge of the wine in the glass as it is tipped against a white background can provide a clue as to quality. A brownish rim may indicate maturity in a red wine of at least six years of age, or it may indicate deterioration due to improper storage in a younger red wine. The rim is not important in white wines, for their total color is readily discernible.

Robust: Big, full-bodied, intensely flavored, full of character.

Sec: Dry. But indicates residual sugar or sweetness when the term appears on a sparkling wine label.

Sheets: Wide rivulets of wine that cling to the inside of a glass and slowly run down after the wine has been swirled around inside. Sheets are wide legs. They indicate a certain amount of glycerine content in the wine.

Shellfish wine: Very dry white wine, with fairly high acidity, although not unpleasant. More austere than the rich, creamy style of white wine that some people prefer. More suitable to drink with raw clams or oysters.

Short: Lacking firmness and aftertaste, suggesting too low acidity.

Soft: Lacking firmness and texture, not robust or intense, yet pleasant in some cases. Also used to connote low alcohol.

Spicy: Suggesting spices and complexity, plus flavor intensity. Pleasing and interesting, sometimes peppery, sometimes minty or any other spice that comes to mind.

Spritz: Effervescence or, in French, *pétillance.* The presence of a very subtle sparkle in the wine.

Stemmy: Tasting of grape stems, or overly woody. A negative charactertistic indicating lack of fruit.

Tannic: The presence of tannic acid that is derived from the aging barrels as well as from the skins, seeds and stems of the grapes. A necessary element in good red wines and in some whites, but it can be harsh in young wines. The tannin abates with bottle aging. The term refers to texture, rather than flavor.

Tar: Certain Cabernet Sauvignons and Zinfandels are said to have the aroma of melting road tar on a hot summer day. A positive trait.

Texture: The feel of the wine on the palate. A textured wine is one that creates the impression of tiny, solid flavor particles in the mouth. A wine with texture may not necessarily be robust, but it will have flavor characteristics that are readily identifiable. The sensation of flavor particles is sometimes referred to as a "dusty" quality.

Tight: Undeveloped, young, unyielding. A wine that is immature and lacks fruitiness, but that is eventually likely to blossom into something complex and interesting. The tightness in red wines generally results from high tannin levels. Tightness in a white is sometimes considered a negative quality, for most whites should be ready for drinking when young.

Vanilla, vanillin: Some whites, especially Chardonnays that have been aged in new oak barrels from France, convey an impression of vanilla-bean extract. This is similar to the creamy or buttery quality also found in these wines.

Varietal: Term used for wines that are named after the grape used to make them, as opposed to generic wines that use names borrowed from the wine regions of other countries. The most popular varietals are Cabernet Sauvignon, Zinfandel, Pinot Noir and Petite Sirah among the reds; and Chardonnay, Pinot Blanc, Sauvignon Blanc, Gewürztraminer, Chenin Blanc and Johannisberg or White Riesling among the whites. Generics are California wines called chablis, claret, burgundy, rhine, and the like, and they may be made from any grapes the winery chooses. They are nearly always inferior to the varietals.

Varietal Intensity: Quality of flavor readily identifiable with a particular varietal. A wine of classic Cabernet Sauvignon flavor, for example, which any expert can readily identify, is said to have varietal intensity.

Vegetal: Grassy, herbaceous, tasting and smelling of freshly mown grass or of vegetable soup. Typical of some wines of Monterey County, California, and of some of the growing areas of southern California. Generally a negative quality.

Vinify: To turn grape juice into wine.

Woody: Tasting of wood, reflecting extended aging in wooden barrels or tanks. A woody quality is not necessarily negative, unless the aroma and flavor of the wood is dominant and prevents the taster from sensing the fruit of the grapes. But barrel aging adds complexity to wines, and some woody nuances are desirable.

MAPS OF THE WINE COUNTRY

Maps have been provided to guide you in your trip through the wine country. To the extent possible, each winery has been identified on one of the maps. But some wineries do not even exist. Rather, they vinify their wines at another winery's facilities. In these cases it is difficult to pinpoint their location, for they may change from one winery to another each year. But the maps are intended as an aid to enable you to travel literally or figuratively through the wine country while you are enjoying your tasting experiences. It is also wise to arm yourself with a detailed road map for each region you explore.

KEY TO MAPS
1. Humboldt County (*page 25*)
2. Mendocino and Lake Counties (*page 25*)
3. Sonoma County (*page 26*)
4. Sonoma Valley (*page 27*)
5. Napa County (*pages 28 & 29*)
6. Sierra Foothills and Northern Central Valley (*page 31*)
7. Bay Area (*page 30*)
8. North Central Coast (*page 32*)
9. South Central Coast (*page 33*)

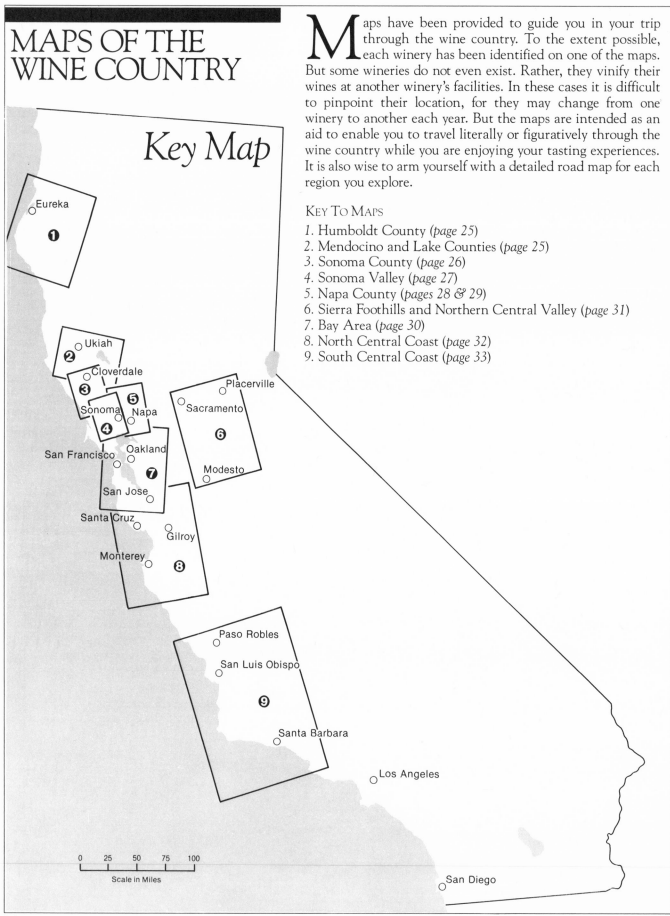

Key Map

Eureka

❶

Ukiah

❷

Cloverdale

❸

Sonoma ❺ Napa

❹

Placerville

Sacramento

❻

San Francisco   Oakland

❼

Modesto

San Jose

Santa Cruz

Gilroy

Monterey

❽

Paso Robles

San Luis Obispo

❾

Santa Barbara

Los Angeles

0   25   50   75   100
Scale in Miles

San Diego

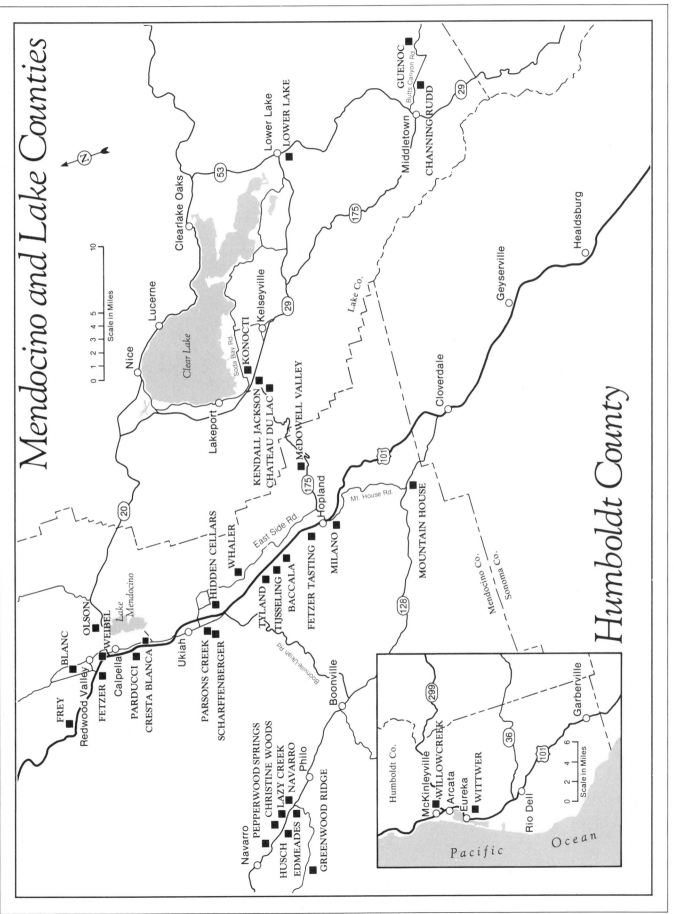

Mendocino and Lake Counties

Humboldt County

GUENOC

Lower Lake
LOWER LAKE

Middletown

CHANNING RUDD

29

175

Healdsburg

53

Clearlake Oaks

Scale in Miles
10
5 4 3 2 1 0

Lucerne

Kelseyville

29

Geyserville

Nice

Clear Lake

KONOCTI

Soda Bay Rd.

Lakeport

KENDALL JACKSON
CHATEAU DU LAC

McDOWELL VALLEY

Lake Co.

Cloverdale

175

Hopland

Mt. House Rd.

101

MOUNTAIN HOUSE

Mendocino Co.
Sonoma Co.

20

HIDDEN CELLARS

WHALER

East Side Rd.

TYLAND
TIJSSELING
BACCALA

FETZER TASTING

MILANO

128

OLSON

WEIBEL

Lake Mendocino

Ukiah

Boonville Ukiah Rd.

FREY
BLANC

Redwood Valley

Calpella

PARDUCCI

CRESTA BLANCA

PARSONS CREEK

SCHARFFENBERGER

FETZER

Boonville

PEPPERWOOD SPRINGS
CHRISTINE WOODS

Philo

Navarro

LAZY CREEK
NAVARRO

GREENWOOD RIDGE

HUSCH
EDMEADES

299

McKinleyville
WILLOWCREEK

Arcata
Eureka
WITTWER

36

Garberville

101

Humboldt Co.

Rio Dell

Scale in Miles
0 2 4 6

Pacific   Ocean

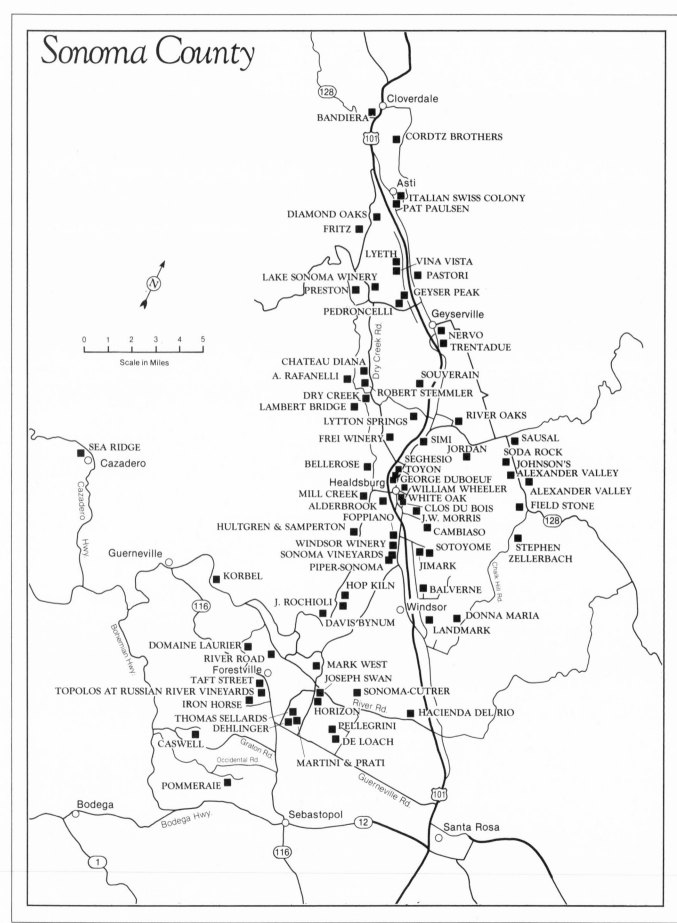

Sonoma County

Cloverdale

BANDIERA

CORDTZ BROTHERS

Asti
ITALIAN SWISS COLONY
PAT PAULSEN

DIAMOND OAKS
FRITZ

LYETH
VINA VISTA
PASTORI

LAKE SONOMA WINERY
PRESTON
GEYSER PEAK

PEDRONCELLI
Geyserville

NERVO
TRENTADUE

CHATEAU DIANA
A. RAFANELLI
SOUVERAIN

DRY CREEK
ROBERT STEMMLER
LAMBERT BRIDGE

LYTTON SPRINGS
RIVER OAKS

FREI WINERY
SIMI
JORDAN
SAUSAL
SODA ROCK

SEA RIDGE
Cazadero

BELLEROSE
SEGHESIO
TOYON
JOHNSON'S
ALEXANDER VALLEY

Healdsburg
GEORGE DUBOEUF
WILLIAM WHEELER
ALEXANDER VALLEY

MILL CREEK
WHITE OAK
FIELD STONE
ALDERBROOK
CLOS DU BOIS
FOPPIANO
J.W. MORRIS

HULTGREN & SAMPERTON
CAMBIASO

Guerneville

WINDSOR WINERY
SOTOYOME
STEPHEN
ZELLERBACH
SONOMA VINEYARDS

KORBEL
PIPER-SONOMA
JIMARK

HOP KILN
BALVERNE

J. ROCHIOLI
Windsor
DONNA MARIA

DAVIS BYNUM
LANDMARK

DOMAINE LAURIER
RIVER ROAD
Forestville
MARK WEST

TAFT STREET
JOSEPH SWAN
TOPOLOS AT RUSSIAN RIVER VINEYARDS
SONOMA-CUTRER

IRON HORSE
HORIZON
HACIENDA DEL RIO
THOMAS SELLARDS
DEHLINGER
PELLEGRINI

CASWELL
DE LOACH

MARTINI & PRATI

POMMERAIE

Bodega

Sebastopol
Santa Rosa

Scale in Miles
0 1 2 3 4 5

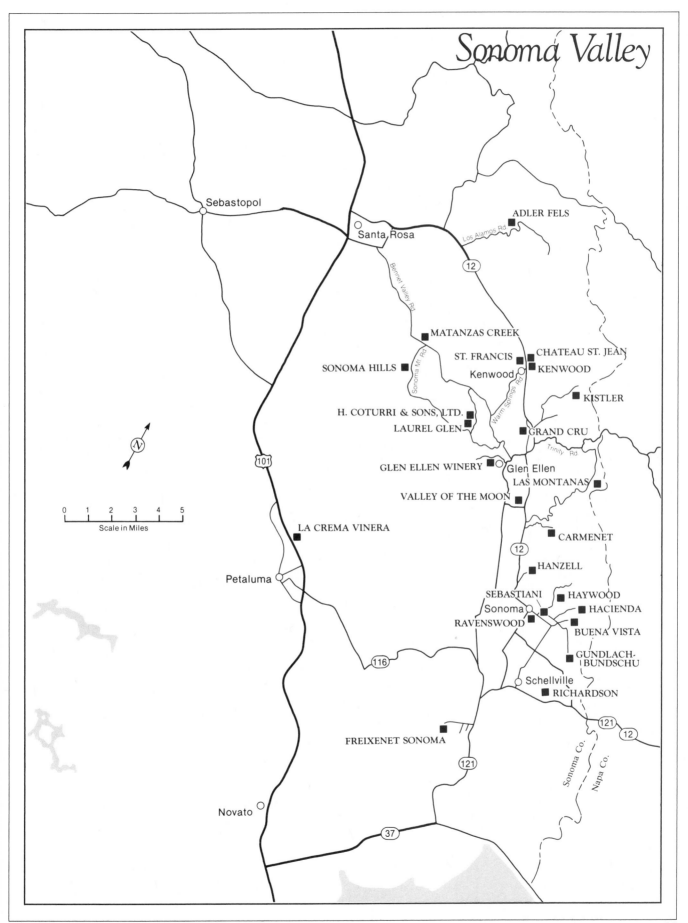

Sonoma Valley

ADLER FELS

Sebastopol

Santa Rosa

Los Alamos Rd

12

Bennet Valley Rd

MATANZAS CREEK

ST. FRANCIS   CHATEAU ST. JEAN

SONOMA HILLS   Kenwood   KENWOOD

Sonoma Mt. Rd

Warm Springs Rd

KISTLER

H. COTURRI & SONS, LTD.

LAUREL GLEN   GRAND CRU

Trinity Rd

N

GLEN ELLEN WINERY   Glen Ellen

LAS MONTANAS

VALLEY OF THE MOON

101

0 1 2 3 4 5
Scale in Miles

LA CREMA VINERA   CARMENET

12

HANZELL

Petaluma

SEBASTIANI   HAYWOOD

Sonoma   HACIENDA

RAVENSWOOD   BUENA VISTA

GUNDLACH-
BUNDSCHU

116   Schellville

RICHARDSON

121   12

FREIXENET SONOMA

121   Sonoma Co.   Napa Co.

Novato

37

27

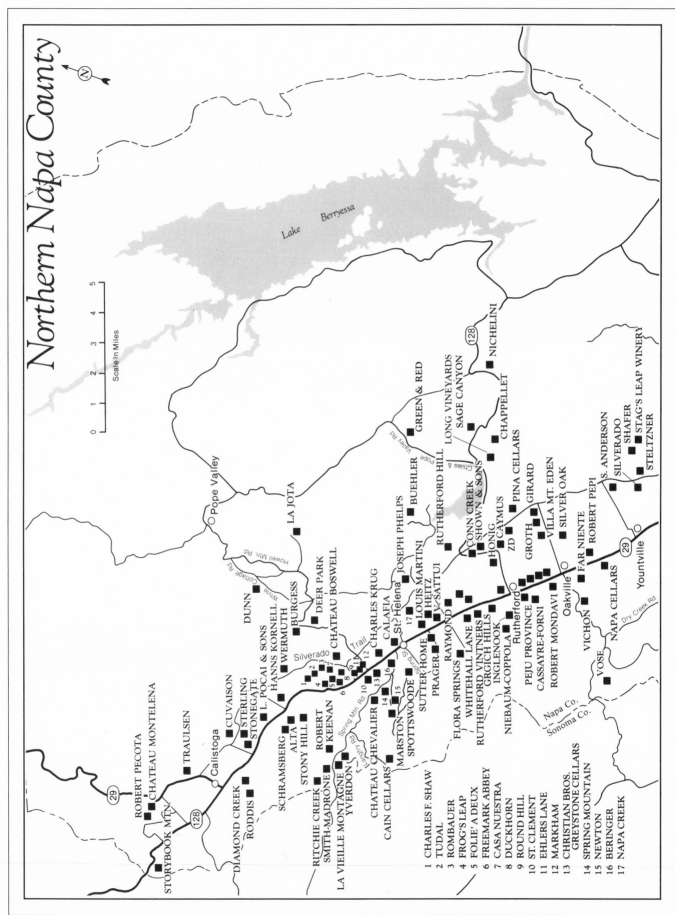

Northern Napa County

Lake Berryessa

Scale in Miles
0 1 2 3 4 5

128 NICHELINI

GREEN & RED
LONG VINEYARDS
SAGE CANYON
CHAPPELLET

BUEHLER
RUTHERFORD HILL
Chiles & Pope Valley Rd
CONN CREEK
SHOWN & SONS
PINA CELLARS
GIRARD
VILLA MT. EDEN
SILVER OAK

S. ANDERSON
SILVERADO
SHAFER
STAG'S LEAP WINERY
STELTZNER

Pope Valley

LA JOTA

JOSEPH PHELPS
LOUIS MARTINI
HEITZ
V. SATTUI
RAYMOND

CAYMUS
HONIG
ZD
GROTH

FAR NIENTE
ROBERT PEPI

29 Yountville

DEER PARK
CHATEAU BOSWELL
CHARLES KRUG
CALAFIA
St. Helena

White Cottage Rd
Howell Mtn Rd

DUNN
HANNS KORNELL
WERMUTH
BURGESS

Silverado Trail

CUVAISON
STERLING
STONEGATE
L. POCAI & SONS

ALTA
STONY HILL
ROBERT KEENAN

SCHRAMSBERG
RITCHIE CREEK
SMITH-MADRONE
LA VIEILLE MONTAGNE
YVERDON

CHATEAU CHEVALIER
CAIN CELLARS

MARSTON
SPOTTSWOODE
SUTTER HOME
PRAGER
FLORA SPRINGS
WHITEHALL LANE
RUTHERFORD VINTNERS
GRGICH HILLS
INGLENOOK
NIEBAUM-COPPOLA
Rutherford
PEJU PROVINCE
CASSAYRE-FORNI
ROBERT MONDAVI
VICHON
VOSE
NAPA CELLARS

Napa Co.
Sonoma Co.
Dry Creek Rd

Oakville

Spring Mtn Rd 10
Langtry Rd

ROBERT PECOTA
CHATEAU MONTELENA
TRAULSEN

29
128
Calistoga

DIAMOND CREEK
RODDIS

STORYBOOK MTN.

CHRISTIAN BROS.
GREYSTONE CELLARS
SPRING MOUNTAIN
NEWTON
BERINGER
NAPA CREEK

1 CHARLES F. SHAW
2 TUDAL
3 ROMBAUER
4 FROG'S LEAP
5 FOLIE A DEUX
6 FREEMARK ABBEY
7 CASA NUESTRA
8 DUCKHORN
9 ROUND HILL
10 ST. CLEMENT
11 EHLERS LANE
12 MARKHAM
13 CHRISTIAN BROS.
   GREYSTONE CELLARS
14 SPRING MOUNTAIN
15 NEWTON
16 BERINGER
17 NAPA CREEK

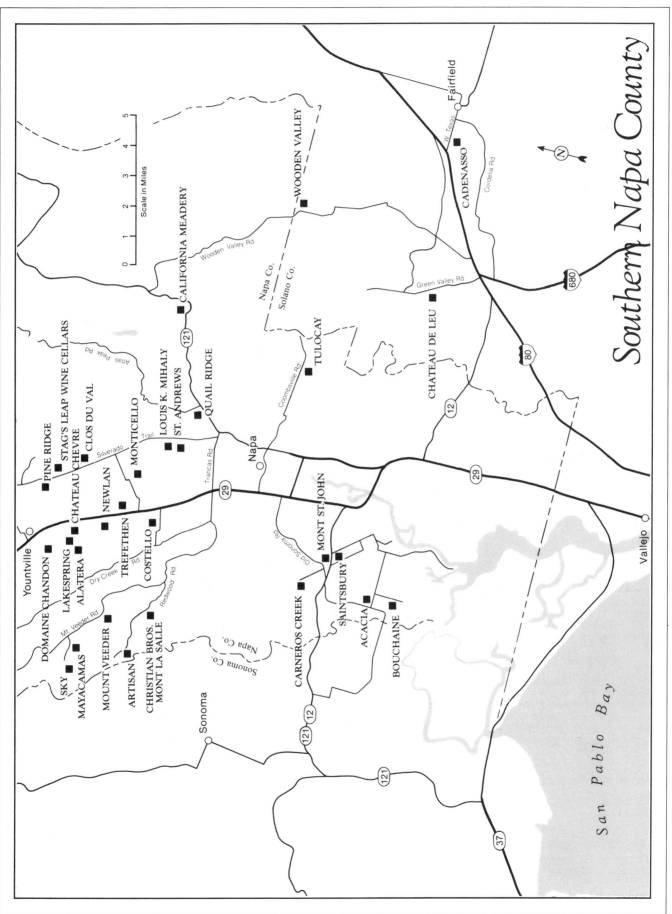

Southern Napa County

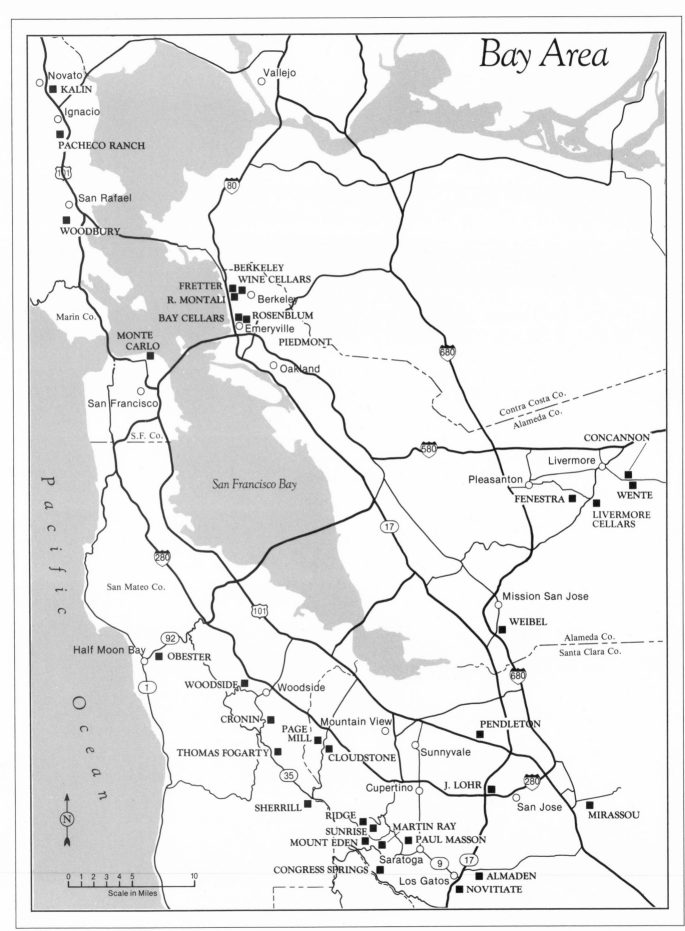

Bay Area

Novato
KALIN
Ignacio
PACHECO RANCH
Vallejo
101
San Rafael
WOODBURY
BERKELEY
WINE CELLARS
FRETTER
R. MONTALI
Berkeley
BAY CELLARS
ROSENBLUM
Emeryville
MONTE
CARLO
PIEDMONT
Marin Co.
Oakland
San Francisco
S.F. Co.
San Francisco Bay
Contra Costa Co.
Alameda Co.
CONCANNON
Livermore
Pleasanton
FENESTRA
WENTE
LIVERMORE
CELLARS
San Mateo Co.
101
17
Mission San Jose
WEIBEL
Alameda Co.
Santa Clara Co.
92
Half Moon Bay
OBESTER
WOODSIDE
Woodside
CRONIN
Mountain View
PAGE
MILL
PENDLETON
THOMAS FOGARTY
CLOUDSTONE
Sunnyvale
35
Cupertino
J. LOHR
280
SHERRILL
San Jose
MIRASSOU
RIDGE
SUNRISE
MARTIN RAY
MOUNT EDEN
PAUL MASSON
CONGRESS SPRINGS
Saratoga
9
17
ALMADEN
Los Gatos
NOVITIATE

Pacific Ocean

1

N

0 1 2 3 4 5   10
Scale in Miles

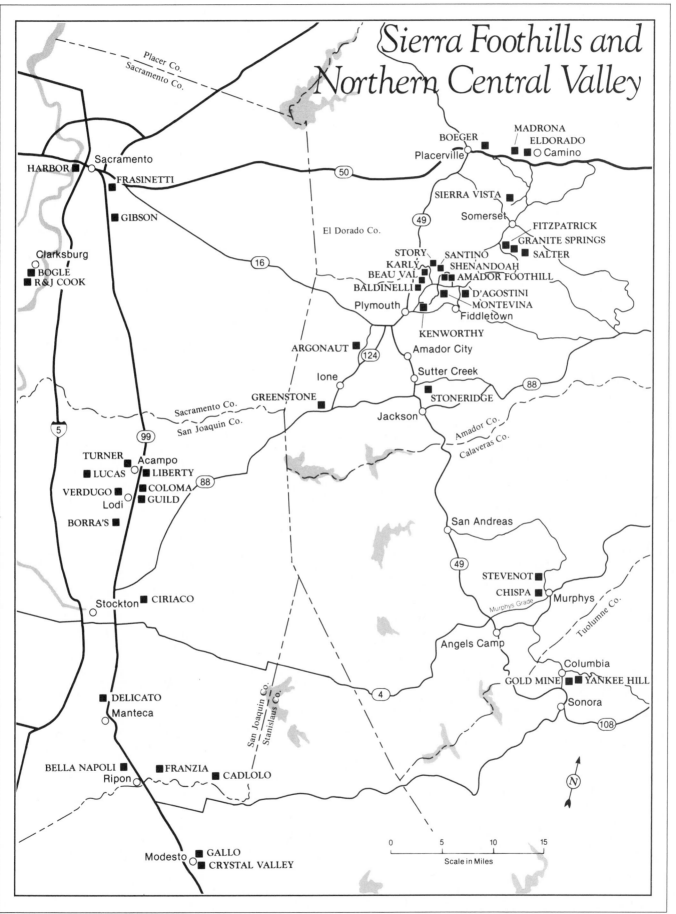

Sierra Foothills and Northern Central Valley

Placer Co.
Sacramento Co.

BOEGER ■

MADRONA
ELDORADO
Placerville ○ ■ ■ ○ Camino

HARBOR ■ Sacramento

FRASINETTI ■

SIERRA VISTA ■

GIBSON ■

Somerset

El Dorado Co.

FITZPATRICK
GRANITE SPRINGS ■
SALTER ■

Clarksburg ○
BOGLE ■
R&J COOK ■

STORY ■ SANTINO ■
KARLY ■ SHENANDOAH ■
BEAU VAL ■ AMADOR FOOTHILL ■
BALDINELLI ■

D'AGOSTINI ■
MONTEVINA ■

Plymouth ○
Fiddletown

KENWORTHY ■

ARGONAUT ■

Amador City ○

Ione ○

Sutter Creek ○

GREENSTONE ■

STONERIDGE ■

Jackson ○

Sacramento Co.
San Joaquin Co.

Amador Co.
Calaveras Co.

TURNER ■ Acampo ○
LUCAS ■ LIBERTY ■
VERDUGO ■ COLOMA ■
Lodi ○ GUILD ■

BORRA'S ■

San Andreas ○

STEVENOT ■
CHISPA ■
Murphys Grade
Murphys ○

Stockton ○ CIRIACO ■

Tuolumne Co.

Angels Camp ○

Columbia ○

DELICATO ■
Manteca ○

GOLD MINE ■ ■ YANKEE HILL

Sonora ○

San Joaquin Co.
Stanislaus Co.

BELLA NAPOLI ■ FRANZIA ■
Ripon ○ CADLOLO ■

N

Modesto ○ GALLO ■
CRYSTAL VALLEY ■

0   5   10   15
Scale in Miles

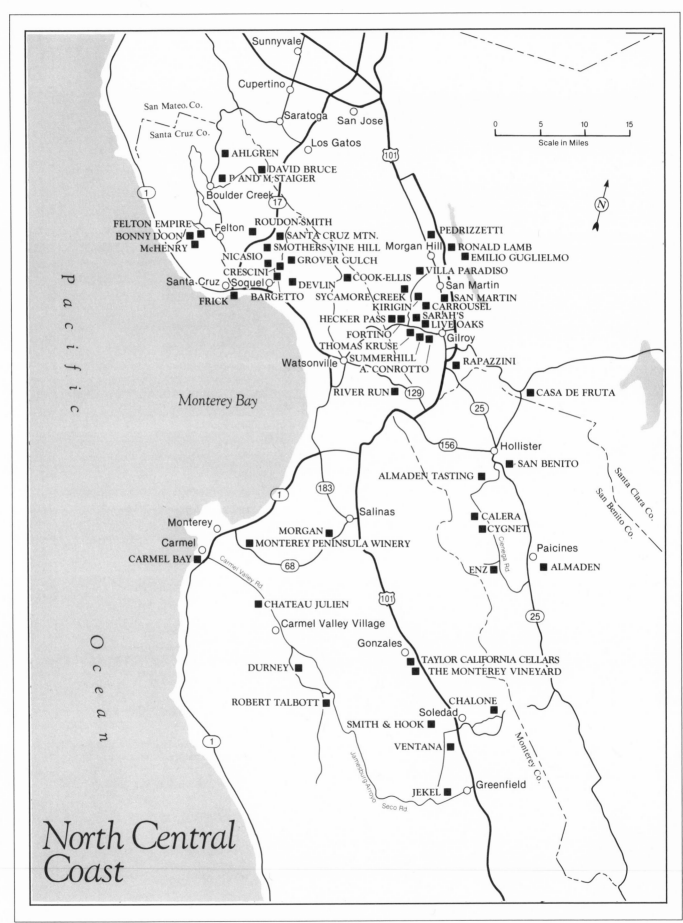

Scale in Miles
0 5 10 15

San Mateo Co.
Santa Cruz Co.

Sunnyvale
Cupertino
Saratoga
San Jose
Los Gatos

AHLGREN
DAVID BRUCE
P AND M STAIGER
Boulder Creek

FELTON EMPIRE
BONNY DOON
McHENRY
Felton
ROUDON-SMITH
SANTA CRUZ MTN.
SMOTHERS VINE HILL
NICASIO
GROVER GULCH
CRESCINI
Santa Cruz
Soquel
DEVLIN
COOK-ELLIS
FRICK
BARGETTO
SYCAMORE CREEK
KIRIGIN
HECKER PASS
FORTINO
THOMAS KRUSE
SUMMERHILL
A. CONROTTO
Watsonville

PEDRIZZETTI
Morgan Hill
RONALD LAMB
EMILIO GUGLIELMO
VILLA PARADISO
San Martin
SAN MARTIN
CARROUSEL
SARAH'S
LIVE OAKS
Gilroy
RAPAZZINI

River Run
RIVER RUN

Monterey Bay

CASA DE FRUTA

Hollister
SAN BENITO

ALMADEN TASTING

CALERA
CYGNET

Paicines

ENZ
ALMADEN

Pacific

Monterey
Carmel
CARMEL BAY

Salinas

MORGAN
MONTEREY PENINSULA WINERY

Carmel Valley Rd

CHATEAU JULIEN

Carmel Valley Village

Gonzales

DURNEY

TAYLOR CALIFORNIA CELLARS
THE MONTEREY VINEYARD

ROBERT TALBOTT

CHALONE
Soledad
SMITH & HOOK

Ocean

VENTANA

Jamesburg-Arroyo

Seco Rd.

JEKEL
Greenfield

Santa Clara Co.
San Benito Co.

Monterey Co.

North Central
Coast

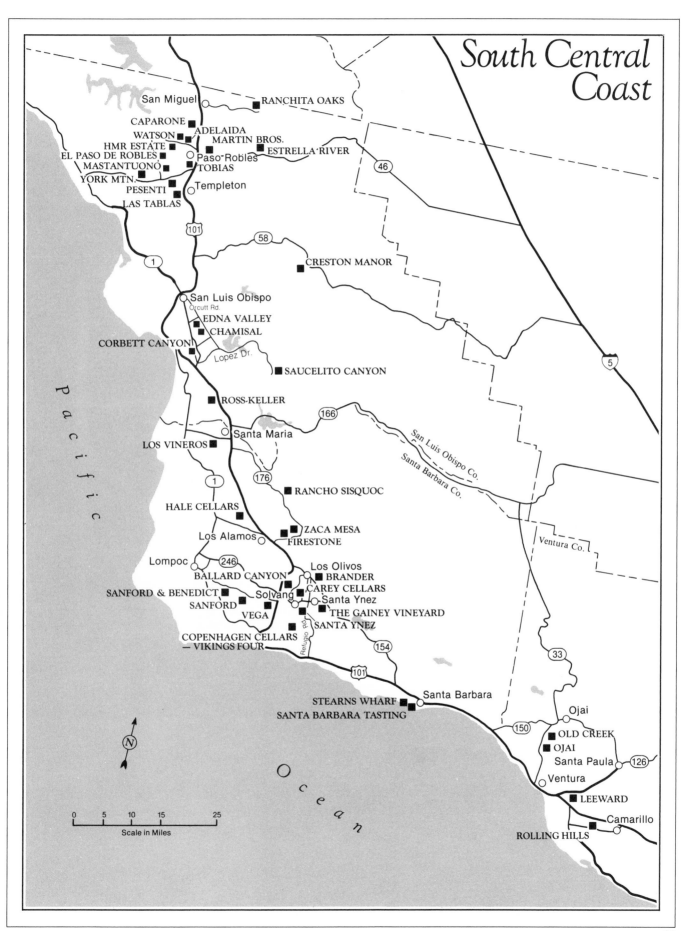

South Central Coast

San Miguel ◯ ■ RANCHITA OAKS

CAPARONE ■
WATSON ■ ■ ADELAIDA
HMR ESTATE ■ MARTIN BROS.
EL PASO DE ROBLES ■ ◯ Paso Robles ■ ESTRELLA RIVER
MASTANTUONO ■ TOBIAS ■
YORK MTN. ■
PESENTI ■ ◯ Templeton
LAS TABLAS ■

(101)

(1)

(58)

■ CRESTON MANOR

(46)

(5)

◯ San Luis Obispo
Orcutt Rd.
■ EDNA VALLEY
■ CHAMISAL
CORBETT CANYON ■

Lopez Dr.

■ SAUCELITO CANYON

■ ROSS-KELLER

(166)

◯ Santa Maria

LOS VINEROS ■

(1)

(176)

San Luis Obispo Co.
Santa Barbara Co.

■ RANCHO SISQUOC

HALE CELLARS ■

■ ZACA MESA
Los Alamos ◯ FIRESTONE

Ventura Co.

Lompoc ◯ (246)
BALLARD CANYON ■ Los Olivos
■ BRANDER
SANFORD & BENEDICT ■ ■ Solvang CAREY CELLARS
SANFORD ■ ◯ Santa Ynez
VEGA ■ THE GAINEY VINEYARD
SANTA YNEZ

COPENHAGEN CELLARS
— VIKINGS FOUR

Refugio Rd.

(154)

(101)

(33)

STEARNS WHARF ■ Santa Barbara
SANTA BARBARA TASTING

(150)

Ojai ◯
■ OLD CREEK
■ OJAI
Santa Paula ◯ (126)
◯ Ventura

■ LEEWARD

Camarillo
◯
ROLLING HILLS ■

P a c i f i c

O c e a n

N

0   5   10   15   25
Scale in Miles

CALI-FORNIA WINE LABEL ALBUM

RED WINES

CABERNET SAUVIGNON

The Cabernet Sauvignon is the basic grape of red Bordeaux in France, the grape that gives us such renowned wines as Château Lafite-Rothschild, Château Latour, Château Margaux, Château Mouton-Rothschild and Château Haut-Brion. These are among the most celebrated red wines made anywhere on earth, wines of great majesty, elegance and finesse.

In California the Cabernet Sauvignon is clearly the most successful European red varietal. It is responsible for the best California red wines and is widely cultivated. California producers have been highly successful in vinifying European-style wines from this grape, and a number of California Cabernets have vanquished the best wines from Bordeaux in blind tastings.

California Cabernets often are big, rich, intensely flavorful wines that require considerable bottle age to achieve the elegance and finesse that they are capable of achieving. A decade is not too much time for many of them, although it is probable that most are drunk when far younger, for they tend to exhibit great charm after only four or five years. At their best, they exude an aroma of cigar-box cedarwood with nuances of raspberries or cassis. This berry quality is also evident on the palate, where a plummy accent often can be detected. Styles vary with each producer, but the Cabernet is without question the finest red varietal made in California.

CONNOISSEUR SELECTION

WINERY:	Beaulieu Vineyard
WINE NAME:	**Cabernet Sauvignon, Georges de Latour Private Reserve**
ORIGIN:	Napa Valley, Estate Bottled
VINTAGE: 1969	**RATING:** 19
ALCOHOL:	12.5 percent
TASTING NOTES:	Garnet/brick color, with brownish edge. Ripe, plummy, road-tar nose, very fragrant. Rich, round, full flavor of raspberries and cassis, with cedary notes. Big and at the same time elegant, with beautiful finesse. At a tasting of great Cabernets, put on by New York City's River Cafe in May 1985, this was the author's favorite B.V. Private Reserve.
DATE TASTED:	
WINERY ADDRESS:	1960 St. Helena Highway Rutherford, CA 94573 (707) 963-2411
WINERY VISITS:	10 AM–4 PM. Appt. not req. Credit cards.
PERSONAL NOTES:	

WINERY:	Beaulieu Vineyard
WINE NAME:	**Cabernet Sauvignon, Georges de Latour Private Reserve**
ORIGIN:	Napa Valley, Estate Bottled
VINTAGE: 1980	**RATING:** 17
ALCOHOL:	13.0 percent
TASTING NOTES:	Deep ruby color. Rich, spicy, herbal nose with mint-chocolate nuances. Very fragrant and enticing. Firm, tannic structure. Rich, opulent cassis flavor, concentrated fruit and fleshy, muscular tone. Slightly stemmy background needs watching. These B.V. bottlings are consistently among the best red wines made in the United States, with great flavor concentration and structure.
DATE TASTED:	
WINERY ADDRESS:	1960 St. Helena Highway Rutherford, CA 94573 (707) 963-2411
WINERY VISITS:	10 AM–4 PM. Appt. not req. Credit cards.
PERSONAL NOTES:	

CABERNET SAUVIGNON

WINERY:	Beaulieu Vineyard
WINE NAME:	**Cabernet Sauvignon, Rutherford**
ORIGIN:	Napa Valley, Estate Bottled
VINTAGE: 1981	**RATING:** 14
ALCOHOL:	12.5 percent
TASTING NOTES:	Ruby color. Briary, smoky nose, fruity undertone. Medium body, tannic, young and awkward. Somewhat stemmy and vegetal. Lacking in generosity and structure and basically austere. A difficult vintage for B.V. and many other producers following the opulent 1980. Should improve with time, but underlying structure seems absent. Probably best in 1987–89.
DATE TASTED:	
WINERY ADDRESS:	1960 St. Helena Highway Rutherford, CA 94573 (707) 963-2411
WINERY VISITS:	10 AM–4 PM. Appt. not req. Credit cards.
PERSONAL NOTES:	

WINERY:	Beringer Vineyards
WINE NAME:	**Cabernet Sauvignon, Private Reserve**
ORIGIN:	Lemmon-Chabot Vineyard
VINTAGE: 1980	**RATING:** 18
ALCOHOL:	13.5 percent
TASTING NOTES:	Deep ruby color. Cigar-box nose, with herbal elements. Tannic, chewy texture, somewhat coarse and undeveloped, but promising. Very concentrated flavor, with cassis showing through tobacco overlay. Much character. Best 1988–90. Lay it down and wait for it. Beringer's Rhine House, on the St. Helena Highway, is a major tourist attraction.
DATE TASTED:	
WINERY ADDRESS:	2000 Main Street St. Helena, CA 94574 (707) 963-7115
WINERY VISITS:	9:30 AM–4:30 PM. Appt. not req. Credit cards. Full tours.
PERSONAL NOTES:	

WINERY:	Jean Claude Boisset Vineyards
WINE NAME:	**Cabernet Sauvignon**
ORIGIN:	Napa Valley
VINTAGE: 1981	**RATING:** 18
ALCOHOL:	13.0 percent

TASTING NOTES: Deep ruby color. Fruity, berry nose, very generous. Very concentrated fruit flavor—cassis and cherry extract. Splendid and complex California Cabernet by a prominent Burgundian *négociant*, demonstrating that the skills of a Burgundy producer can be transferred to another country and another grape variety. Best 1986–89.

DATE TASTED:

WINERY ADDRESS: Winery not yet constructed.

WINERY VISITS:

PERSONAL NOTES:

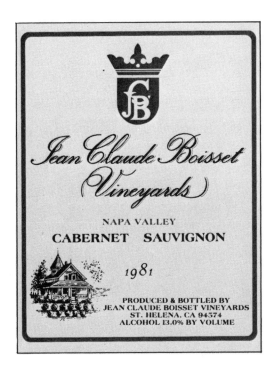

WINERY:	Bonny Doon Vineyard
WINE NAME:	**Claret**
ORIGIN:	Mendocino County
VINTAGE: 1982	**RATING:** 16
ALCOHOL:	11.5 percent

TASTING NOTES: Dark ruby color. Berry fruit nose with tack-room nuances and hints of vanilla extract. Medium body, round; lightly fruited, elegant flavor with a youthful, grapy undertone. Soft tannins prevail. More like a young California Cabernet than a young claret, though the blend of grape varieties is classic Bordeaux—57% Cabernet Sauvignon, 38% Merlot, 2.5% Malbec, 2.5% Cabernet Franc. Best 1986–87.

DATE TASTED:

WINERY ADDRESS: 10 Pine Flat Road
Santa Cruz, CA 95060   (408) 425-3625

WINERY VISITS: Tues.–Sun. noon–6 P.M. Appt. req.
Credit cards.

PERSONAL NOTES:

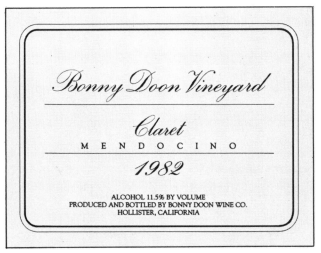

CABERNET SAUVIGNON

CONNOISSEUR SELECTION

WINERY:	Buena Vista Winery
WINE NAME:	**Cabernet Sauvignon, Cask 25**
ORIGIN:	Sonoma County, Estate Bottled
VINTAGE: 1974	**RATING:** 15
ALCOHOL:	12.5 percent

TASTING NOTES: Deep garnet color, with slightly brown edge. Restrained, almost flat nose. Dry in the mouth. Much structure, but lacking fruit extract and somewhat austere. Here is an example of a 1974 Cabernet that has lost its fruit and dried out through aging. It was probably best in 1982–83, but will give ample pleasure through 1986.

DATE TASTED:

WINERY ADDRESS: 18000 Old Winery Road
Sonoma, CA 95476   (707) 938-1266

WINERY VISITS: 10 AM–5 PM. Appt. not req. Credit cards.

PERSONAL NOTES:

WINERY:	Buena Vista Winery
WINE NAME:	**Cabernet Sauvignon, Special Selection**
ORIGIN:	Sonoma Valley, Carneros District, Estate Bottled
VINTAGE: 1980	**RATING:** 18
ALCOHOL:	14.2 percent

TASTING NOTES: Very deep ruby color. Restrained nose of ripe berries, with fruit beginning to emerge. Full, rich, slightly herbaceous, though not grassy. Very chewy and textured. A big wine with much tannin and underlying fruit. Should be superb in 1989–90. The original Sonoma winery, a major tourist attraction, is claimed to be the oldest operating premium winery in California today.

DATE TASTED:

WINERY ADDRESS: 18000 Old Winery Road
Sonoma, CA 95476   (707) 938-1266

WINERY VISITS: 10 AM–5 PM. Appt. not req. Credit cards.

PERSONAL NOTES:

WINERY:	Buena Vista Winery
WINE NAME:	**Cabernet Sauvignon, Private Reserve**
ORIGIN:	Sonoma Valley, Carneros District, Estate Bottled
VINTAGE: 1981	RATING: 17
ALCOHOL:	12.8 percent
TASTING NOTES:	Deep ruby color. Restrained nose of ripe berries, with fruit emerging slowly. Full, rich, slightly herbaceous flavor. Very chewy and textured. Hints of cassis, but young and astringent and less generous than some other Buena Vista Cabernets. Best 1988–90. The old Buena Vista Winery in Sonoma is a major tourist attraction.
DATE TASTED:	
WINERY ADDRESS:	18000 Old Winery Road Sonoma, CA 95476 (707) 938-1266
WINERY VISITS:	10 AM–5 PM. Appt. not req. Credit cards.
PERSONAL NOTES:	

WINERY:	Burgess Cellars
WINE NAME:	**Cabernet Sauvignon, Vintage Selection**
ORIGIN:	Napa Valley
VINTAGE: 1981	RATING: 17
ALCOHOL:	13.0 percent
TASTING NOTES:	Very dark ruby color. Restrained, tight, undeveloped nose with hints of berries. Chewy, tannic, full-bodied, promising. Much flavor extract and concentration, but needs time. Classic example of a young, awkward Cabernet whose enormous potential is evident beneath the hard veneer of tannin. Tom Burgess has found as much success on the ground with his vines as he had in the sky as a corporate pilot.
DATE TASTED:	
WINERY ADDRESS:	1108 Deer Park Road St. Helena, CA 94574 (707) 963-4766
WINERY VISITS:	10 AM–4 PM. Appt. req. Credit cards.
PERSONAL NOTES:	

CABERNET SAUVIGNON

WINERY:	Carneros Creek Winery
WINE NAME:	**Cabernet Sauvignon**
ORIGIN:	Napa Valley
VINTAGE: 1981	**RATING:** 17
ALCOHOL:	12.8 percent

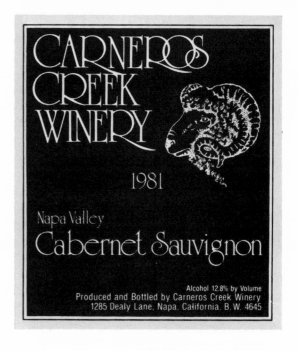

TASTING NOTES: Dark ruby color. Very concentrated nose of road tar, old leather and blackberries, with oaky accents. Tannic texture, though not astringent. Medium body. Some cassis, some raspberries emerge with breathing, but needs time. Best 1987–89. The winery is one of the early Napa boutiques, established in 1972 in the Carneros District to take advantage of the cool breezes blowing off San Pablo Bay.

DATE TASTED:

WINERY ADDRESS: 1285 Dealy Lane
Napa, CA 94559   (707) 253-WINE

WINERY VISITS: Mon.–Fri. 9:30 AM–4:30 PM. Appt req. No credit cards.

PERSONAL NOTES:

CONNOISSEUR SELECTION

WINERY:	Chappellet Vineyard
WINE NAME:	**Cabernet Sauvignon**
ORIGIN:	Napa Valley
VINTAGE: 1970	**RATING:** 19
ALCOHOL:	12.0 percent

TASTING NOTES: Very deep ruby color. Rich, ripe berry nose, very fragrant. Classic cassis, cedar and spice. Concentrated berry flavor, showing very ripe fruit and great complexity. Hint of volatile acidity, but this adds to the complexity and is often present in great clarets. This was the author's favorite in a vertical tasting of Chappellet Cabernets from 1968 through 1982 at the Four Seasons Restaurant in New York in May 1985.

DATE TASTED:

WINERY ADDRESS: 1581 Sage Canyon Road
St. Helena, CA 94574   (707) 963-7136

WINERY VISITS: Appt. req. No credit cards.

PERSONAL NOTES:

WINERY:	Chateau Montelena Winery
WINE NAME:	**Cabernet Sauvignon**
ORIGIN:	Napa Valley, Estate Bottled
VINTAGE: 1980	**RATING:** 17
ALCOHOL:	13.5 percent
TASTING NOTES:	Deep ruby color. Briary, coffee-bean nose. Chewy, full, rich, big, stylish and promising. Lots of stuffing and structure. Tannins obscuring cassis undertone, but fruit will emerge. A big wine, fairly typical of the rich 1980 vintage in the Napa Valley. Best 1988–90.
DATE TASTED:	
WINERY ADDRESS:	1429 Tubbs Lane Calistoga, CA 94515 (707) 942-5105
WINERY VISITS:	10 AM–4 PM. Appt. not req. Credit cards.
PERSONAL NOTES:	

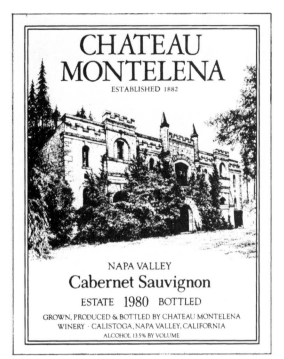

WINERY:	Chateau Montelena Winery
WINE NAME:	**Cabernet Sauvignon, Silverado Cellars**
ORIGIN:	Napa Valley
VINTAGE: 1982	**RATING:** 16
ALCOHOL:	13.5 percent
TASTING NOTES:	Inky, deep ruby hue. Concentrated tobacco and vegetal nose, very intense. Vegetal, herbaceous, tannic flavor. Uncertain how this wine will evolve— could move toward elegance, but now it is quite vegetal for a Napa Cabernet from such a renowned producer. Best 1986–88. (You must read the fine print to know this is the second label of Chateau Montelena.)
DATE TASTED:	
WINERY ADDRESS:	1429 Tubbs Lane Calistoga, CA 94515 (707) 942-5105
WINERY VISITS:	10 AM–4 PM. Appt. not req. Credit cards.
PERSONAL NOTES:	

CABERNET SAUVIGNON

WINERY:	Christian Brothers
WINE NAME:	**Cabernet Sauvignon**
ORIGIN:	Napa Valley
VINTAGE: 1980	**RATING:** 16
ALCOHOL: 13.0 percent	

TASTING NOTES: Deep ruby color. Restrained nose with peppery, spicy notes. Round, rich, ripe, fruity, with spices and oaky accents evident. Soft tannins add texture and firmness, but the wine was basically accessible at age five. Stylish effort from the new Christian Brothers as it attempts to shed its old-fashioned image. Best 1986–87.

DATE TASTED:

WINERY ADDRESS: 2555 Main Street
St. Helena, CA 94574   (707) 226-5566

WINERY VISITS: 10 AM–4:30 PM. Appt. not req. Credit cards.

PERSONAL NOTES:

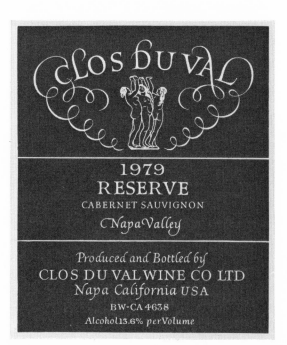

THE
CHRISTIAN
BROTHERS

VINTNERS SINCE 1882

1980

NAPA VALLEY
CABERNET SAUVIGNON

PRODUCED AND BOTTLED BY
THE CHRISTIAN BROTHERS, ST. HELENA, CALIFORNIA
750ML · ALCOHOL 13% BY VOLUME · BW 4497 · PRODUCT OF USA

WINERY:	Clos du Val Wine Co.
WINE NAME:	**Cabernet Sauvignon, Reserve**
ORIGIN:	Napa Valley
VINTAGE: 1979	**RATING:** 18
ALCOHOL: 13.6 percent	

TASTING NOTES: Very deep ruby color, with garnet accents. Tight, concentrated berry nose. Medium body. Soft but tight structure. Elegant and sleek, with hints of cassis and herbal accents. Elusive complexity challenges the palate. Very subtle in the Bernard Portet style. Portet, son of the cellar master at Château Lafite-Rothschild in Bordeaux, strives for elegance in his Napa wines. Best 1988–90.

DATE TASTED:

WINERY ADDRESS: 5330 Silverado Trail
Napa, CA 94558   (707) 252-6711

WINERY VISITS: Mon.–Sat. 10 AM–4 PM. Appt. not req. Credit cards.

PERSONAL NOTES:

CLOS DU VAL

1979
RESERVE
CABERNET SAUVIGNON
Napa Valley

Produced and Bottled by
CLOS DU VAL WINE CO LTD
Napa California USA
BW-CA 4638
Alcohol 13.6% per Volume

WINERY:	Conn Creek Winery
WINE NAME:	**Cabernet Sauvignon**
ORIGIN:	Napa Valley
VINTAGE: 1980	**RATING:** 18
ALCOHOL:	14.0 percent
TASTING NOTES:	Inky, dark ruby color. Tight, concentrated nose, showing subtle black-currant fruit with hints of cigar box. Concentrated flavor of currants, with intense extract. Begins to open up after one hour, but still tightly packed. Legs take forever to run down the sides of the glass. A Cabernet of great concentration and massive fruit. Best 1990–92. Conn Creek is one of the unsung great wineries of the Napa Valley.
DATE TASTED:	
WINERY ADDRESS:	8711 Silverado Trail St. Helena, CA 94574 (707) 963-5133
WINERY VISITS:	Appt. req. Credit cards.
PERSONAL NOTES:	

WINERY:	Cuvaison Vineyard
WINE NAME:	**Cabernet Sauvignon**
ORIGIN:	Napa Valley
VINTAGE: 1980	**RATING:** 17
ALCOHOL:	14.0 percent
TASTING NOTES:	Deep, dark ruby color. Briary, black-currant nose with hints of cigar box. Very tannic and somewhat hot. Astringent, full in body, very young and undeveloped. Very European in aging potential, which is appropriate because the winery is Swiss-owned. Concentrated structure, but fruit largely suppressed beneath tannic texture and heat of alcohol. Best 1990–92.
DATE TASTED:	
WINERY ADDRESS:	4550 Silverado Trail Calistoga, CA 94515 (707) 942-6266
WINERY VISITS:	10 AM–4 PM. Appt. not req. No credit cards.
PERSONAL NOTES:	

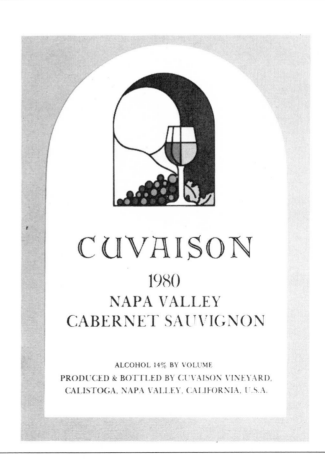

WINERY:	De Loach Vineyards
WINE NAME:	**Cabernet Sauvignon**
ORIGIN:	Sonoma County, Dry Creek Valley
VINTAGE: 1981	**RATING:** 17
ALCOHOL:	14.1 percent
TASTING NOTES:	Deep ruby color. Tight, undeveloped nose, with berry nuances. Spicy, minty flavor with subtle hints of clove. Tannic, astringent texture. Somewhat hot with alcohol, confirming extremely high reading. Could develop nicely, but years will be required. Let it rest until 1988–89 and it should endure into the 1990s. A big wine from Cecil De Loach.
DATE TASTED:	
WINERY ADDRESS:	1791 Olivet Road Santa Rosa, CA 95401 (707) 526-9111
WINERY VISITS:	10 AM–4:30 PM. Appt. not req. Credit cards.
PERSONAL NOTES:	

WINERY:	Diamond Creek Vineyards
WINE NAME:	**Cabernet Sauvignon, Red Rock Terrace**
ORIGIN:	Napa Valley
VINTAGE: 1982	**RATING:** 18
ALCOHOL:	12.0 percent
TASTING NOTES:	Inky, deep ruby color. Briary, peppery cassis nose—undeveloped but fruit wells up with breathing. Tough, tannic texture, very muscular and typical of the various Diamond Creek bottlings. Leathery, spicy elements emerge after 40 minutes in the glass (90 minutes after decanting). Coats the mouth. Classic Cabernet from the vineyards of Al and Boots Brounstein. Best 1995 and after.
DATE TASTED:	
WINERY ADDRESS:	1500 Diamond Mountain Road Calistoga, CA 94515 (707) 942-6926
WINERY VISITS:	Not open to the public.
PERSONAL NOTES:	

WINERY:	Dry Creek Vineyard
WINE NAME:	**Cabernet Sauvignon**
ORIGIN:	Sonoma County
VINTAGE:	1980

RATING: 18

ALCOHOL: 14.4 percent

TASTING NOTES: Inky purple color. Jammy, concentrated cassis nose displaying berry essence. Chewy, concentrated, opulent black-currant flavor. Big, round, deeply fruity. Plums with tobacco nuances. Complex and already charming, but should be much smoother and suppler in 1986–87. Splendid emissary of the rich 1980 vintage by David Stare, an M.I.T. graduate who opted for wine over engineering.

DATE TASTED:

WINERY ADDRESS: 3770 Lambert Bridge Road
Healdsburg, CA 95448   (707) 443-1000

WINERY VISITS: 10:30 AM–4:30 PM. Appt. not req. Credit cards.

PERSONAL NOTES:

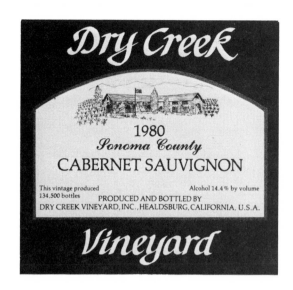

Dry Creek
1980
Sonoma County
CABERNET SAUVIGNON
This vintage produced   Alcohol 14.4% by volume
134,500 bottles   PRODUCED AND BOTTLED BY
DRY CREEK VINEYARD, INC., HEALDSBURG, CALIFORNIA, U.S.A.
Vineyard

WINERY:	Dry Creek Vineyard
WINE NAME:	**Cabernet Sauvignon**
ORIGIN:	Sonoma County
VINTAGE:	1982

RATING: 17

ALCOHOL: 13.0 percent

TASTING NOTES: Deep ruby color. Toasty, cigar-box nose, with undercurrent of cassis. Full, round, rich, raspberry/cassis flavor. Soft, mellow and ready now due to the addition of 24% Merlot, which has a softening impact. A typical Bordeaux blend by David Stare, the winemaker and owner. A wine already accessible that will be best in 1986–87 and will be outlasted by the Dry Creek '80.

DATE TASTED:

WINERY ADDRESS: 3770 Lambert Bridge Road
Healdsburg, CA 95448   (707) 443-1000

WINERY VISITS: 10:30 AM–4:30 PM. Appt. not req. Credit cards.

PERSONAL NOTES:

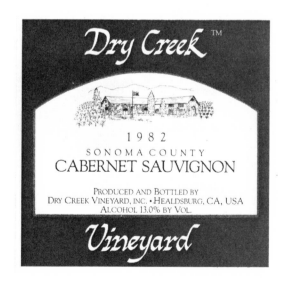

Dry Creek ™
1 9 8 2
SONOMA COUNTY
CABERNET SAUVIGNON
PRODUCED AND BOTTLED BY
DRY CREEK VINEYARD, INC. • HEALDSBURG, CA, USA
ALCOHOL 13.0% BY VOL.
Vineyard

CABERNET SAUVIGNON

WINERY:	Felton-Empire Vineyards
WINE NAME:	**Cabernet Sauvignon**
ORIGIN:	Santa Cruz Mountains
VINTAGE: 1980	**RATING:** 18
ALCOHOL: 12.75 percent	

TASTING NOTES: Deep, dark garnet color, almost opaque. Concentrated nose of blackberries and road tar, though still immature and therefore promising something special in the future. Full, rich, round, fruity Cabernet with abundant texture and dimension—a fleshy, muscular wine promising opulence at maturity in 1988–90. Leo McCloskey went to the Santa Cruz Mountains for these grapes, and the trip paid off.

DATE TASTED:

WINERY ADDRESS: 379 Felton-Empire Road
Felton, CA 95018   (408) 335-3939

WINERY VISITS: Weekends 11 AM–4:30 PM. Appt. not req. Credit cards.

PERSONAL NOTES:

FELTON-EMPIRE 1980
SANTA CRUZ MOUNTAINS
CABERNET SAUVIGNON

Produced and bottled by Felton-Empire Vineyards, **Santa Cruz Mountains**, California, Alcohol 12 3/4% by volume.

WINERY:	Freemark Abbey Winery
WINE NAME:	**Cabernet Sauvignon**
ORIGIN:	Napa Valley
VINTAGE: 1980	**RATING:** 17
ALCOHOL: 13.0 percent	

TASTING NOTES: Very dark ruby color, inky, almost opaque. Minty, woody nose with vanilla accents, but wood is dominant. Concentrated flavor of cassis with tobacco undertone and woody notes masking the Cabernet fruit. Hints of cassis, but barely perceptible under wood and tannin. Potentially a big wine that will take time to develop. Best 1988–90.

DATE TASTED:

WINERY ADDRESS: 3022 St. Helena Highway North
St. Helena, CA 94574   (707) 963-9694

WINERY VISITS: 10 AM–4:30 PM. Appt. not req. Credit cards.

PERSONAL NOTES:

FREEMARK ABBEY ST. HELENA

1980
NAPA VALLEY
CABERNET SAUVIGNON

PRODUCED AND BOTTLED BY
FREEMARK ABBEY WINERY, ST. HELENA, CALIFORNIA, U.S.A.
Alcohol 13.0% by volume

WINERY:	Freemark Abbey Winery
WINE NAME:	**Cabernet Bosché**
ORIGIN:	Napa Valley
VINTAGE: 1981	RATING: 18
ALCOHOL:	13.3 percent

TASTING NOTES:	Deep ruby color. Spicy, briary, smoky nose with cassis undertone. Chewy texture. Big, rich and full. Tannic, with cassis berries bursting through after 30 minutes of breathing. Very concentrated and filled with berry extract. Best 1989–91. This is the premium Cabernet of Freemark Abbey. The winery was established in 1967 by Charles Carpy and several partners.
DATE TASTED:	
WINERY ADDRESS:	3022 St. Helena Highway North St. Helena, CA 94574 (707) 963-9694
WINERY VISITS:	10 AM–4:30 PM. Appt. not req. Credit cards.
PERSONAL NOTES:	

WINERY:	Frog's Leap Winery
WINE NAME:	**Cabernet Sauvignon**
ORIGIN:	Napa Valley
VINTAGE: 1982	RATING: 17
ALCOHOL:	12.7 percent

TASTING NOTES:	Very deep ruby color. Spicy, peppery, tobacco nose. Firm, dusty texture, with soft tannins evident. Cassis berry flavor, oaky accents. Becomes very mellow after one hour of breathing. A restaurant wine, with beguiling fruit and great accessibility at age three. Best 1986–87. Stylish effort from winemaker John Williams. The Frog's Leap motto has become famous: "Time's fun when you're having flies."
DATE TASTED:	
WINERY ADDRESS:	3358 St. Helena Highway St. Helena, CA 94574 (707) 963-4704
WINERY VISITS:	Appt req. No credit cards.
PERSONAL NOTES:	

CABERNET SAUVIGNON

WINERY:	E. & J. Gallo
WINE NAME:	**Cabernet Sauvignon, Limited Release**
ORIGIN:	California
VINTAGE: 1978	**RATING:** 17
ALCOHOL:	13.0 percent

TASTING NOTES: Medium ruby color with a garnet edge, but no brown. Spicy, cedary, tobacco nose with cassis overtones. Cedary, slightly herbaceous, with peppery notes. Very claret-like and still improving in its eighth year. More proof that Ernest and Julio know how to venture beyond jug wines. Best 1985–86. This is a historic wine, the first vintage-dated varietal from Gallo.

DATE TASTED:

WINERY ADDRESS: 600 Yosemite Boulevard
Modesto, CA 95353   (209) 579-3111

WINERY VISITS: Gallo does not offer public tours or tastings.

PERSONAL NOTES:

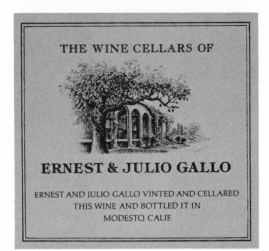

WINERY:	Geyser Peak Winery
WINE NAME:	**Cabernet Sauvignon**
ORIGIN:	Sonoma County, Alexander Valley
VINTAGE: 1980	**RATING:** 17
ALCOHOL:	12.5 percent

TASTING NOTES: Ruby color. Raspberry nose with coffee-box accents. Tannic and textured. Medium body, round, opulent fruit with a hint of herbaceousness. Tannins abate with breathing, leaving a velvety softness. Somewhat short finish, but a pleasure to drink and fairly typical of the '80 Cabernets in general. Best 1986–87.

DATE TASTED:

WINERY ADDRESS: 22281 Chianti Road
Geyserville, CA 95441   (707) 433-6585

WINERY VISITS: 10 AM–5 PM. Appt. not req. No credit cards.

PERSONAL NOTES:

WINERY:	Grand Cru Vineyards
WINE NAME:	**Cabernet Sauvignon, Collector Series**
ORIGIN:	Alexander Valley
VINTAGE: 1980	**RATING:** 17
ALCOHOL:	13.2 percent

TASTING NOTES: Ruby color, garnet accents. Smoky nose, with hints of cranberry and a toasty background. Round, full, rich and chewy, with peppery notes. Generous, ripe Cabernet fruit. Much charm and style. Best 1988–90. Typical of the rich 1980 vintage in California. Grapes were grown at Garden Creek Ranch in the Alexander Valley, one of the top Sonoma appellations.

DATE TASTED:

WINERY ADDRESS: 1 Vintage Lane
Glen Ellen, CA 95442   (707) 996-8100

WINERY VISITS: 10 AM–5 PM. Appt. not req. Credit cards.

PERSONAL NOTES:

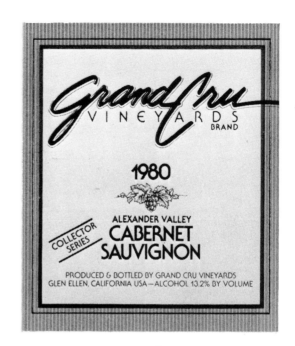

WINERY:	Grand Cru Vineyards
WINE NAME:	**Cabernet Sauvignon**
ORIGIN:	Sonoma County
VINTAGE: 1983	**RATING:** 16
ALCOHOL:	12.9 percent

TASTING NOTES: Medium ruby color. Cassis nose with peppery notes and beguiling berry fruit. Full, round, tannic. Very accessible at age two, with a stylish personality and peppery flavor accents. Best 1986–88, which means it will be useful to restaurants that are reluctant to invest in late-maturing Cabernets. The winery will be celebrating its centennial in 1986.

DATE TASTED:

WINERY ADDRESS: 1 Vintage Lane
Glen Ellen, CA 95442   (707) 996-8100

WINERY VISITS: 10 AM–5 PM. Appt. not req. Credit cards.

PERSONAL NOTES:

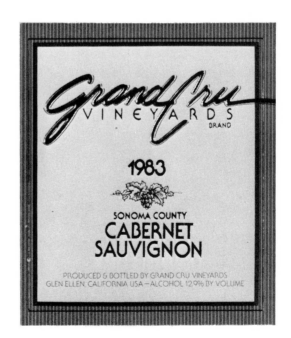

CABERNET SAUVIGNON

WINERY:	Grgich Hills Cellar
WINE NAME:	**Cabernet Sauvignon**
ORIGIN:	Napa Valley
VINTAGE: 1981	**RATING:** 15
ALCOHOL:	13.3 percent
TASTING NOTES:	Deep ruby color. Herbaceous, peppery nose with cigar-box elements. Full, rich, herbaceous flavor, even somewhat vegetal. This Cabernet is not in the same class as the splendid, big Chardonnays that have made Mike Grgich famous. The winery attracts a steady stream of visitors, many of whom are fanatical about the Grgich Chardonnays.
DATE TASTED:	
WINERY ADDRESS:	1829 St. Helena Highway Rutherford, CA 94573 (707) 963-2784
WINERY VISITS:	9:30 AM–4:30 PM. Appt. not req. No credit cards.
PERSONAL NOTES:	

WINERY:	Guenoc Winery
WINE NAME:	**Cabernet Sauvignon**
ORIGIN:	Lake County
VINTAGE: 1982	**RATING:** 16
ALCOHOL:	13.1 percent
TASTING NOTES:	Ruby color. Intense, briary, cedary nose. Chewy, tannic, young. Moderate acid level creates accessibility. A useful restaurant wine in 1986–87. Brothers Orville and Bob Magoon, descendants of a Scottish sea captain who settled in Hawaii, structured a tax deal whereby acreage in downtown Honolulu was traded for the huge Guenoc Ranch, where the country home of Lillie Langtry stands.
DATE TASTED:	
WINERY ADDRESS:	21000 Butts Canyon Road Middletown, CA 95461 (707) 987-2385
WINERY VISITS:	Thurs.–Sun. 10 AM–4:30 PM. Appt. not req. Credit cards.
PERSONAL NOTES:	

Guenoc

1982
Lake County
Cabernet Sauvignon

Produced and Bottled by Guenoc Winery
Middletown, California Alcohol 13.1% by Volume

WINERY:	Gundlach-Bundschu Winery
WINE NAME:	**Cabernet Sauvignon**
ORIGIN:	Sonoma Valley, Batto Ranch
VINTAGE: 1982	**RATING:** 16
ALCOHOL: 12.4 percent	

TASTING NOTES: Deep ruby color. Rich, cigar-box nose with vanilla nuances. Round, rich, full fruit flavor—blackberries. Already accessible at a young age. Perhaps a bit soft and less complex than some earlier Batto Ranch Cabernets, but a pleasant-drinking wine from Jim Bundschu, whose family has been making wine at the same winery since 1858. Best 1986–87.

DATE TASTED:

WINERY ADDRESS: 3775 Thornsberry Road
Sonoma, CA 95487   (707) 938-5277

WINERY VISITS: 11 AM–4:30 PM. Appt. not req. No credit cards.

PERSONAL NOTES:

WINERY:	Hacienda Wine Cellars
WINE NAME:	**Cabernet Sauvignon**
ORIGIN:	Sonoma Valley
VINTAGE: 1981	**RATING:** 17
ALCOHOL: 12.3 percent	

TASTING NOTES: Dark ruby color. Undeveloped nose with hints of road tar and leather. Chewy texture, medium to full body, tannic, but tannins are basically soft. Cassis nuances, but fruit will not fully emerge until 1988–89, though the soft tannins make the wine drinkable in its youth. Try to wait for this one—could be very stylish at maturity.

DATE TASTED:

WINERY ADDRESS: 1000 Vineyard Lane
Sonoma, CA 95476   (707) 938-3220

WINERY VISITS: 10 AM–5 PM. Appt. not req. Credit cards.

PERSONAL NOTES:

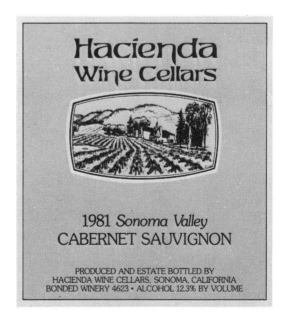

CABERNET SAUVIGNON

WINERY:	Hagafen Cellars
WINE NAME:	**Cabernet Sauvignon, Yountville Selection**
ORIGIN:	Napa Valley
VINTAGE: 1982/5743	**RATING:** 18
ALCOHOL: 12.9 percent	

TASTING NOTES: Deep ruby color. Fragrant berry nose with tobacco and cedar overtones, generously fruity. Full, round, rich, yet textured, with the essence of cassis flavor. Utterly beguiling while also complex. Arguably the best American kosher wine available, from the Hebrew year 5743. Best 1986–89.

DATE TASTED:

WINERY ADDRESS: 4195 Silverado Trail
Napa, CA 94558 (707) 252-0781

WINERY VISITS: Appt. req. Credit cards.

PERSONAL NOTES:

HAGAFEN

הגפן

1982 NAPA VALLEY 5743
CABERNET SAUVIGNON
YOUNTVILLE SELECTION

MADE & BOTTLED BY HAGAFEN CELLARS, NAPA, CA   ALC. 12.9% BY VOL.

WINERY:	Haywood Winery
WINE NAME:	**Cabernet Sauvignon**
ORIGIN:	Sonoma Valley, Estate Bottled
VINTAGE: 1982	**RATING:** 18
ALCOHOL: 12.6 percent	

TASTING NOTES: Deep ruby color. Pungent cigar-box nose with cedary overtones. Chewy texture, but tannins mostly soft, with occasional sharp needles. Long, concentrated, chewy, oaky Cabernet fruit with a blackberry undertone. Very promising. Best 1988–91.

DATE TASTED:

WINERY ADDRESS: 1870 Gehricke Road
Sonoma, CA 95476 (707) 996-4298

WINERY VISITS: 11 AM–5 PM. Appt. not req. Credit cards.

PERSONAL NOTES:

1982
CABERNET SAUVIGNON
SONOMA VALLEY
ESTATE BOTTLED

HAYWOOD

Harvested by hand at an average BRIX of 23.6°
100% Cabernet Sauvignon. Alcohol 12.6% by vol.
Grown, produced and bottled at 18701 Gehricke Rd.
HAYWOOD, WINERY, SONOMA, CALIFORNIA

CONNOISSEUR SELECTION

WINERY: Heitz Cellars

WINE NAME: **Cabernet Sauvignon**

ORIGIN: Napa Valley, Martha's Vineyard

VINTAGE: 1968   **RATING:** 19

ALCOHOL: 13.0 percent

TASTING NOTES: Deep garnet color. Elegant cassis and tobacco nose. Rich, textured, fruity, very full, even young at age 17. Very concentrated cassis flavor, minty accents. Long and complex. The best of the 1968s at a tasting of California classics arranged by New York City's River Cafe in May 1985. All of 745 cases of this wine were made by Joe Heitz from grapes grown by Martha and Tom May. It came out at $11 a bottle—today a bottle would cost hundreds.

DATE TASTED:

WINERY ADDRESS: 436 St. Helena Highway South
St. Helena, CA 94574   (707) 963-3542

WINERY VISITS: 11 AM–4:30 PM. Appt. not req. No credit cards.

PERSONAL NOTES:

WINERY: William Hill Winery

WINE NAME: **Cabernet Sauvignon**

ORIGIN: Napa Valley, Mt. Veeder

VINTAGE: 1981   **RATING:** 17

ALCOHOL: 13.4 percent

TASTING NOTES: Deep, dark ruby color. Very ripe black-currant nose with cigar-box notes. Full, rich, chewy, with long cassis flavor. Tough and muscular, but generous fruit evident beneath the oaky veneer. Hill makes Cabernets of great concentration and style from stressed vines growing high on Mt. Veeder. He is convinced that growing vines at high altitudes and under arid conditions adds to the complexity and concentration of Cabernet fruit.

DATE TASTED:

WINERY ADDRESS: 1775 Lincoln Avenue
Napa, CA 94558   (707) 224-6565

WINERY VISITS: Appt. req. No credit cards.

PERSONAL NOTES:

CABERNET SAUVIGNON

WINERY:	Inglenook Vineyards
WINE NAME:	**Cabernet Sauvignon, Limited Cask Selection**
ORIGIN:	Napa Valley, Estate Bottled
VINTAGE: 1970	**RATING:** 18
ALCOHOL: 12.0 percent	

TASTING NOTES: Deep garnet color, with plenty of ruby left at age 15. Nose of road tar, truffles and spices—classic bottle bouquet, a reason to wait for a wine like this. Big, ripe, rich cassis fruit flavor that clings to the palate. Dusty, chewy texture. In superb condition when tasted at the winery at age 15. Proof that Inglenook belongs in the front ranks of Cabernet producers. Best now to 1988.

DATE TASTED:

WINERY ADDRESS: 1991 St. Helena Highway
Rutherford, CA 94573   (707) 963-2616

WINERY VISITS: 10 AM–5 PM. Appt. not req. Credit cards.

PERSONAL NOTES:

WINERY:	Inglenook Vineyards
WINE NAME:	**Cabernet Sauvignon, Limited Cask Reserve Selection**
ORIGIN:	Napa Valley, Estate Bottled
VINTAGE: 1980	**RATING:** 17
ALCOHOL: 12.5 percent	

TASTING NOTES: Deep ruby color. Fruity, concentrated nose showing cedar, road tar and berries. Tight structure, but the wine rounds off after 30 minutes of breathing. Spicy elements emerge, with cassis berries. A round, generous wine with much charm, vibrance and fruit. It marks a strong comeback by Inglenook, a showcase winery. Best 1988–90.

DATE TASTED:

WINERY ADDRESS: 1991 St. Helena Highway
Rutherford, CA 94573   (707) 963-2616

WINERY VISITS: 10 AM–5 PM. Appt. not req. Credit cards.

PERSONAL NOTES:

WINERY:	Jekel Vineyard
WINE NAME:	**Cabernet Sauvignon**
ORIGIN:	65% Monterey County, 35% San Luis Obispo County
VINTAGE:	1981 RATING: 17
ALCOHOL:	13.0 percent
TASTING NOTES:	Deep, inky, nearly opaque purple color. Nose of tobacco and herbs, with berries in the background and hints of smoke. Tannic, chewy texture. Very slightly herbaceous in the Monterey style, but showing strong cassis overtones. A young, sinewy, very promising Cabernet that probably will not peak before 1988–89. The Jekel twins, Gus and Bill, have pioneered in stripping the grassy flavor out of Monterey varietals.
DATE TASTED:	
WINERY ADDRESS:	40155 Walnut Avenue Greenfield, CA 93927 (408) 674-5522
WINERY VISITS:	Thurs.–Mon. 10 AM–5 PM. Appt. not req. Credit cards.
PERSONAL NOTES:	

WINERY:	Jordan Vineyard and Winery
WINE NAME:	**Cabernet Sauvignon**
ORIGIN:	Alexander Valley, Estate Bottled
VINTAGE:	1979 RATING: 16
ALCOHOL:	12.8 percent
TASTING NOTES:	Medium ruby color. Ripe, jammy nose, with cedary nuances, but less concentrated than the Jordan 1980. Medium body, round, very accessible, apparently low in tannins. Hints of cassis, peppery accents. Very subtle and balanced, a so-called restaurant wine because of its early drinkability. Best 1986–88.
DATE TASTED:	
WINERY ADDRESS:	1474 Alexander Valley Road Healdsburg, CA 95448 (707) 433-6955
WINERY VISITS:	Appt. req. No credit cards.
PERSONAL NOTES:	

CABERNET SAUVIGNON

WINERY:	Jordan Vineyard and Winery
WINE NAME:	**Cabernet Sauvignon**
ORIGIN:	Alexander Valley, Estate Bottled
VINTAGE: 1980	**RATING:** 17
ALCOHOL:	12.8 percent

TASTING NOTES: Medium ruby hue. Cedary, peppery nose with tobacco nuances. Fairly mature at age five. Full-bodied, moderately tannic, accessible. Peppery, slightly herbaceous, with spicy notes. Structured and fleshy, but not overbearing. Stylish effort by winemaker Rob Davis for Tom and Sally Jordan, proprietors. Should peak around 1988–90.

DATE TASTED:

WINERY ADDRESS: 1474 Alexander Valley Road
Healdsburg, CA 95448   (707) 433-6955

WINERY VISITS: Appt. req. No credit cards.

PERSONAL NOTES:

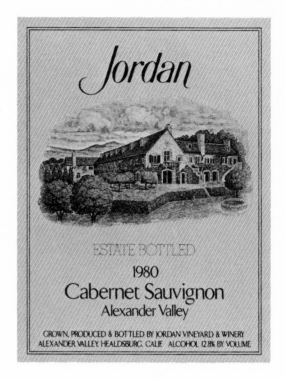

WINERY:	Jordan Vineyard and Winery
WINE NAME:	**Cabernet Sauvignon**
ORIGIN:	Alexander Valley, Estate Bottled
VINTAGE: 1981	**RATING:** 15
ALCOHOL:	12.8 percent

TASTING NOTES: Ruby color. Fruity, herbaceous nose with oaky nuances. Medium to full body, tannic. Peppery, tobacco flavor, herbaceous, even vegetal accents. Lacking richness and not up to the rounder and fuller 1980 Jordan. Best 1988–90. Jordan is one of California's showcase wineries modeled after a French château and built from scratch in the 1970s by Tom Jordan, a Denver oil man.

DATE TASTED:

WINERY ADDRESS: 1474 Alexander Valley Road
Healdsburg, CA 95448   (707) 433-6955

WINERY VISITS: Appt. req. No credit cards.

PERSONAL NOTES:

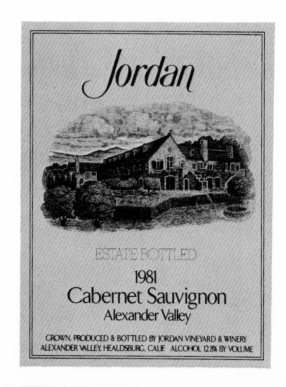

WINERY:	Robert Keenan Winery
WINE NAME:	**Cabernet Sauvignon**
ORIGIN:	Napa Valley
VINTAGE:	1981 RATING: 16
ALCOHOL:	13.1 percent
TASTING NOTES:	Deep ruby/purple color. Cigar-box, cedary nose, with undertone of berries. Full, rich, tannic, astringent and very promising. Fruity elements mostly submerged beneath tannic texture, but hints of cassis come out with breathing. Very concentrated. Best 1988–90.
DATE TASTED:	
WINERY ADDRESS:	3660 Spring Mountain Road St. Helena, CA 94574 (707) 963-9177
WINERY VISITS:	Mon.–Fri. 8 AM–4 PM. Appt. req. No credit cards.
PERSONAL NOTES:	

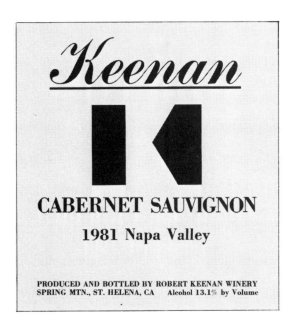

WINERY:	Kendall-Jackson Vineyards and Winery
WINE NAME:	**Cabernet Sauvignon**
ORIGIN:	Lake County, Clear Lake
VINTAGE:	1982 RATING: 15
ALCOHOL:	13.1 percent
TASTING NOTES:	Deep ruby color. Immature, tight nose with hints of cassis, but only hints. Medium-bodied, firm, somewhat tannic. Blackberry nuances in the flavor, but needs time to evolve. Could be nice. Best 1988–89. So far, Kendall-Jackson has shown superior abilities with white wines.
DATE TASTED:	
WINERY ADDRESS:	600 Mathews Road Lakeport, CA 95453 (707) 263-9333
WINERY VISITS:	10:30 AM–5:30 PM. Appt. req. Credit cards.
PERSONAL NOTES:	

CABERNET SAUVIGNON

WINERY:	Konocti Winery
WINE NAME:	**Cabernet Sauvignon**
ORIGIN:	Lake County
VINTAGE: 1980	**RATING:** 14
ALCOHOL:	12.5 percent

TASTING NOTES: Ruby/garnet color. Earthy nose, hinting of barnyard. Medium body, tannic, with fruit trying to emerge, but may be defeated by more awkward components. Less rich than an '80 should be and has a vegetal element that needs watching. Best 1986–88. Konocti has been operated as a cooperative, but now John and George Parducci of Parducci Wine Cellars have acquired a 50-percent interest.

DATE TASTED:

WINERY ADDRESS: Highway 29 at Thomas Drive
Kelseyville, CA 95451   (707) 279-8861

WINERY VISITS: 10 AM–5 PM. Appt. not req. Credit cards.

PERSONAL NOTES:

WINERY:	Lambert Bridge
WINE NAME:	**Cabernet Sauvignon**
ORIGIN:	Sonoma County
VINTAGE: 1981	**RATING:** 16
ALCOHOL:	13.0 percent

TASTING NOTES: Medium ruby color. Briary, peppery nose with herbaceous background. Peppery flavor. Round, full, textured. A wine of dimension, though the peppery elements could become unbalanced with time. Soft tannins abound, and the wine was accessible by age four. Best 1986–87. This bottle was splendid with a steak dinner.

DATE TASTED:

WINERY ADDRESS: 4085 West Dry Creek Road
Healdsburg, CA 95448   (707) 433-5855

WINERY VISITS: Appt. req. No credit cards.

PERSONAL NOTES:

WINERY:	Louis M. Martini Winery
WINE NAME:	**Cabernet Sauvignon**
ORIGIN:	North Coast
VINTAGE:	1982 RATING: 15
ALCOHOL:	12.5 percent
TASTING NOTES:	Medium ruby color. Fragrant, ripe, jammy nose with peppery and cedary notes. Firm, slightly tannic texture. Concentrated ripe fruit flavor—black currants with spicy accents. Coats the mouth, yet the tannins are mostly soft. Already accessible at age three, as is typical of most Martini Cabernets. Best 1987–89. The winery is a popular tourist stop on the St. Helena Highway.
DATE TASTED:	
WINERY ADDRESS:	St. Helena Highway South St. Helena, CA 94574 (707) 963-2736
WINERY VISITS:	10 AM–4:30 PM. Appt. not req. Credit cards.
PERSONAL NOTES:	

CONNOISSEUR SELECTION	
WINERY:	Mayacamas Vineyards
WINE NAME:	**Cabernet Sauvignon**
ORIGIN:	Napa Valley
VINTAGE:	1974 RATING: 19
ALCOHOL:	13.0 percent
TASTING NOTES:	Very deep ruby color with purple accents—looks incredibly young. Tight, concentrated, briary, cedary nose. Very concentrated cassis and herbal flavors. The youngest of all the 1974s at a tasting of the greatest Cabernets arranged by the River Cafe in New York in 1985. The Cabernets of Mayacamas may well be the longest-lived of all California reds. Grapes are grown high in the Mayacamas Mountains.
DATE TASTED:	
WINERY ADDRESS:	1155 Lokoyo Road Napa, CA 94558 (707) 224-4030
WINERY VISITS:	Appt. req. No credit cards. (Very steep drive to the winery.)
PERSONAL NOTES:	

CABERNET SAUVIGNON

WINERY:	Michtom Vineyards
WINE NAME:	**Cabernet Sauvignon**
ORIGIN:	Sonoma County, Alexander Valley
VINTAGE: 1981	**RATING:** 18
ALCOHOL: 12.0 percent	

TASTING NOTES: Very deep ruby color. Spicy, briary nose with peppery notes. Chewy with soft tannins initially, but it mellows out after 30 minutes. Spicy cassis and raspberry flavors emerge, accompanied by bursts of tobacco and coffee bean. A marvelous Cabernet from a young winery that did everything right with this one. Best 1986–87, possibly 1988. The Michtom '81 Cabernet is one of the best early-maturing Cabernets of that vintage.

DATE TASTED:

WINERY ADDRESS: Jimark Winery, 602 Limerick Lane Healdsburg, CA 95448   (707) 433-3118

WINERY VISITS: Wed.–Sun. 10 AM–4 PM. Appt. not req. No credit cards.

PERSONAL NOTES:

CONNOISSEUR SELECTION

WINERY:	Robert Mondavi Winery
WINE NAME:	**Cabernet Sauvignon, Reserve**
ORIGIN:	Napa Valley
VINTAGE: 1973	**RATING:** 19
ALCOHOL: 12.0 percent	

TASTING NOTES: Deep garnet color. Tight, young nose with cedar and cigar-box accents—classic claret fragrance. Full, rich, spicy, minty flavor. Long, complex finish. A big wine at its peak. The best of the 1973s and just as good as the heralded Mondavi Reserve '74. This wine was 12% Merlot. Bob Mondavi was the winemaker; his head oenologist was Zelma Long, more recently the winemaker at the Simi Winery.

DATE TASTED:

WINERY ADDRESS: 7801 St. Helena Highway St. Helena, CA 94562   (707) 963-9611

WINERY VISITS: 9 AM–5 PM. Appt. not req. Credit cards.

PERSONAL NOTES:

WINERY:	Robert Mondavi Winery
WINE NAME:	**Opus One**
ORIGIN:	Napa Valley
VINTAGE: 1979	**RATING:** 17
ALCOHOL:	12.5 percent

TASTING NOTES: Deep ruby color. Tight, lightly spiced, briary, undeveloped nose. Full and tannic on the palate, with a racy, elegant personality. Already quite drinkable, but structure suggests the wine will also last. Hints of black currants emerge with breathing. This was the first vintage of the joint venture of Robert Mondavi and Baron Philippe de Rothschild, of Château Mouton-Rothschild in Bordeaux. Best around 1990.

DATE TASTED:

WINERY ADDRESS: 7801 St. Helena Highway
St. Helena, CA 94562 (707) 963-9611

WINERY VISITS: 9 AM–5 PM. Appt. not req. Credit cards.

PERSONAL NOTES:

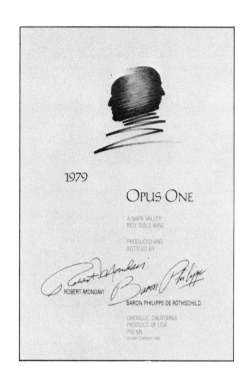

WINERY:	Robert Mondavi Winery
WINE NAME:	**Opus One**
ORIGIN:	Napa Valley
VINTAGE: 1980	**RATING:** 19
ALCOHOL:	12.5 percent

TASTING NOTES: Very deep ruby color. Grapy, rich, opulently fruity nose. Tannic, chewy texture. Massive fruit showing through tannic veneer. Very concentrated flavor, suggesting raspberries. Superb balance of fruit and texture. Much bigger and more generous than the first Opus One. The 1980 finished first in a blind tasting of that vintage, at the International Wine Center in New York, almost justifying the $45–$50 price. Best 1993–95.

DATE TASTED:

WINERY ADDRESS: 7801 St. Helena Highway
St. Helena, CA 94562 (707) 963-9611

WINERY VISITS: 9 AM–5 PM. Appt. not req. Credit cards.

PERSONAL NOTES:

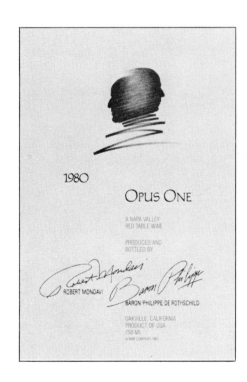

CABERNET SAUVIGNON

WINERY:	Robert Mondavi Winery
WINE NAME:	**Cabernet Sauvignon**
ORIGIN:	Napa Valley
VINTAGE:	1981 RATING: 16
ALCOHOL:	12.5 percent
TASTING NOTES:	Deep ruby color. Concentrated, black-currant nose with coffee nuances. Very full and round, yet tannic. Structured and reaching for richness, yet more austere than some earlier Mondavi efforts, reflecting the efforts of Tim Mondavi, Bob's younger son, to develop a sleeker style. Some critics say this is the wave of the future; others lament the passing of the big wines of character and personality. This one still needs time. Best 1987–89.
DATE TASTED:	
WINERY ADDRESS:	7801 St. Helena Highway St. Helena, CA 94562 (707) 963-9611
WINERY VISITS:	9 AM–5 PM. Appt. not req. Credit cards.
PERSONAL NOTES:	

1981
Napa Valley
CABERNET SAUVIGNON
ALCOHOL 12.5% BY VOLUME
PRODUCED AND BOTTLED BY
ROBERT MONDAVI WINERY
OAKVILLE, CALIFORNIA

WINERY:	Robert Mondavi Winery
WINE NAME:	**Cabernet Sauvignon**
ORIGIN:	Napa Valley
VINTAGE:	1982 RATING: 17
ALCOHOL:	13.0 percent
TASTING NOTES:	Brilliant ruby color. Cassis and tobacco nose. Full, rich, textured Cabernet, with berry undertone beneath a tannic overlay. Somewhat austere, but structure is evident. Stylish, complex. A less aggressive Cabernet from Tim Mondavi, winemaker, who seeks a sleeker, racier style.
DATE TASTED:	
WINERY ADDRESS:	7801 St. Helena Highway St. Helena, CA 94562 (707) 963-9611
WINERY VISITS:	9 AM–5 PM. Appt. not req. Credit cards.
PERSONAL NOTES:	

1982
Napa Valley
CABERNET SAUVIGNON
ALCOHOL 13% BY VOLUME
PRODUCED AND BOTTLED BY
ROBERT MONDAVI WINERY
OAKVILLE, CALIFORNIA

WINERY:	Monterey Vineyard
WINE NAME:	**Classic California Red**
ORIGIN:	California
VINTAGE:	1980 RATING: 18
ALCOHOL:	13.5 percent
TASTING NOTES:	Ruby hue. Spicy, road-tar nose, tobacco accents. Full, round, rich cedar and blackberry flavor. Stylish and complex, belying the simple generic name. Composition is 75% Cabernet Sauvignon, 14% Zinfandel, 11% Pinot Noir. The Zinfandel spiciness and Pinot Noir cherry-extract can be detected beneath the Cabernet overlay. Very claret-like—could be mistaken for a good, young Bordeaux red. Best 1986–87.
DATE TASTED:	
WINERY ADDRESS:	800 South Alta Street Gonzales, CA 93926 (408) 675-2481
WINERY VISITS:	10 AM–5 PM. Appt. not req. Credit cards.
PERSONAL NOTES:	

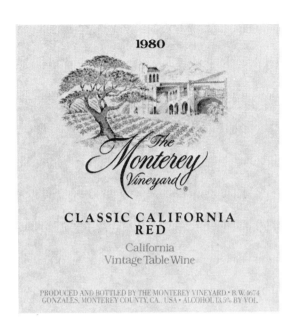

WINERY:	Monticello Cellars
WINE NAME:	**Cabernet Sauvignon, Jefferson Cuvée**
ORIGIN:	Napa Valley
VINTAGE:	1982 RATING: 17
ALCOHOL:	12.5 percent
TASTING NOTES:	Medium ruby color. Peppery, tobacco nose. Medium body. Cedary, fruity, with cassis flavor accents. Much charm, though astringent, tannic background confirms the wine's youth. Very tight, sleek and promising. Should peak around 1990.
DATE TASTED:	
WINERY ADDRESS:	4242 Big Ranch Road Napa, CA 94558 (707) 253-2802
WINERY VISITS:	10 AM–4 PM. Appt. not req. Credit cards.
PERSONAL NOTES:	

CABERNET SAUVIGNON

WINERY:	Monticello Cellars
WINE NAME:	**Cabernet Sauvignon, Corley Reserve**
ORIGIN:	Napa Valley
VINTAGE: 1982	**RATING:** 17
ALCOHOL: 12.5 percent	
TASTING NOTES:	Deep ruby/purple color. Tight, concentrated, undeveloped, fairly austere nose. Full, firm and textured on the palate. Rich, big, chewy and stylish. Very concentrated peppery, cassis flavor. Young and promising. Should be superb in 1990.
DATE TASTED:	
WINERY ADDRESS:	4242 Big Ranch Road Napa, CA 94558 (707) 253-2802
WINERY VISITS:	10 AM–4 PM. Appt. not req. Credit cards.
PERSONAL NOTES:	

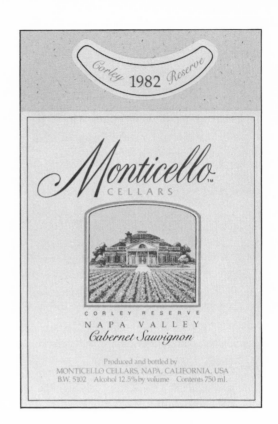

WINERY:	Parducci Wine Cellars
WINE NAME:	**Cabernet Sauvignon**
ORIGIN:	Mendocino County
VINTAGE: 1980	**RATING:** 17
ALCOHOL: 12.5 percent	
TASTING NOTES:	Very deep ruby/garnet color. Restrained briary, cedary nose. Soft, round, elegant, accessible Cabernet, with cassis nuances. A restaurant wine with excellent balance and the generosity of the 1980 vintage. This is a superior Mendocino Cabernet from one of the top Mendocino producers.
DATE TASTED:	
WINERY ADDRESS:	501 Parducci Road Ukiah, CA 95482 (707) 462-3828
WINERY VISITS:	9 AM–6 PM. Appt. not req. Credit cards.
PERSONAL NOTES:	

WINERY:	Robert Pecota Winery
WINE NAME:	**Cabernet Sauvignon**
ORIGIN:	Napa Valley
VINTAGE: 1983	**RATING:** 17
ALCOHOL:	12.0 percent
TASTING NOTES:	Very deep, inky ruby hue. Fruity cassis nose with oaky accents and peppery, minty notes. Young, fruity, berry-quality, stylish Cabernet, with cigar-box notes and complexity beginning to show. A bit awkward in its youth, as expected, but very promising. Should be superb in 1988–90.
DATE TASTED:	
WINERY ADDRESS:	3299 Bennett Lane Calistoga, CA 94515 (707) 942-6625
WINERY VISITS:	9 AM–5 PM. Appt. req. No credit cards.
PERSONAL NOTES:	

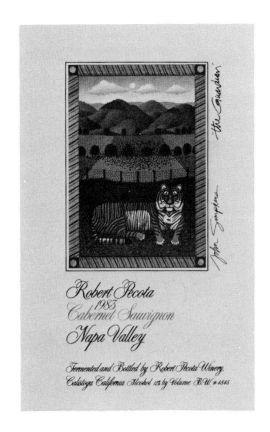

WINERY:	Joseph Phelps Vineyards
WINE NAME:	**Insignia**
ORIGIN:	Napa Valley
VINTAGE: 1980	**RATING:** 18
ALCOHOL:	13.8 percent
TASTING NOTES:	Inky, almost opaque ruby color. Deeply concentrated blackberry nose with tobacco undertone. Young, astringent texture due to strong tannins. Oaky flavor with cassis nuances, but fruit is mostly suppressed beneath a youthful tannic crust. This is a wine to wait for— big, briary and filled with promise. It is 85% Cabernet and 15% Merlot, but Joe Phelps simply calls it Insignia—his premium bottling. Best 1990–93.
DATE TASTED:	
WINERY ADDRESS:	200 Taplin Road St. Helena, CA 94574 (707) 963-2745
WINERY VISITS:	Appt. req. Credit cards.
PERSONAL NOTES:	

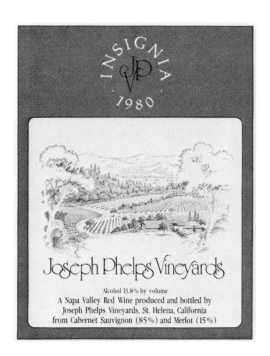

CABERNET SAUVIGNON

WINERY:	Raymond Vineyard and Cellar
WINE NAME:	**Cabernet Sauvignon**
ORIGIN:	Napa Valley, Estate Bottled
VINTAGE: 1981	**RATING:** 18
ALCOHOL: 13.7 percent	

TASTING NOTES: Ruby color. Briary, peppery nose with fruity accents. Deeply concentrated cassis and road tar, with hints of old leather. Chewy, textured, fruity. A big, intense, concentrated and stylish Cabernet that will steadily improve until reaching its peak in 1988–90. Roy Raymond Jr. and his brother Walter are establishing benchmark after benchmark at their Zinfandel Lane winery.

DATE TASTED:

WINERY ADDRESS: 849 Zinfandel Lane
St. Helena, CA 94574   (707) 963-3141

WINERY VISITS: 10 AM–4 PM. Appt. not req. No credit cards.

PERSONAL NOTES:

CONNOISSEUR SELECTION

WINERY:	Ridge Vineyards
WINE NAME:	**Cabernet Sauvignon**
ORIGIN:	Santa Cruz Mountains, Monte Bello Vineyard, Estate Bottled
VINTAGE: 1968	**RATING:** 19
ALCOHOL: 12.7 percent	

TASTING NOTES: Very deep garnet color. Concentrated road-tar and cassis nose, very fragrant, but needs much breathing. Tannic, round and huge in the mouth. Should peak around 1990. The Monte Bello bottlings are among the longest-lived Cabernets, and Paul Draper, the winemaker, is acknowledged as a master at this varietal.

DATE TASTED:

WINERY ADDRESS: 17100 Monte Bello Road
Cupertino, CA 95015   (408) 867-3233

WINERY VISITS: November–May, Sat. 11 AM–3 PM; June–October, Mon.–Sat. 11 AM–5 PM. Appt. not req. Credit cards.

PERSONAL NOTES:

WINERY:	Rombauer Vineyards
WINE NAME:	**Cabernet Sauvignon**
ORIGIN:	Napa Valley
VINTAGE: 1981	RATING: 18
ALCOHOL: 13.4 percent	

TASTING NOTES: Deep, dark ruby color. Nose of black currants with a hint of mint, even perfumy. Chewy texture, but tannins are basically soft and balanced by Cabernet fruit. Rich and full, like a young Pomerol. Long finish. Pleasant to drink at age four, better at five or six. Best 1986–87. Splendid first effort from Koerner Rombauer, an airline pilot with a custom-crushing winery on the Silverado Trail.

DATE TASTED:

WINERY ADDRESS: 3522 Silverado Trail
St. Helena, CA 94574   (707) 963-5170

WINERY VISITS: Mon.–Fri. 8:30 AM–5 PM. Appt. req. No credit cards.

PERSONAL NOTES:

WINERY:	Rutherford Hill Winery
WINE NAME:	**Cabernet Sauvignon**
ORIGIN:	Napa Valley
VINTAGE: 1980	RATING: 18
ALCOHOL: 12.8 percent	

TASTING NOTES: Ruby hue. Concentrated cassis nose, though undeveloped. Rich, ripe cassis flavor with tannic undertone. Full-bodied, rich fruit flavor. Very concentrated, even dense, yet tannins are soft and meld well with the other components. The winery was once the property of Pillsbury, and it's now owned by some of the people behind nearby Freemark Abbey. Picnic area for visitors.

DATE TASTED:

WINERY ADDRESS: 200 Rutherford Hill Road
St. Helena, CA 94574   (707) 963-9694

WINERY VISITS: 10:30 AM–4:30 PM. Appt. not req. Credit cards.

PERSONAL NOTES:

CABERNET SAUVIGNON

WINERY:	Rutherford Hill Winery
WINE NAME:	**Cabernet Sauvignon**
ORIGIN:	Napa Valley
VINTAGE: 1981	**RATING:** 17
ALCOHOL: 13.3 percent	
TASTING NOTES:	Deep ruby color. Smoky cranberry nose with tobacco nuances. Spicy, even chocolaty flavor, with full, firm body and soft texture. Dusty dry, but chocolate accents keep emerging as it breathes. Very beguiling Cabernet, best 1987–89.
DATE TASTED:	
WINERY ADDRESS:	200 Rutherford Hill Road St. Helena, CA 94574 (707) 963-9694
WINERY VISITS:	10:30 AM–4:30 PM. Appt. not req. Credit cards.
PERSONAL NOTES:	

RUTHERFORD HILL

1981
Napa Valley
CABERNET SAUVIGNON

PRODUCED AND BOTTLED BY RUTHERFORD HILL WINERY
RUTHERFORD, CALIF., USA • BW 4591 • ALCOHOL 13.3% BY VOLUME

WINERY:	Sebastiani Vineyards
WINE NAME:	**Cabernet Sauvignon**
ORIGIN:	Sonoma Valley, Eagle Vineyard
VINTAGE: 1981	**RATING:** 18
ALCOHOL: 12.7 percent	
TASTING NOTES:	Deep, dark ruby color. Concentrated cassis berry nose. Very fragrant, with hot road-tar accents. Rich, textured, spicy/peppery flavor, displaying much concentrated fruit extract. Coats the mouth. Very fleshy and full. First in a line of superpremium wines planned by Sam Sebastiani, who took over the winery after his father, August, died in 1980.
DATE TASTED:	
WINERY ADDRESS:	389 Fourth Street East Sonoma, CA 95476 (707) 938-5532
WINERY VISITS:	10 AM–5 PM. Appt. not req. Credit cards.
PERSONAL NOTES:	

1981
SEBASTIANI VINEYARDS • SONOMA VALLEY • CABERNET SAUVIGNON

"Building"   William Downey

GROWN, PRODUCED & BOTTLED BY SEBASTIANI VINEYARDS, SONOMA, CA
BONDED WINERY 876 ALC. 12.7% BY VOL. BOTTLED FEBRUARY 15, 1984

WINERY:	Shafer Vineyards
WINE NAME:	**Cabernet Sauvignon**
ORIGIN:	Napa Valley
VINTAGE: 1983	RATING: 17
ALCOHOL:	12.4 percent

TASTING NOTES: Inky, very deep ruby color. Intense cassis nose, almost flowery. Medium-bodied, elegant, complex fruit. Needs time, but already drinkable in 1985 because the tannins are soft and nicely melded with the other components. Nice Cabernet from the famous Stag's Leap area of the Napa Valley. Best 1987–89.

DATE TASTED:

WINERY ADDRESS: 6154 Silverado Trail
Napa, CA 94558   (707) 944-2877

WINERY VISITS: 8 AM–5 PM. Appt. req. No credit cards.

PERSONAL NOTES:

WINERY:	Simi Winery
WINE NAME:	**Cabernet Sauvignon**
ORIGIN:	Alexander Valley
VINTAGE: 1980	RATING: 18
ALCOHOL:	13.3 percent

TASTING NOTES: Very dark ruby color. Rich, full nose combining cassis with a hint of grassy vegetation. Full body, firm, long texture with tannins melded nicely into the fruit. A classic, opulent offering from the rich 1980 vintage. Best 1988–90. Made by Zelma Long, one of the leading women of California wine. Winery owned by Moët & Chandon of France, the world's largest Champagne producer.

DATE TASTED:

WINERY ADDRESS: 16275 Healdsburg Avenue
Healdsburg, CA 95448   (707) 433-6981

WINERY VISITS: 10 AM–4:30 PM. Appt. not req. Credit cards.

PERSONAL NOTES:

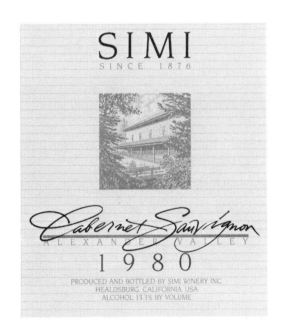

CABERNET SAUVIGNON

WINERY:	Sonoma Vineyards
WINE NAME:	**Cabernet Sauvignon, Rodney Strong**
ORIGIN:	Alexander Valley, Alexander's Crown Vineyard
VINTAGE: 1979	**RATING:** 17
ALCOHOL:	13.0 percent
TASTING NOTES:	Medium ruby color. Smoky cedar and tobacco nose, herbal background. Chewy texture with soft tannins. Herbal, spicy flavor with cassis berry elements. Long cassis finish. Stylish effort by Rod Strong, whose name is replacing Sonoma Vineyards on the labels. Best 1987–90. Strong, a former dancer and choreographer, gave up the stage to go west and make wine.
DATE TASTED:	
WINERY ADDRESS:	11455 Old Redwood Highway Healdsburg, CA 95448 (707) 433-6511
WINERY VISITS:	10 AM–5 PM. Appt. not req. Credit cards.
PERSONAL NOTES:	

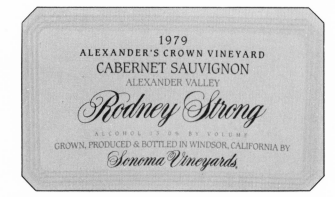

1979
ALEXANDER'S CROWN VINEYARD
CABERNET SAUVIGNON
ALEXANDER VALLEY
Rodney Strong
ALCOHOL 13.0% BY VOLUME
GROWN, PRODUCED & BOTTLED IN WINDSOR, CALIFORNIA BY
Sonoma Vineyards

CONNOISSEUR SELECTION

WINERY:	Stag's Leap Wine Cellars
WINE NAME:	**Cabernet Sauvignon**
ORIGIN:	Napa Valley, Stag's Leap Vineyards
VINTAGE: 1973	**RATING:** 19
ALCOHOL:	13.0 percent
TASTING NOTES:	Deep brick color. Fragrant, concentrated, truffle nose, with raspberry underlay. Very chewy texture, with long, rich flavor of cassis. This is the famous wine that finished first in the bicentennial tasting in Paris in 1976, topping the most celebrated Bordeaux and awakening the world to California Cabernets. Warren Winiarski is the owner and winemaker.
DATE TASTED:	
WINERY ADDRESS:	5766 Silverado Trail Napa, CA 94558 (707) 944-2020
WINERY VISITS:	10 AM–4 PM. Appt. not req. Credit cards.
PERSONAL NOTES:	

WINERY:	Sterling Vineyards
WINE NAME:	**Cabernet Sauvignon**
ORIGIN:	Napa Valley, Estate Bottled
VINTAGE: 1980	RATING: 17
ALCOHOL:	12.5 percent

TASTING NOTES: Deep ruby color, with hints of garnet at the rim. Cedary, tobacco nose with spicy accents. Round, full, rich flavor, already very accessible, with berry elements bursting through the tannin and oak overlay. Very claret-like and fully the equal of the Sterling Reserve bottling from the same vintage, at least at age five. Sterling, once owned by Coca-Cola, is now owned by the House of Seagram.

DATE TASTED:

WINERY ADDRESS: 1111 Dunaweal Lane
Calistoga, CA 94515   (707) 942-5151

WINERY VISITS: 10:30 AM–4:30 PM. Appt. not req. Credit cards.

PERSONAL NOTES:

WINERY:	Sterling Vineyards
WINE NAME:	**Cabernet Sauvignon, Sterling Reserve**
ORIGIN:	Napa Valley, Estate Bottled
VINTAGE: 1980	RATING: 17
ALCOHOL:	13.0 percent

TASTING NOTES: Deep ruby color. Concentrated raspberry nose, undeveloped but promising. Rich, spicy, full. Moderately tannic texture. Ripe and rich, yet with acidity behind the ripeness to carry the wine as it matures. Best 1988–90. Sterling is one of the spectacular visitor attractions of the Napa, with a tramway that carries tourists from the valley floor to the tasting room and winery.

DATE TASTED:

WINERY ADDRESS: 1111 Dunaweal Lane
Calistoga, CA 94515   (707) 942-5151

WINERY VISITS: 10:30 AM–4:30 PM. Appt. not req. Credit cards.

PERSONAL NOTES:

CABERNET SAUVIGNON

WINERY:	Sterling Vineyards
WINE NAME:	**Cabernet Sauvignon**
ORIGIN:	Napa Valley, Diamond Mountain Ranch, Estate Bottled
VINTAGE: 1982	**RATING:** 18
ALCOHOL:	13.5 percent
TASTING NOTES:	Very deep ruby color. Tight, undeveloped nose, with hints of berries and cedary accents. Very concentrated fruit, with cassis notes emerging after 40 minutes of breathing. Big and stylish. The first single-vineyard Cabernet for Sterling, from the Diamond Mountain vineyard where the vines are stressed by the altitude and the dry soil. Best 1992–95.
DATE TASTED:	
WINERY ADDRESS:	1111 Dunaweal Lane Calistoga, CA 94515 (707) 942-5151
WINERY VISITS:	10:30 AM–4:30 PM. Appt. not req. Credit cards.
PERSONAL NOTES:	

WINERY:	Stonegate Winery
WINE NAME:	**Cabernet Sauvignon**
ORIGIN:	Napa Valley
VINTAGE: 1981	**RATING:** 17
ALCOHOL:	12.5 percent
TASTING NOTES:	Deep ruby color. Strong cedar and tobacco nose, promising much. Chewy and tannic, briary, young and undeveloped, but complex. Muscular and tightly knit, with undertone of cassis. Best in 1988–91. The grapes are from Stonegate's vineyard in the Mayacamas Mountains, and this Cabernet includes 17% Merlot, typical of some Bordeaux blends.
DATE TASTED:	
WINERY ADDRESS:	1183 Dunaweal Lane Calistoga, CA 94515 (707) 942-6500
WINERY VISITS:	10:30 AM–4 PM. Appt. not req. Credit cards.
PERSONAL NOTES:	

WINERY:	Wente Bros.
WINE NAME:	**Cabernet Sauvignon, 100th Anniversary**
ORIGIN:	California
VINTAGE:	1980 RATING: 18
ALCOHOL:	12.5 percent
TASTING NOTES:	Deep ruby color. Nose of cedar and berries. Very concentrated fruit flavor, fleshy and full and rich, with abundant cassis and spices. An opulent, generous Cabernet from Wente, showing magnificent style and complexity. Wente is perhaps better known for its white wines, but this red puts it firmly on the red-wine map. Extensive visitor facilities.
DATE TASTED:	
WINERY ADDRESS:	5050 Arroyo Road Livermore, CA 94550 (415) 447-3023
WINERY VISITS:	Mon.–Sat. 9 AM–4:30 PM; Sun. 11 AM–4:30 PM. Appt. not req. Credit cards.
PERSONAL NOTES:	

WINERY:	William Wheeler Vineyards
WINE NAME:	**Cabernet Sauvignon**
ORIGIN:	Sonoma County, Dry Creek Valley
VINTAGE:	1982 RATING: 15
ALCOHOL:	13.2 percent
TASTING NOTES:	Ruby color, garnet highlights. Vegetal, peppery nose with hints of tobacco and cedar. Tannic, chewy, big and full. Vegetal notes submerge in fruit flavor, but raw oak is also evident. Difficult to assess, but wood and herbaceous notes dominate, raising questions about future development of fruit. Best 1986–88.
DATE TASTED:	
WINERY ADDRESS:	130 Plaza Street Healdsburg, CA 95448 (707) 433-8786
WINERY VISITS:	Appt. req. No credit cards.
PERSONAL NOTES:	

GAMAY AND GAMAY BEAUJOLAIS

The grape used to make Beaujolais in the southern part of the French Burgundy country is the Gamay, which yields wines rich in fruit, with much charm. Beaujolais is a wine meant to be drunk young, with few exceptions, and in the region of production it is usually drunk chilled.

For many years two kinds of Gamay have been cultivated in California, and only in recent years have they been properly identified. The grape that is basically the same as the one that grows in Beaujolais is called the Napa Gamay. Another one, called the Gamay Beaujolais, has been identified as a clone of Pinot Noir. At many wineries the distinction is lost. The wines from either grape in California tend to lack the fresh and readily accessible charm of the Beaujolais of France, but occasionally a California version of the Gamay rises to Beaujolais levels.

WINERY:	Buena Vista Winery
WINE NAME:	**Gamay Beaujolais**
ORIGIN:	Sonoma Valley, Carneros District, Estate Bottled
VINTAGE: 1984	**RATING:** 14
ALCOHOL:	12.0 percent
TASTING NOTES:	Medium cherry color, very bright. Muted nose, with very subtle fruit. Briary, slightly vegetal flavor. Crisp texture. Fruit quite subdued in a varietal whose hallmark is supposed to be fruitiness. Drink before 1987.
DATE TASTED:	
WINERY ADDRESS:	18000 Old Winery Road Sonoma, CA 95476 (707) 938-1266
WINERY VISITS:	10 AM–5 PM. Appt. not req. Credit cards.
PERSONAL NOTES:	

WINERY:	J. Lohr Winery
WINE NAME:	**Gamay**
ORIGIN:	Monterey County, Greenfield Vineyards
VINTAGE: 1984	**RATING:** 17
ALCOHOL:	12.0 percent
TASTING NOTES:	Ruby/purple color. Ripe cranberry nose with candy accents. Rich, ripe, firm, cherry flavor. Crisp and textured, yet not hard. Much charm, like a young Beaujolais, with the fruit up front. Best when served chilled, as Beaujolais is best served. Drink before 1987.
DATE TASTED:	
WINERY ADDRESS:	1000 Lenzen Avenue San Jose, CA 95126 (408) 288-5057
WINERY VISITS:	10 AM–5 PM. Appt. not req. Credit cards.
PERSONAL NOTES:	

WINERY:	Preston Vineyards and Winery
WINE NAME:	**Gamay Beaujolais**
ORIGIN:	Sonoma County, Dry Creek Valley, Estate Bottled
VINTAGE: 1984	**RATING:** 16
ALCOHOL: 12.5 percent	

TASTING NOTES: Ruby color. Classic grapy, fresh-fruit nose. Textured, full-bodied, rich Gamay flavor. Like a very stylish *Grand Cru* of Beaujolais, perhaps a Fleurie. Much charm, though lower acid level than most Beaujolais and thus lacking the crisp finish of a true Beaujolais. Nevertheless, a nice wine that should be drunk slightly chilled.

DATE TASTED:

WINERY ADDRESS: 9282 West Dry Creek Road
Healdsburg, CA 95448   (707) 433-3372

WINERY VISITS: Appt. req. No credit cards.

PERSONAL NOTES:

ESTATE BOTTLED

1984

PRESTON
VINEYARDS & WINERY

Gamay Beaujolais

DRY CREEK VALLEY
SONOMA COUNTY

GROWN, PRODUCED AND BOTTLED BY PRESTON WINERY
HEALDSBURG, CALIFORNIA   ALCOHOL 12.5% BY VOLUME

MERLOT

The Merlot is the principal grape of the Pomerol district of Bordeaux in France and is used liberally, along with Cabernet Sauvignon, in the great noble reds of St. Emilion. It ripens before Cabernet Sauvignon and tends to impart a softer, mellower quality, although the great Château Pétrus of Pomerol, vinified more than 90 percent from Merlot grapes, can hardly be called a soft wine.

In California the Merlot is not nearly as widely cultivated as the Cabernet Sauvignon or Zinfandel, but a number of wineries have begun to bottle varietal versions. These tend to lack the charm and finesse of the best Cabernets or Zinfandels, but they provide interesting counterpoints. The Merlot is also widely used to blend with Cabernet Sauvignon for added complexity. A mixture of 80 percent Cabernet and 20 percent Merlot is unusual neither in California nor in Bordeaux.

MERLOT

WINERY:	Boeger Winery
WINE NAME:	**Merlot, G.B.V.**
ORIGIN:	El Dorado County, Estate Bottled
VINTAGE: 1982	**RATING:** 19
ALCOHOL: 13.3 percent	
TASTING NOTES:	Deep, dark purple color. Cassis and cranberry nose. Rich, mellow, full-bodied, yet satin soft, with the essence of berries in the flavor. A superb Merlot. The White House discovered this Merlot and served it at state dinners. (The G.B.V. initials in the name stand for George Babbin Vintage, in honor of a founder of the winery.) Best now through 1987.
DATE TASTED:	
WINERY ADDRESS:	1709 Carson Road Placerville, CA 95667 (916) 622-8094
WINERY VISITS:	Wed.–Sun. 10 AM–5 PM. Appt. not req. Credit cards.
PERSONAL NOTES:	

WINERY:	Gundlach-Bundschu Winery
WINE NAME:	**Merlot**
ORIGIN:	Sonoma Valley, Rhinefarm Vineyards, Estate Bottled
VINTAGE: 1982	**RATING:** 18
ALCOHOL: 13.8 percent	
TASTING NOTES:	Deep ruby color. Spicy, cigar-box nose with chocolaty accents. Big, tannic, chewy texture. Full, rich, briary flavor. A big Merlot with berries emerging after 20 minutes of breathing. Very stylish claret-style wine from Jim Bundschu, whose family has been making wine here since 1858.
DATE TASTED:	
WINERY ADDRESS:	3775 Thornsberry Road Sonoma, CA 95487 (707) 938-5277
WINERY VISITS:	11 AM–4:30 PM. Appt. not req. No credit cards.
PERSONAL NOTES:	

WINERY:	Inglenook Vineyards
WINE NAME:	**Merlot, Limited Cask Reserve Selection**
ORIGIN:	Napa Valley, Estate Bottled
VINTAGE: 1981	RATING: 17
ALCOHOL:	12.5 percent
TASTING NOTES:	Deep ruby color, with garnet edge. Chocolaty, cigar-box aroma. Full, tannic, structured. Cedary and cassis elements in the flavor. Stylish Merlot from an old Napa winery that is once more producing serious wines. Best 1988–90.
DATE TASTED:	
WINERY ADDRESS:	1991 St. Helena Highway Rutherford, CA 94573 (707) 963-2616
WINERY VISITS:	10 AM–5 PM. Appt. not req. Credit cards.
PERSONAL NOTES:	

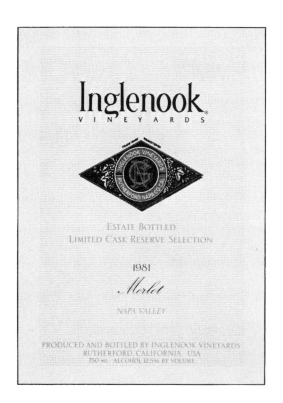

WINERY:	Robert Keenan Winery
WINE NAME:	**Merlot**
ORIGIN:	Napa Valley
VINTAGE: 1982	RATING: 17
ALCOHOL:	13.6 percent
TASTING NOTES:	Deep ruby color. Smoky, cigar-box nose, but subtle and restrained. Hints of berries in the mouth. Medium body, soft, fruity, raspberry undertone. Basically elegant and stylish. Accessible at a young age, which is typical of Merlots in general. Best 1986–87.
DATE TASTED:	
WINERY ADDRESS:	3660 Spring Mountain Road St. Helena, CA 94574 (707) 963-9177
WINERY VISITS:	Mon.–Fri. 8 AM–4 PM. Appt. req. No credit cards.
PERSONAL NOTES:	

MERLOT

WINERY:	Lambert Bridge
WINE NAME:	**Merlot**
ORIGIN:	Sonoma County
VINTAGE: 1982	**RATING:** 16
ALCOHOL:	13.1 percent

TASTING NOTES: Deep ruby color. Berries, cherries in the nose with hints of cigar box—promises much. Medium body, lightly tannic and fruity, with a raspberry undertone. Very beguiling, but lacking complexity. Best 1986–88. The wines of Gerry Lambert have shown considerable improvement in recent vintages.

DATE TASTED:

WINERY ADDRESS: 4085 West Dry Creek Road
Healdsburg, CA 95448   (707) 433-5855

WINERY VISITS: Appt. req. No credit cards.

PERSONAL NOTES:

WINERY:	Lambert Bridge
WINE NAME:	**Merlot**
ORIGIN:	Sonoma County
VINTAGE: 1983	**RATING:** 18
ALCOHOL:	13.0 percent

TASTING NOTES: Ruby color, with a touch of onion skin on the edge. Cigar-box nose with road-tar accents, promising much. Berries evident—cassis and raspberries. Ready now, confirming Merlot's reputation for early evolution. This one is especially charming and clearly superior to the 1982 Merlot from the same winery.

DATE TASTED:

WINERY ADDRESS: 4085 West Dry Creek Road
Healdsburg, CA 95448   (707) 433-5855

WINERY VISITS: Appt. req. No credit cards.

PERSONAL NOTES:

WINERY:	Louis M. Martini Winery
WINE NAME:	**Merlot**
ORIGIN:	North Coast
VINTAGE:	1982
RATING:	16
ALCOHOL:	12.5 percent

TASTING NOTES: Medium ruby color. Cedary, smoky, peppery nose, with berries emerging after 15 minutes of breathing. Crisp, tannic veneer initially evident atop a fruity undertone. It mellows out as it breathes, with cassis poking through the surface. Full, rich flavor, round and beguiling in the classic, accessible Martini style. Best 1986–88.

DATE TASTED:

WINERY ADDRESS: St. Helena Highway South
St. Helena, CA 94574   (707) 963-2736

WINERY VISITS: 10 AM–4:30 PM. Appt. not req. Credit cards.

PERSONAL NOTES:

Louis M. Martini

1982
North Coast
Merlot

PRODUCED AND BOTTLED AT THE WINERY BY LOUIS M. MARTINI
ST. HELENA, NAPA VALLEY, CALIF., U.S.A.   BONDED WINERY 3596
ALCOHOL 12.5% BY VOLUME

PINOT NOIR

The Pinot Noir is the basic grape of red Burgundy in France. It provides the character, charm and finesse of Romanée-Conti, Pommard, Chambertin, Bonnes Mares, Musigny, Clos de Vougeot and all the other great Burgundy reds. At its best it yields spicy, rich, complex wines of great finesse and elegance.

In California the Pinot Noir has proven less successful. It is widely cultivated, but wines of Burgundy style and character have been difficult to achieve from the Pinot Noir in the Golden State. Nobody is quite sure why, and intensive efforts are under way to overcome this grape's stubbornness.

At its best in California the Pinot Noir yields wines with an aroma of violets and honeysuckle and an intense berry flavor evocative of cherries or cranberries. Yet even the best California Pinot Noirs lack the grace and finesse of the finest red Burgundies. Nevertheless the search will go on, and eventually there will be a breakthrough confirming that California producers are capable of doing with the Pinot Noir what they have already accomplished with the Cabernet Sauvignon.

WINERY:	Belvedere Winery
WINE NAME:	**Pinot Noir, Bacigalupi**
ORIGIN:	Sonoma County
VINTAGE:	1982 RATING: 16
ALCOHOL:	13.9 percent

TASTING NOTES: Ruby color. Briary, slightly smoky nose. Smooth, refined, lightly tannic but elegant texture. Some cherry/apple notes, but lacking Burgundy intensity. Another single-vineyard bottling from Peter Friedman of Belvedere Winery. Charles and Helen Bacigalupi also sell their grapes to other wineries, which usually do not put the Bacigalupi name on the label as Belvedere does.

DATE TASTED:

WINERY ADDRESS: 4035 Westside Road
Healdsburg, CA 95448   (707) 433-8236

WINERY VISITS: Mon.–Fri. 8 AM–5 PM. Appt. req. No credit cards.

PERSONAL NOTES:

WINERY:	Clos du Bois Winery
WINE NAME:	**Pinot Noir, Proprietor's Reserve**
ORIGIN:	Dry Creek Valley
VINTAGE:	1980 RATING: 16
ALCOHOL:	13.6 percent

TASTING NOTES: Medium garnet color. Nose of cherries, elegantly fruity. Spicy, peppery flavor, like a light Rhone wine, with briary nuances, yet light-bodied and lacking flesh. Elegance at the expense of character, but a decent effort at one of California's most difficult varietals by Frank Woods, whose last name translates to *bois* in French. Best 1986–87.

DATE TASTED:

WINERY ADDRESS: 5 Fitch Street
Healdsburg, CA 95448   (707) 433-5576

WINERY VISITS: Mon.–Fri. noon–4 PM; weekends 10 AM–4 PM. Appt. not req. Credit cards.

PERSONAL NOTES:

PINOT NOIR

WINERY:	De Loach Vineyards
WINE NAME:	**Pinot Noir**
ORIGIN:	Sonoma County, Russian River Valley, Estate Bottled
VINTAGE: 1982	**RATING:** 17
ALCOHOL:	13.8 percent
TASTING NOTES:	Deep ruby color. Undeveloped cherry nose, still young and awkward, immature. Full-bodied, textured, slightly hot, confirming fairly high alcohol level. Concentrated cherry/raspberry fruit, though much more time needed for the parts to meld. Very stylish and showing much potential for a varietal notoriously difficult to produce in California.
DATE TASTED:	
WINERY ADDRESS:	1791 Olivet Road Santa Rosa, CA 95401 (707) 526-9111
WINERY VISITS:	10 AM–4:30 PM. Appt. not req. Credit cards.
PERSONAL NOTES:	

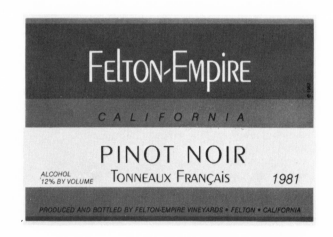

WINERY:	Felton-Empire Vineyards
WINE NAME:	**Pinot Noir**
ORIGIN:	California
VINTAGE: 1981	**RATING:** 15
ALCOHOL:	12.0 percent
TASTING NOTES:	Garnet hue. Spicy nose, with fruity notes and some barnyard accents. Round, textured, slightly astringent with tannin. Cherry accents beneath the hard veneer. Tastes better than it smells, like many young Burgundies. Could be something special, but only time will tell. Best 1988–90. The notation *Tonneaux Français* on the label indicates aging in French oak barrels.
DATE TASTED:	
WINERY ADDRESS:	379 Felton-Empire Road Felton, CA 95018 (408) 335-3939
WINERY VISITS:	Weekends 11 AM–4:30 PM. Appt. not req. Credit cards.
PERSONAL NOTES:	

WINERY:	Gundlach-Bundschu Winery
WINE NAME:	**Pinot Noir**
ORIGIN:	Sonoma Valley, Rhinefarm Vineyards, Estate Bottled
VINTAGE:	1982 RATING: 15
ALCOHOL:	14.3 percent
TASTING NOTES:	Medium ruby color. Spicy nose. Medium body, slightly tannic, pleasant Pinot Noir fruit with cherry notes. Charming, simple, pleasant wine that marries well with red meats and poultry, but not up to Burgundy standards. Surprisingly high alcohol level is well integrated with the fruit and tannins.
DATE TASTED:	
WINERY ADDRESS:	3775 Thornsberry Road Sonoma, CA 95487 (707) 938-5277
WINERY VISITS:	11 AM–4:30 PM. Appt. not req. No credit cards.
PERSONAL NOTES:	

WINERY:	Iron Horse Vineyards
WINE NAME:	**Pinot Noir**
ORIGIN:	Sonoma County, Green Valley, Estate Bottled
VINTAGE:	1982 RATING: 15
ALCOHOL:	13.0 percent
TASTING NOTES:	Ruby color. Briary, slightly smoky, fruity nose. Medium body, firm texture. Crisp, cherry flavor. Interesting style, but not a breakthrough Pinot Noir. Lacking depth and flavor concentration. Chief trait seems to be structure, with fruit submerged. Could evolve nicely, but doubtful that any more fruit will come out. Best 1986–88.
DATE TASTED:	
WINERY ADDRESS:	9786 Ross Station Road Sebastopol, CA 95472 (707) 887-1507
WINERY VISITS:	Mon.–Fri. 8 AM–5 PM. Appt. req. No credit cards.
PERSONAL NOTES:	

PINOT NOIR

WINERY:	Robert Mondavi Winery
WINE NAME:	**Pinot Noir**
ORIGIN:	Napa Valley
VINTAGE: 1981	**RATING:** 15
ALCOHOL:	13.5 percent

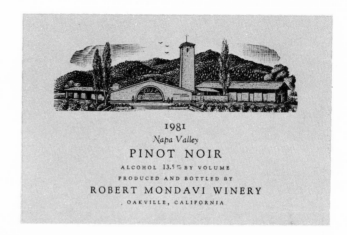

TASTING NOTES: Medium brick red color. Smoky nose with hint of fruit, but mostly smoky. Medium body, crisp, tannic. Nice acid balance, firm texture. Cherry extract in the flavor, but most of this wine's personality is in its texture, which is fairly typical of California Pinot Noirs. Mondavi probably will be among the first to make a Pinot Noir comparable to a true Burgundy, but this is not the breakthrough wine. Best 1986–88.

DATE TASTED:

WINERY ADDRESS: 7801 St. Helena Highway
St. Helena, CA 94562   (707) 963-9611

WINERY VISITS: 9 AM–5 PM. Appt. not req. Credit cards.

PERSONAL NOTES:

WINERY:	Robert Mondavi Winery
WINE NAME:	**Pinot Noir, Reserve**
ORIGIN:	Napa Valley
VINTAGE: 1981	**RATING:** 16
ALCOHOL:	13.5 percent

TASTING NOTES: Bright garnet color. Vanilla-extract nose, very concentrated, with hints of fruit compote, although oak dominates aroma. Firm, dusty texture. Round, rich, yet lacking Burgundy fullness. A nice wine, but not up to the Pinot Noir grape's achievements in the Côte d'Or. Lacks deep flavor extract, though very decent effort by one of California's foremost producers. This wine will be interesting to watch. Best 1987–88.

DATE TASTED:

WINERY ADDRESS: 7801 St. Helena Highway
St. Helena, CA 94562   (707) 963-9611

WINERY VISITS: 9 AM–5 PM. Appt. not req. Credit cards.

PERSONAL NOTES:

WINERY:	Parducci Wine Cellars
WINE NAME:	**Pinot Noir**
ORIGIN:	Mendocino County
VINTAGE: 1981	**RATING:** 13
ALCOHOL:	12.5 percent
TASTING NOTES:	Medium ruby/garnet color. Vegetal nose. Medium body, slightly awkward, tannic, hints of mushrooms, but texture dominates and fruit is not forward. Best 1986 (a guess). It is no disgrace to be unable to make a good Pinot Noir in California—this has proven to be the most stubborn of European grapes to cultivate in the Golden State.
DATE TASTED:	
WINERY ADDRESS:	501 Parducci Road Ukiah, CA 95482 (707) 462-3828
WINERY VISITS:	9 AM–6 PM. Appt. not req. Credit cards.
PERSONAL NOTES:	

WINERY:	Sanford Winery
WINE NAME:	**Pinot Noir**
ORIGIN:	Central Coast
VINTAGE: 1983	**RATING:** 17
ALCOHOL:	13.9 percent
TASTING NOTES:	Medium to pale ruby color, with garnet edge, indicating surprising maturity. Very concentrated cherry extract, perfumy nose. Full, ripe, rich cherry/cranberry flavor. Some soft tannins evident, but fruit extract is dominant. One of the few California Pinot Noirs to achieve finesse. It would have an even higher rating if not for the early maturity. Best 1986–88.
DATE TASTED:	
WINERY ADDRESS:	7250 Santa Rosa Road Buellton, CA 93427 (805) 688-3300
WINERY VISITS:	Mon.–Fri. 10 AM–4 PM. Appt. req. No credit cards.
PERSONAL NOTES:	

ZINFANDEL

The most mysterious grape cultivated in California is the Zinfandel. It is from the European species known as *Vitis vinifera*, but precisely where it came from in Europe is not known. According to legend, it was among the vine cuttings carried to the Golden State by Count Agoston Haraszthy in the middle of the last century to establish European viticulture in this country. The tag bearing the name of this varietal was said to have been damaged in transit and thus was not legible, although the letters seemed to read "Zinfandel." But no such wine existed in Europe, so its origins remained uncertain.

Then in 1967, Dr. Austin Goheen, a plant pathologist, discovered that the Primitivo grape cultivated in the Puglia region of Italy was the same. This seemed to solve the mystery, but only for a while. Doubts were cast on the discovery when it was demonstrated that the Primitivo's origins in Italy postdated the Zinfandel's arrival in California. Moreover, the grape apparently was cultivated in the eastern United States before it reached California. Now some theorists believe it came originally from eastern Europe.

Regardless of its origins, the Zinfandel yields wines of great depth, texture, and fundamental charm. Often they have a chewy quality, thick with tannins and spices, with great body. They tend to mature earlier than Cabernet Sauvignons and often are accessible by age three or four, although more time is needed for the best versions.

WINERY:	Boeger Winery
WINE NAME:	**Zinfandel**
ORIGIN:	El Dorado County
VINTAGE: 1981	RATING: 18
ALCOHOL:	14.6 percent
TASTING NOTES:	Medium ruby color. Spicy, cedary, cigar-box nose. Full, round, yet sleek and spicy Zinfandel with chocolate-mint and coffee nuances in the flavor. Chewy, tannic texture, but generosity of fruit dominates the impression. Best 1987–88. Another big, round, opulent red from Boeger's winery in the gold rush country.
DATE TASTED:	
WINERY ADDRESS:	1709 Carson Road Placerville, CA 95667 (916) 622-8094
WINERY VISITS:	Wed.–Sun. 10 AM–5 PM. Appt. not req. Credit cards.
PERSONAL NOTES:	

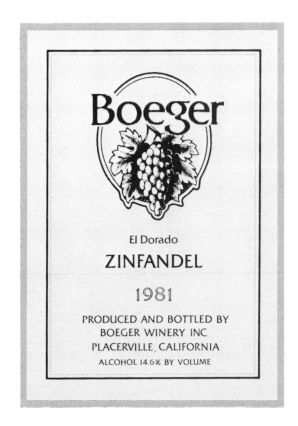

WINERY:	Buehler Vineyards
WINE NAME:	**Zinfandel**
ORIGIN:	Napa Valley
VINTAGE: 1982	RATING: 18
ALCOHOL:	13.0 percent
TASTING NOTES:	Deep, dark ruby color. Spicy, opulent berries in the nose, with tobacco accents. Round, mellow texture. Very full and ripe, with minty essences and black raspberry jam. Rich and mouth-filling. Fruit intensifies after 30 minutes of breathing, becomes even more concentrated and stylish. Splendid, from a Napa producer with a history of splendid Zinfandels. Best 1986–88.
DATE TASTED:	
WINERY ADDRESS:	820 Greenfield Road St. Helena, CA 94574 (707) 963-2155
WINERY VISITS:	Mon.–Fri. 8 AM–5 PM. Appt. req. No credit cards.
PERSONAL NOTES:	

ZINFANDEL

WINERY:	Buena Vista Winery
WINE NAME:	**Zinfandel**
ORIGIN:	Sonoma County
VINTAGE: 1982	**RATING:** 15
ALCOHOL:	12.8 percent

TASTING NOTES: Ruby color. Restrained, herbal nose with briary notes. Firm, crisp texture. Undeveloped fruit flavor—most of the personality is in the texture. Relatively low alcohol level for a Zinfandel suggests early harvest. Peppery elements emerge with breathing, along with hints of raspberry, but the wine is less developed than expected. Buena Vista is best at Cabernet Sauvignons.

DATE TASTED:

WINERY ADDRESS: 18000 Old Winery Road
Sonoma, CA 95476   (707) 938-1266

WINERY VISITS: 10 AM–5 PM. Appt. not req. Credit cards.

PERSONAL NOTES:

WINERY:	Chateau Montelena Winery
WINE NAME:	**Zinfandel**
ORIGIN:	Napa Valley, Estate Bottled
VINTAGE: 1982	**RATING:** 15
ALCOHOL:	13.5 percent

TASTING NOTES: Garnet color. Briary nose, with alcoholic overtones, aromatic. Full, chewy, tannic, with fruit submerged beneath overlay of tannin and alcohol, which makes it hot—possibly more alcoholic than the 13.5% indicates. The wine may settle down with time. Best 1987–89.

DATE TASTED:

WINERY ADDRESS: 1429 Tubbs Lane
Calistoga, CA 94515   (707) 942-5105

WINERY VISITS: 10 AM–4 PM. Appt. not req. Credit cards.

PERSONAL NOTES:

WINERY:	Conn Creek Winery
WINE NAME:	**Zinfandel**
ORIGIN:	Napa Valley, Estate Bottled
VINTAGE:	1980 RATING: 17
ALCOHOL:	14.0 percent

TASTING NOTES: Ruby color. Spicy, fruity nose, herbal accents. Medium body (for a Zinfandel), textured and young. Raspberry fruit is concentrated and waiting to emerge. Spicy background. Fairly restrained style, especially for a 1980 made from 62-year-old vines, but should evolve nicely and be accessible by 1987–89. High alcohol is well integrated and scarcely noticeable.

DATE TASTED:

WINERY ADDRESS: 8711 Silverado Trail
St. Helena, CA 94574   (707) 963-5133

WINERY VISITS: Appt. req. Credit cards.

PERSONAL NOTES:

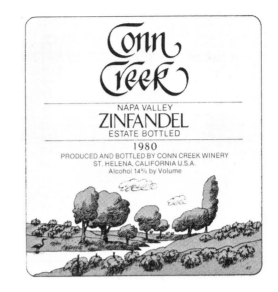

WINERY:	De Loach Vineyards
WINE NAME:	**Zinfandel**
ORIGIN:	Sonoma County, Russian River Valley, Estate Bottled
VINTAGE:	1981 RATING: 17
ALCOHOL:	14.7 percent

TASTING NOTES: Ruby color. Very spicy, concentrated, rich, alcoholic nose. Chewy, tannic, astringent texture. Full, rich, even opulent fruity flavor, but hot with alcohol. This wine is splendid for game—wild boar, venison, buffalo, even wild duck or grouse. Another old-fashioned Zinfandel that has been allowed to reach its natural, high-alcohol, savage state. Best 1987–88.

DATE TASTED:

WINERY ADDRESS: 1791 Olivet Road
Santa Rosa, CA 95401   (707) 526-9111

WINERY VISITS: 10 AM–4:30 PM. Appt. not req. Credit cards.

PERSONAL NOTES:

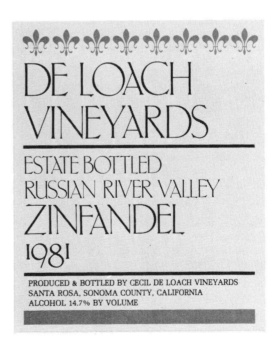

ZINFANDEL

WINERY:	Guenoc Winery
WINE NAME:	**Zinfandel**
ORIGIN:	Lake County
VINTAGE: 1982	**RATING:** 17
ALCOHOL:	14.7 percent
TASTING NOTES:	Ruby/brick color. Spicy, alcoholic nose. Rich, full, textured, road-tar spicy flavor. Big, powerful and fruity, with raspberry essence. Chewy, astringent. An old-fashioned, briary Zinfandel from a northern California region destined to become fashionable. Best 1987–89. Walter Raymond, of Raymond Vineyard in the Napa Valley, is the Guenoc winemaker and he knows what to do with those Lake County grapes.
DATE TASTED:	
WINERY ADDRESS:	21000 Butts Canyon Road Middletown, CA 95461 (707) 987-2385
WINERY VISITS:	Thurs.–Sun. 10 AM–4:30 PM. Appt. not req. Credit cards.
PERSONAL NOTES:	

Guenoc

1982
Lake County
Zinfandel

Produced and Bottled by Guenoc Winery
Middletown, California Alcohol 14.7% by Volume

WINERY:	Hacienda Wine Cellars
WINE NAME:	**Zinfandel**
ORIGIN:	California
VINTAGE: 1981	**RATING:** 15
ALCOHOL:	12.8 percent
TASTING NOTES:	Medium ruby color. Subtle, quiet nose for a Zinfandel, lacking spice or heat. Elegant, even austere flavor showing little of classic Zinfandel spices or briars and muscle. Moderate tannins, almost soft. Already drinkable. Hints of chocolate emerge with breathing, but pronounced flavor seems unlikely to develop. Best 1986. This is a Zinfandel trying to be a Cabernet Sauvignon, which is difficult at best.
DATE TASTED:	
WINERY ADDRESS:	1000 Vineyard Lane Sonoma, CA 95476 (707) 938-3220
WINERY VISITS:	10 AM–5 PM. Appt. not req. Credit cards.
PERSONAL NOTES:	

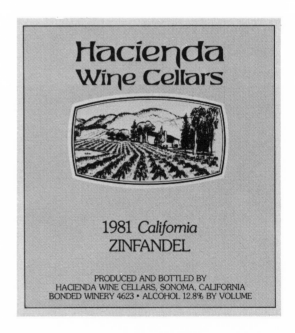

Hacienda Wine Cellars

1981 *California*
ZINFANDEL

PRODUCED AND BOTTLED BY
HACIENDA WINE CELLARS, SONOMA, CALIFORNIA
BONDED WINERY 4623 • ALCOHOL 12.8% BY VOLUME

WINERY:	McDowell Valley Vineyards
WINE NAME:	**Zinfandel, Reserve**
ORIGIN:	McDowell Valley, Estate Bottled
VINTAGE:	1980 RATING: 16
ALCOHOL:	13.4 percent
TASTING NOTES:	Ruby color. Raspberry and spice nose. Chewy, tannic texture. Berry fruit flavor—raspberries and cassis—with spicy nuances. Medium body, less concentration and flavor extract than some 1980s, but pleasant and fruity. Best 1987–88.
DATE TASTED:	
WINERY ADDRESS:	3811 Highway 175 Hopland, CA 95449 (707) 744-1053
WINERY VISITS:	10 AM–5 PM. Appt. req. Credit cards.
PERSONAL NOTES:	

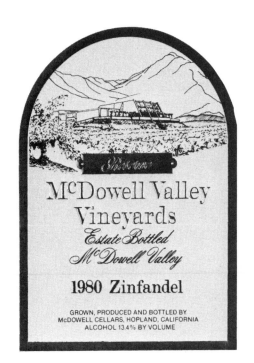

WINERY:	Parducci Wine Cellars
WINE NAME:	**Zinfandel**
ORIGIN:	Mendocino County
VINTAGE:	1982 RATING: 14
ALCOHOL:	12.5 percent
TASTING NOTES:	Brick color. Smoky, briary nose. Fruit and tannin fighting for dominance. Medium body. Some berry fruit evident, but still quite astringent. Texture dominates and fruit is suppressed. Not a Zinfandel that will develop into something special over time. Lacking concentrated fruit underpinnings. Parducci has done better. Best 1986–87.
DATE TASTED:	
WINERY ADDRESS:	501 Parducci Road Ukiah, CA 95482 (707) 462-3828
WINERY VISITS:	9 AM–6 PM. Appt. not req. Credit cards.
PERSONAL NOTES:	

ZINFANDEL

WINERY:	Preston Vineyards and Winery
WINE NAME:	**Zinfandel**
ORIGIN:	Sonoma County, Dry Creek Valley, Estate Bottled
VINTAGE: 1982	**RATING:** 18
ALCOHOL: 13.8 percent	
TASTING NOTES:	Deep ruby/purple color. Strongly scented, spicy, fruity nose with cedary accents. Round, fruity, concentrated flavor. Filled with berries—strawberries—and showing a chocolaty background. Very stylish, mouth-filling, old-fashioned Zinfandel that will delight the Zinfandel fanatics who lament the passing of the old style. High alcohol is masked by concentrated flavor. Best 1986–87.
DATE TASTED:	
WINERY ADDRESS:	9282 West Dry Creek Road Healdsburg, CA 95448 (707) 433-3372
WINERY VISITS:	Appt. req. No credit cards.
PERSONAL NOTES:	

WINERY:	Ridge Vineyards
WINE NAME:	**Zinfandel**
ORIGIN:	Napa County, Howell Mountain
VINTAGE: 1982	**RATING:** 15
ALCOHOL: 12.6 percent	
TASTING NOTES:	Very deep ruby color. Spicy, minty, cedary nose. Very fragrant, with vegetal notes emerging after 40 minutes of breathing. Round, full, rich, cedary, briary flavor. Berries hidden beneath soft tannin. Not one of Ridge's big Zinfandels. Already accessible at age three. Elegant in style, which is contrary to customary Zinfandel personality. Best 1986–88.
DATE TASTED:	
WINERY ADDRESS:	17100 Monte Bello Road Cupertino, CA 95015 (408) 867-3233
WINERY VISITS:	November–May, Sat. 11 AM–3 PM; June–October, Mon.–Sat. 11 AM–5 PM. Appt. not req. Credit cards.
PERSONAL NOTES:	

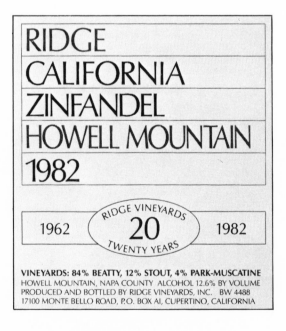

WINERY:	Simi Winery
WINE NAME:	**Zinfandel**
ORIGIN:	Alexander Valley
VINTAGE:	1981 RATING: 17
ALCOHOL:	13.5 percent
TASTING NOTES:	Ruby color. Fruity, spicy nose. Full-bodied, textured, chocolaty flavor with tobacco accents. Not overly powerful despite relatively high alcohol level. Charming, yet ample in character. A nice Zinfandel from Zelma Long.
DATE TASTED:	
WINERY ADDRESS:	16275 Healdsburg Avenue Healdsburg, CA 95448 (707) 433-6981
WINERY VISITS:	10 AM–4:30 PM. Appt. not req. Credit cards.
PERSONAL NOTES:	

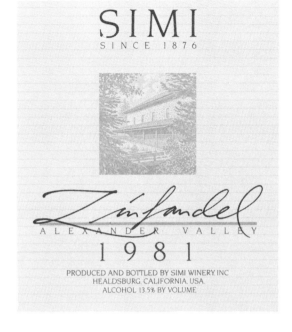

WINERY:	Sutter Home Winery
WINE NAME:	**Zinfandel**
ORIGIN:	Amador County
VINTAGE:	1982 RATING: 15
ALCOHOL:	13.5 percent
TASTING NOTES:	Medium ruby, surprisingly light in color for an Amador Zinfandel. Fruity nose with chocolaty notes. Very fruity flavor. Charming, even beguiling, but lacking in structure and character. A far cry from the Sutter Home Amador Zinfandels of the mid-1970s. The lighter, fruitier style probably has broader consumer appeal, but it will not arouse the passions of card-carrying Zinfandel fanatics. Best 1986–87.
DATE TASTED:	
WINERY ADDRESS:	277 St. Helena Highway South St. Helena, CA 94574 (707) 963-3104
WINERY VISITS:	10 AM–4 PM. Appt. not req. Credit cards.
PERSONAL NOTES:	

ZINFANDEL

WINERY:	Sutter Home Winery
WINE NAME:	**Dessert Zinfandel**
ORIGIN:	El Dorado County, Twin Rivers Vineyard
VINTAGE: 1983	**RATING:** 18
ALCOHOL:	18.0 percent

TASTING NOTES: Deep purple color. Cedar and road-tar nose, with a spicy overlay. Sweet, rich, Port-like. Very hot. Big, round and chewy, to be savored after the meal just as the British sip Port. Some wineries would call this Port, but Sutter Home's Bob Trinchero decided to demonstrate what Zinfandel can accomplish in a late-harvested form. Best 1987–90, though will last much longer due to preservative qualities of the alcohol.

DATE TASTED:

WINERY ADDRESS: 277 St. Helena Highway South
St. Helena, CA 94574   (707) 963-3104

WINERY VISITS: 10 AM–4 PM. Appt. not req. Credit cards.

PERSONAL NOTES:

CALI-
FORNIA
WINE
LABEL
ALBUM

WHITE
WINES

BLUSH WINES

America is a white-wine country. Two-thirds of wine consumed is white. As a result there is a surplus of red grapes, especially in California, which produces more than 90 percent of all the wine made in the United States. One way to remedy this situation is to replant the red-grape vineyards with white varieties. But it takes four years to obtain a commercial crop from new vines, and the replanting is costly and labor-intensive. Another way is to graft white-grape vines onto red stalks. This is less labor-intensive and can yield commercial crops sooner.

But there is yet another way. That is to make white wines from red grapes. This is possible because the pigment is entirely in the grape skins. If the skins are filtered out of the white juice immediately after the grapes are crushed, very little pigment enters the wine. But some invariably does, especially with varieties like Zinfandel, and the result is a very pale coral, salmon or pink color.

What to call this wine? Rosés have been out of fashion in this country for years, as Americans have learned that they are really not a good compromise between red and white. So California producers avoid calling their pink wines rosés. They came up with the term "blush," which is entirely appropriate, for the color is indeed like a blush. Yet because of the unpopularity of rosés, they do not even put the word blush on their labels, at least not very often.

Legalities also enter the picture with blush wines. One small winery, Mill Creek Vineyards in Sonoma County, registered "blush" as a trademark in 1981. Ever since, Mill Creek has been trying to fight off its unauthorized use. Other wineries had been using the name prior to 1981, but they had to stop. The giant House of Seagram, which owns Taylor California Cellars, Monterey Vineyard and Sterling Vineyards, challenged Mill Creek's right to the name in a lawsuit—but then decided it would be less expensive to pay Mill Creek a royalty for the use of the name. Now all wineries using "blush" to name their pink wines must pay royalties to Mill Creek, although in practice the term is used generically and few wineries print it on their labels.

Instead, most wineries call their blush wines "White Zinfandel" or "Pinot Noir Blanc" or "Cabernet Blanc." Thus, the impression is created that these wines are not really pink or rosé or blush, when most of them do have a certain level of color. American consumers like to think they are drinking white wines, even when they are not. So we have the blush-wine phenomenon, which is the biggest trend to hit the California wine industry since the nation's taste shifted from sweet to dry. In 1985 Sutter Home Winery sold an estimated 600,000 cases of White Zinfandel, and numerous other producers, including all of the biggest (Gallo, Paul Masson, Almadén) also began marketing White Zinfandels. Production in 1985 probably surpassed two million cases in all—an enormous quantity. Most of these wines are slightly sweet, with 1 to 2 percent residual sugar. They are excellent as aperitifs, and some go well with a meal. They are the wave of the present, and probably of the foreseeable future as well.

WINERY:	Bandiera Winery
WINE NAME:	**White Zinfandel**
ORIGIN:	North Coast
VINTAGE:	1984 RATING: 15
ALCOHOL:	10.2 percent

TASTING NOTES: Light salmon hue. Fruity nose with herbaceous notes. Somewhat sweet, with residual sugar of 2.45% listed on label. Textured, crisp citric flavors, but subtle. The overall impression is sweetish. Finish slightly viscous. Another in a seemingly endless flow of White Zinfandel blush wines.

DATE TASTED:

WINERY ADDRESS: 555 South Cloverdale Boulevard Cloverdale, CA 95425   (707) 894-4298

WINERY VISITS: 10 AM–5 PM. Appt. not req. Credit cards.

PERSONAL NOTES:

Bandiera
White-Zinfandel 1984
North Coast

Produced & Bottled by Bandiera Winery; Cloverdale, CA
BW3998; ALC. 10.2% VOL.

WINERY:	Belvedere Winery
WINE NAME:	**White Zinfandel, Discovery Series**
ORIGIN:	California
VINTAGE:	1984 RATING: 16
ALCOHOL:	11.0 percent

TASTING NOTES: Light coral blush. Restrained, elegant nose with a fruity undertone. Elegantly fruity flavor, crisp finish. Hint of sweetness, but drier than most blush wines. Medium body, pleasant drinking. Nice aperitif, also good with pasta and poultry.

DATE TASTED:

WINERY ADDRESS: 4035 Westside Road Healdsburg, CA 95448   (707) 433-8236

WINERY VISITS: Mon.–Fri. 8 AM–5 PM. Appt. req. No credit cards.

PERSONAL NOTES:

Belvedere Winery
DISCOVERED AND BOTTLED BY BELVEDERE WINERY
HEALDSBURG, SONOMA COUNTY, CALIFORNIA. ALCOHOL 11% BY VOLUME

Belvedere Winery

Discovery Series
1984
California
White Zinfandel

BLUSH WINES

WINERY:	Boeger Winery
WINE NAME:	**White Zinfandel**
ORIGIN:	El Dorado County
VINTAGE: 1984	**RATING:** 15
ALCOHOL:	11.5 percent
TASTING NOTES:	Very pale coral hue, just barely a blush. Muted, restrained nose. Hints of citrus. Firm, crisp texture. Slightly sweet, but sufficient acidity to balance. Clean finish. Pleasant drinking from a winery in the rugged Sierra foothills, scene of the gold rush in the 19th century and still fairly bucolic.
DATE TASTED:	
WINERY ADDRESS:	1709 Carson Road Placerville, CA 95667 (916) 622-8094
WINERY VISITS:	Wed.–Sun. 10 AM–5 PM. Appt. not req. Credit cards.
PERSONAL NOTES:	

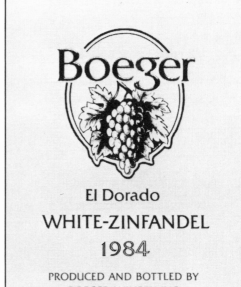

WINERY:	Buehler Vineyards
WINE NAME:	**White Zinfandel**
ORIGIN:	Napa Valley
VINTAGE: 1984	**RATING:** 17
ALCOHOL:	11 percent
TASTING NOTES:	Coral pink color. Grapy, citric nose. Rich, round and slightly sweet flavor of grapefruit, with a touch of earthiness. Full-bodied and stylish. One of the more charming White (rosé-colored) Zinfandels from a producer better known for its brawny red Zins.
DATE TASTED:	
WINERY ADDRESS:	820 Greenfield Road St. Helena, CA 94574 (707) 963-2155
WINERY VISITS:	Mon.–Fri. 8 AM–5 PM. Appt. req. No credit cards.
PERSONAL NOTES:	

WINERY:	De Loach Vineyards
WINE NAME:	**White Zinfandel**
ORIGIN:	Sonoma County, Russian River Valley
VINTAGE:	1984 RATING: 15
ALCOHOL:	12.0 percent
TASTING NOTES:	Elegant coral blush. Rich, fruity, citric nose. Round, full-bodied, richly fruity flavor. Soft, slightly sweet and slightly spritzy, with spicy accents. Pleasant aperitif, but too sweet (1.1% residual sugar) as a food wine except perhaps with dessert.
DATE TASTED:	
WINERY ADDRESS:	1791 Olivet Road Santa Rosa, CA 95401 (707) 526-9111
WINERY VISITS:	10 AM–4:30 PM. Appt. not req. Credit cards.
PERSONAL NOTES:	

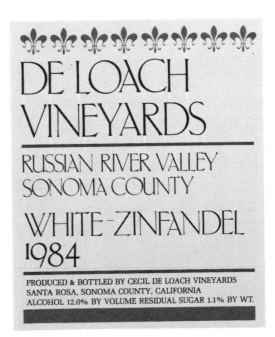

WINERY:	Geyser Peak Winery
WINE NAME:	**White Zinfandel**
ORIGIN:	Sonoma County, Russian River Valley
VINTAGE:	1984 RATING: 14
ALCOHOL:	12.0 percent
TASTING NOTES:	Extra pale coral hue with rosy accents. Subtle green-apple nose. Light to medium body. Very subtle fruit, with slightly odd finish. Fairly soft, with hints of sweetness. Lacking complexity, but pleasant as an aperitif.
DATE TASTED:	
WINERY ADDRESS:	22281 Chianti Road Geyserville, CA 95441 (707) 433-6585
WINERY VISITS:	10 AM–5 PM. Appt. not req. No credit cards.
PERSONAL NOTES:	

BLUSH WINES

WINERY:	Hagafen Cellars
WINE NAME:	**Pinot Noir Blanc**
ORIGIN:	Napa Valley
VINTAGE:	1984/5745 **RATING:** 15
ALCOHOL:	10.5 percent
TASTING NOTES:	Very light brick hue with orange accents. Citric nose. Very crisp, firm texture with full red-wine structure, but flavor is more subtle, with hints of cherry extract in combination with citrus. An intriguing kosher wine and one of the better whites from black grapes. Hagafen is Hebrew for "the vine," and this kosher bottling was made from the vintage of 5745 on the Hebrew calendar.
DATE TASTED:	
WINERY ADDRESS:	4195 Silverado Trail Napa, CA 94558 (707) 252-0781
WINERY VISITS:	Appt. req. Credit cards.
PERSONAL NOTES:	

WINERY:	Konocti Winery
WINE NAME:	**Cabernet Blanc**
ORIGIN:	Lake County
VINTAGE:	1983 **RATING:** 15
ALCOHOL:	12.0 percent
TASTING NOTES:	Totally white—no blush—though this is a white wine from red grapes. Subtly earthy nose, with hints of underlying fruit. Also a hint of sweetness. Medium body, very crisp, pleasant, but lacking complexity. Konocti is an important Lake County winery, with two members of the Parducci family from nearby Mendocino County now involved in ownership.
DATE TASTED:	
WINERY ADDRESS:	Highway 29 at Thomas Drive Kelseyville, CA 95451 (707) 279-8861
WINERY VISITS:	10 AM–5 PM. Appt. not req. Credit cards.
PERSONAL NOTES:	

WINERY:	Charles Lefranc Cellars
WINE NAME:	**White Zinfandel**
ORIGIN:	California
VINTAGE:	1984 RATING: 15
ALCOHOL:	11.0 percent
TASTING NOTES:	Coral blush, rosy accents. Subtle, restrained nose with hints of apple. Very fruity flavor, round, soft, somewhat sweet but very beguiling. Nice aperitif, but level of sweetness means use with food is limited, except for consumers who really prefer sweetish wines at all times. (Lefranc is the premium line of Almadén.)
DATE TASTED:	
WINERY ADDRESS:	1530 Blossom Hill Road San Jose, CA 95118 (408) 269-1312
WINERY VISITS:	9 AM–4 PM. Appt. not req. Credit cards.
PERSONAL NOTES:	

WINERY:	Paul Masson Vineyards
WINE NAME:	**White Zinfandel**
ORIGIN:	California
VINTAGE:	1984 RATING: 14
ALCOHOL:	10.5 percent
TASTING NOTES:	Very pale coral blush. Restrained, elegant nose, fruity accents. Medium body, fruity flavor, semi-dry. Aperitif style with crisp finish, but slightly too sweet for most food and lacking in complexity. The blush entry from one of California's largest wineries, owned by the House of Seagram.
DATE TASTED:	
WINERY ADDRESS:	13150 Saratoga Avenue Saratoga, CA 95070 (408) 257-7800
WINERY VISITS:	Fri.–Sun. 10 AM–4 PM. Appt. not req. Credit cards.
PERSONAL NOTES:	

BLUSH WINES

WINERY:	Sterling Vineyards
WINE NAME:	**Cabernet Blanc**
ORIGIN:	Napa Valley, Estate Bottled
VINTAGE:	1984 RATING: 15
ALCOHOL:	11.6 percent

TASTING NOTES: Pale coral blush. Citric nose. Flavor of apples combined with grapefruit. Hint of residual sugar, but not heavily sweet. Crisp finish suggests balancing acidity to mask the sweetness. An aperitif wine. (Actual residual sugar: 1.3%.) Use of Cabernet Sauvignon, a red grape, to make a blush wine confirms the surplus of red California grapes. Sterling is one of the more spectacular wineries to visit in the Napa Valley.

DATE TASTED:

WINERY ADDRESS: 1111 Dunaweal Lane
Calistoga, CA 94515   (707) 942-5151

WINERY VISITS: 10:30 AM–4:30 PM. Appt. not req. Credit cards.

PERSONAL NOTES:

WINERY:	Sutter Home Winery
WINE NAME:	**White Zinfandel**
ORIGIN:	California
VINTAGE:	1984 RATING: 15
ALCOHOL:	10.0 percent

TASTING NOTES: Very pale salmon blush. Fruity nose with honeydew accents. Intensely fruity flavor, with hints of grapefruit. Slightly sweet—at least 1% residual sugar. A charming aperitif and now the biggest-selling cork-finished premium American wine. Bob Trinchero, proprietor and winemaker at Sutter Home, almost single-handedly created the blush-wine category with his White Zinfandel.

DATE TASTED:

WINERY ADDRESS: 277 St. Helena Highway South
St. Helena, CA 94574   (707) 963-3104

WINERY VISITS: 10 AM–4 PM. Appt. not req. Credit cards.

PERSONAL NOTES:

CHARDONNAY

The basic grape of French white Burgundies is the Chardonnay, which is responsible for the richness and complexity of such celebrated wines as Le Montrachet, Bâtard-Montrachet, Meursault, Corton-Charlemagne, Pouilly-Fuissé and Chablis. It is also the basic grape of Blanc de Blancs Champagne and exists blended with Pinot Noir grapes in virtually all other Champagnes.

The Chardonnay is also clearly the most noble and successful white grape cultivated in California. From modest beginnings only a decade or so ago, it has evolved into the dominant grape for premium California white wines. Dozens of wineries now produce it with great success, attesting to its versatility and adaptability. Styles vary according to the region where it is cultivated and the methods of cultivation. Often it yields big, rich, buttery, creamy wines of intense flavor concentration and great complexity. Sometimes it is vinified more austerely, in the Chablis or Mâconnais style, so that it yields crisply dry, more elegant wines.

The best Chardonnays tend to be aged for one to six months in new oak barrels from France. The oak aging imparts complexity and some of the vanilla-extract flavor nuances that are responsible for the wine's complexity. Because oak aging is expensive and because the yield of Chardonnay grapes per acre of vineyard tends to be modest for the best wines, Chardonnays are usually expensive. But most connoisseurs agree they are worth the price.

CHARDONNAY

WINERY:	Acacia Winery
WINE NAME:	**Chardonnay**
ORIGIN:	Napa Valley, Carneros, Winery Lake Vineyard
VINTAGE: 1983	**RATING:** 18
ALCOHOL: 13.0 percent	
TASTING NOTES:	Medium straw color, brassy glints. Very fully fruited nose with vanilla accents and hints of toast. Concentrated, buttery flavor. Mellow and oaky, but fruit sufficiently concentrated to carry the wood. A big, brawny, characterful Chardonnay.
DATE TASTED:	
WINERY ADDRESS:	2750 Las Amigas Road Napa, CA 94558 (707) 226-9991
WINERY VISITS:	Mon.–Fri. 9 AM–5 PM. Appt. req. No credit cards.
PERSONAL NOTES:	

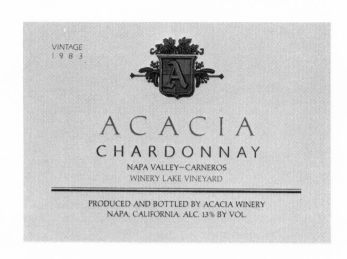

WINERY:	Alexander Valley Vineyards
WINE NAME:	**Chardonnay**
ORIGIN:	Alexander Valley, Estate Bottled
VINTAGE: 1983	**RATING:** 16
ALCOHOL: 13.8 percent	
TASTING NOTES:	Medium straw color. Concentrated apple and vanilla nose. Tight, chewy, concentrated vanilla-extract flavor with oaky undertone and hot notes from the alcohol. A big wine with much character and perhaps too much alcohol, though devotees of big Chardonnays will be delighted with this one. The winery took the name of the valley where it is located.
DATE TASTED:	
WINERY ADDRESS:	8644 Highway 128 Healdsburg, CA 95448 (707) 433-7209
WINERY VISITS:	10 AM–5 PM. Appt. not req. Credit cards.
PERSONAL NOTES:	

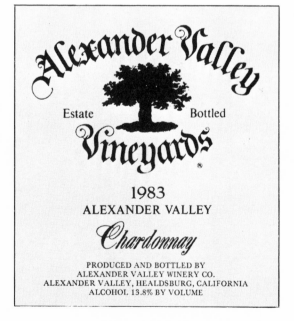

WINERY:	Belvedere Winery
WINE NAME:	**Chardonnay, Wine Discovery Series**
ORIGIN:	Monterey County
VINTAGE:	1983 RATING: 15
ALCOHOL:	12.5 percent
TASTING NOTES:	Medium straw color. Vanilla-bean nose, pure cream soda with oaky accents. Medium body, lightly oaked flavor at first impression, but oak comes on strong after breathing and begins to dominate. Citric accents peek through, but not enough fruit to support the oak. Still, a well-made wine at an inexpensive price, as are most of Belvedere's Discovery Series bottlings.
DATE TASTED:	
WINERY ADDRESS:	4035 Westside Road Healdsburg, CA 95448 (707) 433-8236
WINERY VISITS:	Mon.–Fri. 8 AM–5 PM. Appt. req. No credit cards.
PERSONAL NOTES:	

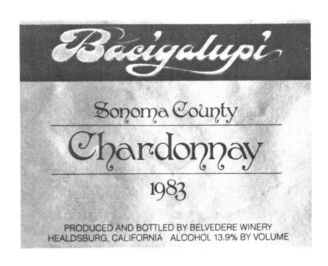

Belvedere Winery

DISCOVERED AND BOTTLED BY BELVEDERE WINERY
HEALDSBURG, SONOMA COUNTY, CALIFORNIA. ALCOHOL 12.5% BY VOLUME

Belvedere Winery
Wine Discovery Series
1983
Monterey County
Chardonnay

WINERY:	Belvedere Winery
WINE NAME:	**Chardonnay, Bacigalupi**
ORIGIN:	Sonoma County
VINTAGE:	1983 RATING: 18
ALCOHOL:	13.9 percent
TASTING NOTES:	Pale gold color. Spicy, aromatic nose. Apples and citrus fruit on the palate, with oak evident but not aggressive. Very firm, crisp and clean, with spicy accents. Stylish bottle from grapes grown by Charles and Helen Bacigalupi, who have been cultivating Chardonnay vines in the Russian River Valley since 1956. The wine was made by Peter Friedman, of Belvedere Winery, a specialist in single-vineyard bottlings.
DATE TASTED:	
WINERY ADDRESS:	4035 Westside Road Healdsburg, CA 95448 (707) 433-8236
WINERY VISITS:	Mon.–Fri. 8 AM–5 PM. Appt. req. No credit cards.
PERSONAL NOTES:	

Bacigalupi

Sonoma County

Chardonnay

1983

PRODUCED AND BOTTLED BY BELVEDERE WINERY
HEALDSBURG, CALIFORNIA   ALCOHOL 13.9% BY VOLUME

WINERY:	Beringer Vineyards
WINE NAME:	**Chardonnay, Private Reserve**
ORIGIN:	Napa Valley, Estate Bottled
VINTAGE: 1982	RATING: 16
ALCOHOL: 13.3 percent	

TASTING NOTES:	Straw color. Restrained nose hinting of vanilla. Medium body, dry, elegant, even austere. Chablis style, though less crisp than genuine Chablis. A very balanced, elegant wine, but lacking the drama anticipated from a Private Reserve bottling. One of the most hospitable wineries. The Rhine House, built in 1876 by Jacob and Frederich Beringer, is a Napa Valley landmark open to the public.
DATE TASTED:	
WINERY ADDRESS:	2000 Main Street St. Helena, CA 94574 (707) 963-7115
WINERY VISITS:	9:30 AM–4:30 PM. No appt. req. Full tours. Credit cards.
PERSONAL NOTES:	

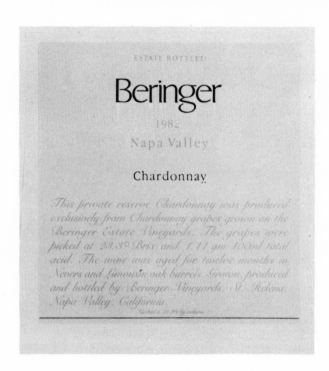

WINERY:	Beringer Vineyards
WINE NAME:	**Chardonnay**
ORIGIN:	Napa Valley, Gamble Vineyard
VINTAGE: 1983	RATING: 15
ALCOHOL: 12.7 percent	

TASTING NOTES:	Pale gold color. Lightly toasty, citric nose. Fruity flavor, but fairly austere for a barrel-fermented Chardonnay. Vanilla background, but the wood is muted. Perhaps this is a representative of the so-called "food wine" swing of the pendulum, whereby character has been sacrificed for blandness. Pleasant drinking, but not exciting.
DATE TASTED:	
WINERY ADDRESS:	2000 Main Street St. Helena, CA 94574 (707) 963-7115
WINERY VISITS:	9:30 AM–4:30 PM. Appt. not req. Full tours. Credit cards.
PERSONAL NOTES:	

WINERY:	Jean Claude Boisset Vineyards
WINE NAME:	**Chardonnay**
ORIGIN:	Napa Valley
VINTAGE: 1983	RATING: 16
ALCOHOL:	12.5 percent

TASTING NOTES:	Pale gold color. Very subtle nose, with hints of smoke and vanilla. Full, subtly fruity, elegant Chardonnay with vanilla nuances. Oak balanced by fruit. A nice effort in California by one of the leading Burgundy dealers in France. Fruit lacks concentration, but the balance and elegance of this wine are pleasant. Citric notes emerge with breathing. Not in the French white Burgundy style, though more similar to a Mâcon Blanc than to any other white Burgundy.
DATE TASTED:	
WINERY ADDRESS:	Winery not yet constructed.
WINERY VISITS:	
PERSONAL NOTES:	

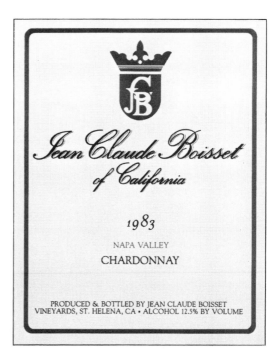

WINERY:	David Bruce Winery
WINE NAME:	**Chardonnay**
ORIGIN:	California
VINTAGE: 1983	RATING: 17
ALCOHOL:	12.5 percent

TASTING NOTES:	Pale straw color. Very concentrated, fragrant nose showing vanilla beans, with a toasty overlay. Concentrated flavor melding butter and oak, with fruity notes. Sleek, almost elegant, which is a departure from the big, overbearing Chardonnays of David Bruce in years past. This is a more balanced, more stylish wine.
DATE TASTED:	
WINERY ADDRESS:	21439 Bear Creek Road Los Gatos, CA 95030 (408) 354-4214
WINERY VISITS:	Sat. 11 AM–4 PM. Appt. req. Credit cards.
PERSONAL NOTES:	

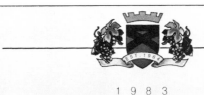

CHARDONNAY

WINERY:	Burgess Cellars
WINE NAME:	**Chardonnay, Vintage Reserve**
ORIGIN:	Napa Valley
VINTAGE: 1983	**RATING:** 18
ALCOHOL: 12.9 percent	

TASTING NOTES: Pale gold color. Smoky, ripe, vanilla nose. Full, round, ripe, buttery flavor. Big but not overwhelming. Chewy texture, complex. A few oaky needles, but they add to the complexity. Splendid citric undertone, though the overall impression is basically toasty and buttery in the Corton-Charlemagne style. Very stylish wine from Tom Burgess, who left piloting corporate aircraft to take up nurturing vines in the Napa Valley.

DATE TASTED:

WINERY ADDRESS: 1108 Deer Park Road
St. Helena, CA 94574   (707) 963-4766

WINERY VISITS: 10 AM–4 PM. Appt. req. Credit cards.

PERSONAL NOTES:

BURGESS
1983
Napa Valley
Chardonnay
Vintage Reserve

FROM GRAPES PICKED IN SEPT. AND OCT. WITH A SUGAR OF 23.1°
BRIX. ALCOHOL 12.9% BY VOLUME PRODUCED AND BOTTLED
BY BURGESS CELLARS, ST. HELENA, CA. NET CONTENTS 750 ML.

WINERY:	Callaway Vineyard and Winery
WINE NAME:	**Chardonnay**
ORIGIN:	Temecula
VINTAGE: 1983	**RATING:** 16
ALCOHOL: 13.2 percent	

TASTING NOTES: Medium straw color, gold accents. Smoky nose—light, elegant, clean. Clean, subtle fruit flavor with a hint of vanilla. A very smooth, subtle wine made from excellent fruit that has not been exposed to oak, reflecting the decision of Ely Callaway to keep oak away from his Chardonnays. This winery, in southern California not far from San Diego, has extensive visitor facilities.

DATE TASTED:

WINERY ADDRESS: 32720 Rancho California Road
Temecula, CA 92390   (714) 676-4001

WINERY VISITS: 10 AM–5 PM. Appt. not req. Credit cards.

PERSONAL NOTES:

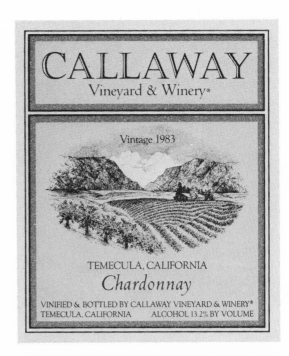

CALLAWAY
Vineyard & Winery®

Vintage 1983

TEMECULA, CALIFORNIA
Chardonnay

VINIFIED & BOTTLED BY CALLAWAY VINEYARD & WINERY®
TEMECULA, CALIFORNIA   ALCOHOL 13.2% BY VOLUME

WINERY:	Carneros Creek Winery
WINE NAME:	**Chardonnay**
ORIGIN:	Napa Valley
VINTAGE:	1982 RATING: 15
ALCOHOL:	13.5 percent
TASTING NOTES:	Light gold color, with brassy highlights. Citric nose with smoky accents. Oaky needles concentrated in moderately citric flavor. Wood and alcohol seem to dominate flavor after 10 minutes of breathing. Crisp, tight finish. Lacking in typical Chardonnay butter and cream, but a big, even overpowering, Chardonnay from one of the early wineries in the cool Carneros District. (Note the phone number.)
DATE TASTED:	
WINERY ADDRESS:	1285 Dealy Lane Napa, CA 94559 (707) 253-WINE
WINERY VISITS:	Mon.–Fri. 9:30 AM–4:30 PM. Appt. req. No credit cards.
PERSONAL NOTES:	

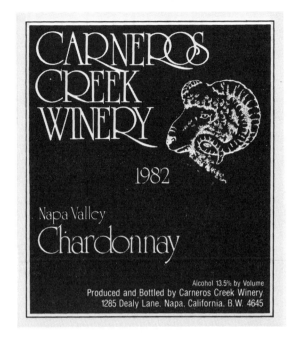

WINERY:	Carneros Creek Winery
WINE NAME:	**Chardonnay**
ORIGIN:	Napa Valley
VINTAGE:	1983 RATING: 17
ALCOHOL:	13.2 percent
TASTING NOTES:	Pale straw color, greenish glints. Smoky vanilla-bean nose. Full, textured, oaky flavor. Tightly knit, chewy, with buttery nuances emerging after 15 minutes of breathing. Complex wine from one of the original Carneros District producers, where cool breezes from San Pablo Bay have a beneficial impact on the vines.
DATE TASTED:	
WINERY ADDRESS:	1285 Dealy Lane Napa, CA 94559 (707) 253-WINE
WINERY VISITS:	Mon.–Fri. 9:30 AM–4:30 PM. Appt. req. No credit cards.
PERSONAL NOTES:	

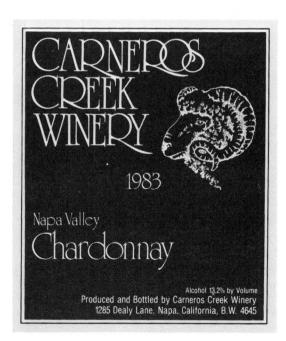

CHARDONNAY

WINERY:	Chateau Montelena Winery
WINE NAME:	**Chardonnay**
ORIGIN:	Napa Valley
VINTAGE: 1982	**RATING:** 18
ALCOHOL:	13.0 percent

TASTING NOTES: Medium straw color. Smoky nose, fruity accents, aromatic. Very concentrated fruit flavor. Round, full, intense, buttery—the Montrachet style, though without quite the same complexity and richness. This is a Chardonnay that will keep improving into the late 1980s.

DATE TASTED:

WINERY ADDRESS: 1429 Tubbs Lane
Calistoga, CA 94515   (707) 942-5105

WINERY VISITS: 10 AM–4 PM. Appt. not req. Credit cards.

PERSONAL NOTES:

WINERY:	Chateau Montelena Winery
WINE NAME:	**Chardonnay**
ORIGIN:	Alexander Valley
VINTAGE: 1983	**RATING:** 17
ALCOHOL:	13.0 percent

TASTING NOTES: Medium straw color. Citric fruit nose, very concentrated, with oaky accents. Ripe, buttery, vanilla flavor. Very concentrated, full and rich. A stylish Chardonnay from Sonoma grapes by a Napa producer.

DATE TASTED:

WINERY ADDRESS: 1429 Tubbs Lane
Calistoga, CA 94515   (707) 942-5105

WINERY VISITS: 10 AM–4 PM. Appt. not req. Credit cards.

PERSONAL NOTES:

WINERY:	Chateau St. Jean
WINE NAME:	**Chardonnay**
ORIGIN:	Alexander Valley, Robert Young Vineyards
VINTAGE: 1983	**RATING:** 17
ALCOHOL: 13.8 percent	

TASTING NOTES: Medium straw color. Restrained creamy nose, smoky accents. Firm and crisp. Citric flavor, even lemony. Round, full and characterful, but less toasty than past St. Jean Chardonnays. St. Jean, under Dick Arrowood, winemaker, made Robert Young the best known premium grape farmer in California by putting his name on the labels. The winery is now owned by Suntory of Japan.

DATE TASTED:

WINERY ADDRESS: 8555 Sonoma Highway
Kenwood, CA 95452   (707) 833-4134

WINERY VISITS: 10:30 AM–4:30 PM. Appt. not req. Credit cards.

PERSONAL NOTES:

1983
Chateau St. Jean
ALEXANDER VALLEY
Chardonnay
ROBERT YOUNG VINEYARDS

PRODUCED AND BOTTLED BY
CHATEAU ST. JEAN • KENWOOD, SONOMA VALLEY, CALIFORNIA, USA
BONDED WINERY NO. 4710 • ALCOHOL 13.8% BY VOLUME

WINERY:	Chateau St. Jean
WINE NAME:	**Chardonnay**
ORIGIN:	Sonoma County
VINTAGE: 1984	**RATING:** 16
ALCOHOL: 13.5 percent	

TASTING NOTES: Medium straw color, greenish glints. Smoky nose with oaky needles. Hints of apple. Chewy, full and textured. Less buttery than the Robert Young bottling, but almost as stylish. A crisp, tight Chardonnay with citric notes—Chablis style, but more concentrated. This bottling is the least costly of the various St. Jean Chardonnays. The winery is now Japanese-owned.

DATE TASTED:

WINERY ADDRESS: 8555 Sonoma Highway
Kenwood, CA 95452   (707) 833-4134

WINERY VISITS: 10:30 AM–4:30 PM. Appt. not req. Credit cards.

PERSONAL NOTES:

1984
Chateau St. Jean
SONOMA COUNTY
Chardonnay

PRODUCED AND BOTTLED BY
CHATEAU ST. JEAN • KENWOOD, SONOMA VALLEY, CALIFORNIA, USA
BONDED WINERY NO. 4710 • ALCOHOL 13.5% BY VOLUME

CHARDONNAY

WINERY:	Christian Brothers
WINE NAME:	**Chardonnay**
ORIGIN:	Napa Valley
VINTAGE: 1981	**RATING:** 14
ALCOHOL:	13.7 percent

TASTING NOTES: Pale gold color. Very concentrated, fruity nose. Round, melony flavor, very smooth, but lacking complexity. Short finish. Christian Brothers is one of the showcase wineries of the Napa Valley, attracting tourists by the busload. The Brothers are among the largest landholders of the valley and now produce a line of vintage-dated premium varietal wines, although they are still best known for their jugs.

DATE TASTED:

WINERY ADDRESS: 2555 Main Street
St. Helena, CA 94574   (707) 226-5566

WINERY VISITS: 10 AM–4:30 PM. Appt. not req. Credit cards.

PERSONAL NOTES:

WINERY:	Clos du Bois Winery
WINE NAME:	**Chardonnay**
ORIGIN:	Alexander Valley, Calcaire Vineyard
VINTAGE: 1982	**RATING:** 17
ALCOHOL:	13.5 percent

TASTING NOTES: Light gold color. Subtle fruit in the nose. Elegantly fruity in the mouth, with lemony accents and subtle notes of oak from aging barrels. Fruit intensity sufficient to balance big alcohol level. A well-made, big yet elegant Chardonnay of considerable finesse. The name of this winery is appropriate because the proprietor is Frank Woods, and *bois* means "woods" in French.

DATE TASTED:

WINERY ADDRESS: 5 Fitch Street
Healdsburg, CA 95448   (707) 433-5576

WINERY VISITS: Mon.–Fri. noon–4 PM; weekends 10 AM–4 PM. Appt. not req. Credit cards.

PERSONAL NOTES:

WINERY:	Clos du Bois Winery
WINE NAME:	**Chardonnay**
ORIGIN:	Dry Creek Valley, Flintwood Vineyard
VINTAGE: 1982	**RATING:** 18
ALCOHOL: 12.9 percent	

TASTING NOTES: Pale gold color. Smoky vanilla nose. Intensely buttery in the mouth, with citric fruit nuances, but butter is dominant, as in a Corton-Charlemagne from the Côte de Beaune. A rich, full Chardonnay with toasty buttery accents. Splendid with sea trout, turbot, bluefish or Atlantic lobster.

DATE TASTED:

WINERY ADDRESS: 5 Fitch Street
Healdsburg, CA 95448   (707) 433-5576

WINERY VISITS: Mon.–Fri. noon–4 PM; weekends 10 AM–4 PM. Appt. not req. Credit cards.

PERSONAL NOTES:

CLOS DU BOIS

1982

FLINTWOOD
Vineyard

DRY CREEK VALLEY
100% Chardonnay

PRODUCED & BOTTLED BY CLOS DU BOIS WINERY
HEALDSBURG, CALIFORNIA, U.S.A. ALCOHOL 12.9% BY VOLUME

WINERY:	Concannon Vineyard
WINE NAME:	**Chardonnay**
ORIGIN:	62% Tepusquet Vineyards of Santa Maria Valley; 38% Mistral Vineyard of Santa Clara County
VINTAGE: 1983	**RATING:** 16
ALCOHOL: 12.5 percent	

TASTING NOTES: Pale straw color. Smoky nose with toasty accents. Full, rich, smoky flavor, perhaps lacking somewhat in fruit intensity, but the most stylish Concannon Chardonnay yet. Sergio Traverso, formerly winemaker at Sterling Vineyards, is now making the wine at Concannon, and all of this winery's varietals seem to be improving.

DATE TASTED:

WINERY ADDRESS: 4590 Tesla Road
Livermore, CA 94550   (415) 447-3760

WINERY VISITS: Mon.–Sat. 9 AM–4:30 PM; Sun. noon–4:30 PM. Appt. not req. Credit cards.

PERSONAL NOTES:

SELECTED VINEYARDS

SINCE 1883

Concannon

1983

CALIFORNIA

CHARDONNAY

38% MISTRAL VINEYARD, SANTA CLARA COUNTY
62% TEPUSQUET VINEYARDS, SANTA MARIA VALLEY

PRODUCED & BOTTLED BY
CONCANNON VINEYARD, LIVERMORE,
CALIFORNIA, U.S.A., ALC. 12.5% BY VOL.

CHARDONNAY

WINERY:	Concannon Vineyard
WINE NAME:	**Chardonnay**
ORIGIN:	74% Tepusquet Vineyards of Santa Maria Valley; 26% Mistral Vineyard of Santa Clara County
VINTAGE: 1984	**RATING:** 17
ALCOHOL:	13.1 percent
TASTING NOTES:	Pale straw color. Lemony/apple nose, with smoky accents. Ripe, rich flavor, yet sleek and racy in style, with a long, complex finish. Abundant fruit, with hints of cream. Best Chardonnay yet under the revived Concannon.
DATE TASTED:	
WINERY ADDRESS:	4590 Tesla Road Livermore, CA 94550 (415) 447-3760
WINERY VISITS:	Mon.–Sat. 9 AM–4:30 PM. Sun. noon–4:30 PM. Appt. not req. Credit cards.
PERSONAL NOTES:	

SELECTED VINEYARDS
1984
Concannon
SINCE 1883
CHARDONNAY
26% Mistral Vineyard, Santa Clara County
74% Tepusquet Vineyards, Santa Maria Valley
PRODUCED & BOTTLED BY
CONCANNON VINEYARD, LIVERMORE,
CALIFORNIA, U.S.A., ALC. 13.1% BY VOL.

WINERY:	Corbett Canyon Vineyards
WINE NAME:	**Chardonnay**
ORIGIN:	Central Coast
VINTAGE: 1984	**RATING:** 16
ALCOHOL:	12.5 percent
TASTING NOTES:	Medium gold color. Herbal bouquet with citric nuances. Firm, clean, austere fruit flavor, with only a hint of wood. Very elegant, what some would call an excellent "food wine." Winery was called Lawrence Winery before takeover by Glenmore Distilleries. Winemaker is Cary Gott, who moved from Amador County, where his richly flavored Zinfandels made his reputation.
DATE TASTED:	
WINERY ADDRESS:	2195 Corbett Canyon Road San Luis Obispo, CA 93403 (805) 544-5800
WINERY VISITS:	8 AM–5 PM. (Thurs. from 9:30 AM). Appt. not req. Credit cards.
PERSONAL NOTES:	

CORBETT CANYON
V I N E Y A R D S

1984

Central Coast

CHARDONNAY

PRODUCED AND BOTTLED BY CORBETT CANYON VINEYARDS
EDNA VALLEY, SAN LUIS OBISPO, CA ALCOHOL 12.5% BY VOL.

WINERY:	Corbett Canyon Vineyards
WINE NAME:	**Chardonnay, Coastal Classic**
ORIGIN:	Central Coast
VINTAGE: 1984	**RATING:** 17
ALCOHOL:	13.0 percent
TASTING NOTES:	Straw color. Fruity nose with smoky accents. Textured, chewy, full, oaky. Surprising complexity for a Chardonnay that comes in a one-liter bottle called "special European carafe size," implying jug quality. Nice, inexpensive effort from the former Lawrence Winery, where Cary Gott is now the winemaker.
DATE TASTED:	
WINERY ADDRESS:	2195 Corbett Canyon Road San Luis Obispo, CA 93403 (805) 544-5800
WINERY VISITS:	8 AM–5 PM. (Thurs. from 9:30 AM). Appt. not req. Credit cards.
PERSONAL NOTES:	

WINERY:	Crystal Valley Cellars, Cosentino Wine Co.
WINE NAME:	**Chardonnay, Reserve Edition**
ORIGIN:	Sacramento County, Deer Creek Vineyard
VINTAGE: 1983	**RATING:** 15
ALCOHOL:	12.2 percent
TASTING NOTES:	Light gold color. Oaky nose. Oaky flavor with citric accents, but the basic fruit is no match for the oak. Crisp finish. Oaky aftertaste. This wine will appeal to oenophiles who love heavily oaked Chardonnays, but the only foods it would readily marry with are walnuts, hazelnuts or sharp cheeses.
DATE TASTED:	
WINERY ADDRESS:	417 Hosmer Avenue Modesto, CA 95351 (209) 577-0556
WINERY VISITS:	Mon.–Fri. 10 AM–5 PM. Appt. not req. Sat. appt. req. Credit cards.
PERSONAL NOTES:	

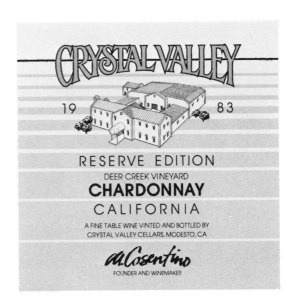

CHARDONNAY

WINERY:	Cuvaison Vineyard
WINE NAME:	**Chardonnay**
ORIGIN:	Napa Valley
VINTAGE: 1982	**RATING:** 17
ALCOHOL:	13.0 percent
TASTING NOTES:	Light to medium brass hue. Creamy vanilla nose. Round, rich, complex flavor. Buttery, with hints of caramel balanced by oaky, smoky accents. Classic Chardonnay from a Swiss-owned winery that always strives for the highest quality.
DATE TASTED:	
WINERY ADDRESS:	4550 Silverado Trail Calistoga, CA 94515 (707) 942-6266
WINERY VISITS:	10 AM–4 PM. Appt. not req. No credit cards.
PERSONAL NOTES:	

WINERY:	De Loach Vineyards
WINE NAME:	**Chardonnay**
ORIGIN:	Sonoma County, Russian River Valley
VINTAGE: 1983	**RATING:** 17
ALCOHOL:	13.6 percent
TASTING NOTES:	Pale gold color. Subtle nose with creamy/vanilla nuances. Creamy, complex, almost buttery flavor with citric accents. Full, rich and toasty in the Corton-Charlemagne style. A fleshy, opulent wine with a vigorous personality. Fairly heavily oaked, but ample fruit to support the wood.
DATE TASTED:	
WINERY ADDRESS:	1791 Olivet Road Santa Rosa, CA 95401 (707) 526-9111
WINERY VISITS:	10 AM–4:30 PM. Appt. not req. Credit cards.
PERSONAL NOTES:	

WINERY:	De Loach Vineyards
WINE NAME:	**Chardonnay O.F.S.**
ORIGIN:	Russian River Valley
VINTAGE:	1984
RATING:	17
ALCOHOL:	13.8 percent

TASTING NOTES: Medium straw color. Creamy nose with citric and oaky/smoky accents. Full, rich, round Chardonnay with lemony undertone and a very tight, crisp finish. A toasty personality. Should evolve toward sleekness by the end of 1986. (O.F.S. means "our finest selection." Cecil De Loach keeps the vineyard location a secret.)

DATE TASTED:

WINERY ADDRESS: 1791 Olivet Road
Santa Rosa, CA 95401   (707) 526-9111

WINERY VISITS: 10 AM–4:30 PM. Appt. not req. Credit cards.

PERSONAL NOTES:

© 1985 Navajo Mountain by Sally Baker

DE LOACH VINEYARDS
RUSSIAN RIVER VALLEY
1984 CHARDONNAY O.F.S.
PRODUCED & BOTTLED BY DE LOACH VINEYARDS, INC.
SANTA ROSA, SONOMA COUNTY, CA • ALC. 13.8% BY VOL.

WINERY:	Domaine Laurier
WINE NAME:	**Chardonnay**
ORIGIN:	Sonoma County
VINTAGE:	1982
RATING:	17
ALCOHOL:	13.4 percent

TASTING NOTES: Medium straw color. Fruity, citric nose. Big, full, almost tartly fruity. Long, expansive finish. A fully fleshed Chardonnay of concentrated, opulent fruit. Very stylish.

DATE TASTED:

WINERY ADDRESS: 8075 Martinelli Road
Forestville, CA 95436   (707) 887-2176

WINERY VISITS: Mon.–Fri. 9 AM–4 PM. Appt. req. No credit cards.

PERSONAL NOTES:

Domaine Laurier

1982
Chardonnay

Sonoma County

Produced and bottled by
Domaine Laurier, Forestville, Ca U.S.A.
Alcohol 13.4% by volume. BW #4840

CHARDONNAY

WINERY:	Dry Creek Vineyard
WINE NAME:	**Chardonnay**
ORIGIN:	Sonoma County
VINTAGE: 1983	**RATING:** 17
ALCOHOL:	13.0 percent

TASTING NOTES: Pale gold color. Buttery nose with toasty accents. Full and textured, with citric notes and buttery accents, though not intense. Oaky background yields to the fruit up front. Crisp, tight finish. On the borderline between the big, rich blockbusters of yesteryear and the overly austere "food wines" advocated by some critics.

DATE TASTED:

WINERY ADDRESS: 3770 Lambert Bridge Road
Healdsburg, CA 95448   (707) 443-1000

WINERY VISITS: 10:30 AM–4:30 PM. Appt. not req. Credit cards.

PERSONAL NOTES:

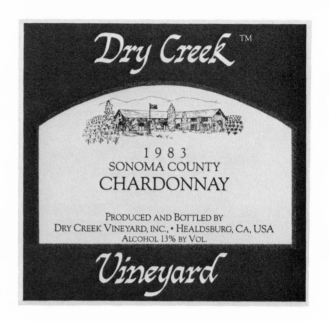

WINERY:	Far Niente Winery
WINE NAME:	**Chardonnay**
ORIGIN:	Napa Valley
VINTAGE: 1983	**RATING:** 17
ALCOHOL:	13.5 percent

TASTING NOTES: Medium straw color with brassy tones. Smoky, lightly fruited nose. Big, oaky, vanilla-extract Chardonnay fruit. Extremely concentrated and structured, with marvelous long fruit. Huge style. Here's one for devotees of the big style who want their Chardonnays to knock their socks off. Showcase winery in the heart of the Napa Valley, built in 1885 and restored nearly a century later by Gil Nickel.

DATE TASTED:

WINERY ADDRESS: 1 Acacia Drive
Oakville, CA 94562   (707) 944-2861

WINERY VISITS: Mon.–Fri. 8:30 AM–4:30 PM. Appt. req. No credit cards.

PERSONAL NOTES:

WINERY:	Felton-Empire Vineyards
WINE NAME:	**Chardonnay**
ORIGIN:	Santa Barbara, Tepusquet Vineyard
VINTAGE: 1983	RATING: 16
ALCOHOL:	13.0 percent

TASTING NOTES: Pale straw color. Smoky nose. Lightly creamy flavor, firm texture. Citric nuances. Full-bodied, complex, with a subtle oakiness. Beguiling. The winery is in the Santa Cruz Mountains, a picturesque area worth a detour, but be sure to plan your visit for a weekend. Leo McCloskey is the president and winemaker. The notation *Tonneaux Français* on the label indicates aging in French oak barrels.

DATE TASTED:

WINERY ADDRESS: 379 Felton-Empire Road
Felton, CA 95018   (408) 335-3939

WINERY VISITS: Weekends 11 AM–4:30 PM. Appt. not req. Credit cards.

PERSONAL NOTES:

FELTON-EMPIRE

SANTA BARBARA

CHARDONNAY

ALCOHOL
13% BY VOLUME   TONNEAUX FRANÇAIS   1983

TEPUSQUET VINEYARD

PRODUCED AND BOTTLED BY FELTON-EMPIRE VINEYARDS • FELTON • CALIFORNIA

WINERY:	Fetzer Vineyards
WINE NAME:	**Chardonnay, Barrel Select**
ORIGIN:	California
VINTAGE: 1983	RATING: 15
ALCOHOL:	13.0 percent

TASTING NOTES: Pale straw color. Fruity nose with woody nuances. Stylish citric flavors, with the wood largely submerged but peeking through. Lemony accents. Another excellent value from the Fetzer family— 10 brothers and sisters working in the business.

DATE TASTED:

WINERY ADDRESS: 13500 South Highway 101
Hopland, CA 95449   (707) 744-1737

WINERY VISITS: 9 AM–5 PM. Appt. not req. Credit cards.

PERSONAL NOTES:

fetzer

1983
Barrel Select
California

chardonnay

PRODUCED AND BOTTLED BY FETZER VINEYARDS
REDWOOD VALLEY, CALIFORNIA, U.S.A. ALCOHOL 13.0% BY VOLUME

CHARDONNAY

WINERY:	Fisher Vineyards
WINE NAME:	**Chardonnay**
ORIGIN:	Sonoma County
VINTAGE: 1982	**RATING:** 17
ALCOHOL:	13.0 percent
TASTING NOTES:	Pale straw color. Elegant, fruity nose. Buttery, rich, concentrated flavor with oaky accents, but the oak and the fruit are nicely integrated. Complex flavor essences, with fruit alternating with occasional oaky splinters. Intense. A big Chardonnay from an heir to the Fisher Body (General Motors) empire. Prize-winning winery, but visits by appointment only.
DATE TASTED:	
WINERY ADDRESS:	6200 St. Helena Road Santa Rosa, CA 95404 (707) 539-7511
WINERY VISITS:	Mon.–Fri. 8 AM–5 PM. Appt. req. No credit cards.
PERSONAL NOTES:	

1982
Sonoma County
CHARDONNAY

PRODUCED & BOTTLED BY FISHER VINEYARDS
MAYACAMAS MOUNTAINS, SANTA ROSA, CALIFORNIA
ALCOHOL 13% BY VOLUME • BW 4926

WINERY:	Fisher Vineyards
WINE NAME:	**Chardonnay**
ORIGIN:	Sonoma County 65%, Napa County 35%
VINTAGE: 1983	**RATING:** 18
ALCOHOL:	13.6 percent
TASTING NOTES:	Straw color, with glint of gold. Buttery nose, showing concentrated fruit, with citric notes. Terrifically concentrated buttery flavor. Rich, full, deep, complex, in the old-fashioned Meursault style. A big wine, but not overdone, with a long, rich finish. Very stylish Chardonnay from Fred Fisher.
DATE TASTED:	
WINERY ADDRESS:	6200 St. Helena Road Santa Rosa, CA 95404 (707) 539-7511
WINERY VISITS:	Mon.–Fri. 8 AM–5 PM. Appt. req. No credit cards.
PERSONAL NOTES:	

1983
CHARDONNAY
NAPA COUNTY 35%
SONOMA COUNTY 65%

PRODUCED & BOTTLED BY FISHER VINEYARDS
MAYACAMAS MOUNTAINS, SANTA ROSA, CALIFORNIA
TABLE WINE • BW 4926

WINERY:	Flora Springs Wine Co.
WINE NAME:	**Chardonnay**
ORIGIN:	Napa Valley
VINTAGE: 1983	RATING: 17
ALCOHOL:	13.0 percent
TASTING NOTES:	Medium straw color. Big, smoky, oaky nose, suggesting buttered toast. Full, rich, opulently fruity and woody. Chewy texture. A big, old-fashioned Chardonnay that got that way by fermentation in the aging barrels.
DATE TASTED:	
WINERY ADDRESS:	1978 West Zinfandel Lane St. Helena, CA 94574 (707) 963-5711
WINERY VISITS:	Mon.–Fri. 8 AM–5 PM. Appt. req. No credit cards.
PERSONAL NOTES:	

WINERY:	Franciscan Vineyards
WINE NAME:	**Chardonnay, Reserve**
ORIGIN:	Napa Valley, Carneros Vineyard, Estate Bottled
VINTAGE: 1982	RATING: 17
ALCOHOL:	13.8 percent
TASTING NOTES:	Very pale straw color. Smoky nose, citric and apple notes. Fruity, full, round, rich flavor. Superb fruit quality completely balances oak, though there are creamy accents for added complexity. Stylish and long.
DATE TASTED:	
WINERY ADDRESS:	1178 Galleron Road Rutherford, CA 94573 (707) 963-7111
WINERY VISITS:	10 AM–5 PM. Appt. not req. Credit cards.
PERSONAL NOTES:	

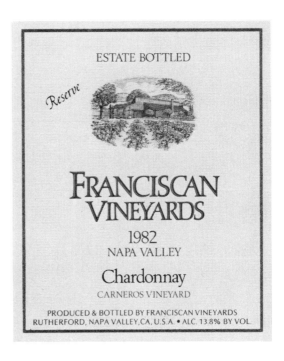

CHARDONNAY

WINERY:	Freemark Abbey Winery
WINE NAME:	**Chardonnay**
ORIGIN:	Napa Valley
VINTAGE: 1982	RATING: 14
ALCOHOL:	12.5 percent

TASTING NOTES: Straw color, with brassy glints. Ripe, smoky, herbal nose with oaky/toasty accents. Very oaky flavor, with wood the dominant trait when tasted in mid-1985. Probably much better a year or so earlier, before the fruit had subsided. Classic example of how oak can take over a Chardonnay after the fruit of youth drops out. Freemark Abbey can do better, although some consumers adore very oaky Chardonnays.

DATE TASTED:

WINERY ADDRESS: 3022 St. Helena Highway North St. Helena, CA 94574   (707) 963-9694

WINERY VISITS: 10 AM–4:30 PM. Appt. not req. Credit cards.

PERSONAL NOTES:

FREEMARK ABBEY

1982

NAPA VALLEY

CHARDONNAY

PRODUCED AND BOTTLED BY
FREEMARK ABBEY WINERY, ST. HELENA, CALIFORNIA, U.S.A.
Alcohol 12.5% by volume

WINERY:	E. & J. Gallo
WINE NAME:	**Chardonnay, Limited Release**
ORIGIN:	California
VINTAGE: N.V.	RATING: 16
ALCOHOL:	12.5 percent

TASTING NOTES: Pale straw color. Lightly spiced nose with citric and smoky elements. Medium body, textured, with elegant citric flavors. Fruit intensifies with breathing—this wine must be waited for. Firm finish. It is Ernest and Julio Gallo's first entry in the premium-wine sweepstakes, proving that the nation's largest winery, producing over a million cases per week, can rise above the jug-wine level.

DATE TASTED:

WINERY ADDRESS: 600 Yosemite Boulevard Modesto, CA 95353   (209) 579-3111

WINERY VISITS: Gallo does not offer tours or tastings to the public.

PERSONAL NOTES:

LIMITED RELEASE
CHARDONNAY
of California

THE WINE CELLARS OF

ERNEST & JULIO GALLO

ERNEST AND JULIO GALLO VINTED AND CELLARED
THIS WINE AND BOTTLED IT IN
MODESTO, CALIF.

WINERY:	Geyser Peak Winery
WINE NAME:	**Chardonnay**
ORIGIN:	Sonoma County, Los Carneros
VINTAGE: 1982	**RATING:** 15
ALCOHOL: 12.5 percent	
TASTING NOTES:	Pale straw color. Fresh apple nose with honeydew melon notes and a touch of vanilla bean. Appley flavor with slightly earthy undertone, though not aggressive. Crisp texture. Austere in the mouth, with an elusive, short finish.
DATE TASTED:	
WINERY ADDRESS:	22281 Chianti Road Geyserville, CA 95441 (707) 433-6585
WINERY VISITS:	10 AM–5 PM. Appt. not req. No credit cards.
PERSONAL NOTES:	

WINERY:	Grgich Hills Cellar
WINE NAME:	**Chardonnay**
ORIGIN:	Napa Valley
VINTAGE: 1982	**RATING:** 18
ALCOHOL: 13.4 percent	
TASTING NOTES:	Pale brass color. Fruity, smoky nose. Huge, full, smoky, toasty, rich Chardonnay that virtually explodes in the mouth. Classic Grgich. Mouth-filling, with a long, complex finish. Fruit is extremely concentrated, balancing strong French oak. Another blockbuster from Mike Grgich, though probably too intense and concentrated for some tasters.
DATE TASTED:	
WINERY ADDRESS:	1829 St. Helena Highway Rutherford, CA 94573 (707) 963-2784
WINERY VISITS:	9:30 AM–4:30 PM. Appt. not req. No credit cards.
PERSONAL NOTES:	

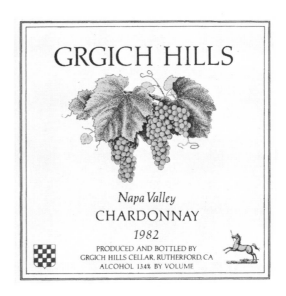

CHARDONNAY

WINERY:	Grgich Hills Cellar
WINE NAME:	**Chardonnay**
ORIGIN:	Napa Valley
VINTAGE: 1983	**RATING:** 19
ALCOHOL: 13.3 percent	

TASTING NOTES: Medium straw color. Fully blown, ripe, fruity, slightly oaky nose. Big, chewy texture. Rich, opulent, minty, spicy flavor, with a long, complex finish. Less concentrated than some of Mike Grgich's previous offerings, but more elegant and stylish and still a very big Chardonnay. This one is clearly in the very structured, very concentrated style that is a Grgich hallmark. It will be a big hit with the Grgich fan club.

DATE TASTED:

WINERY ADDRESS: 1829 St. Helena Highway
Rutherford, CA 94573   (707) 963-2784

WINERY VISITS: 9:30 AM–4:30 PM. Appt. not req. No credit cards.

PERSONAL NOTES:

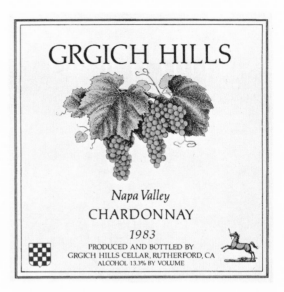

GRGICH HILLS

Napa Valley
CHARDONNAY
1983
PRODUCED AND BOTTLED BY
GRGICH HILLS CELLAR, RUTHERFORD, CA
ALCOHOL 13.3% BY VOLUME

WINERY:	Guenoc Winery
WINE NAME:	**Chardonnay**
ORIGIN:	North Coast
VINTAGE: 1983	**RATING:** 16
ALCOHOL: 13.6 percent	

TASTING NOTES: Medium straw color. Smoky, vanilla-extract nose. Oaky, buttery, chewy. Much character, though perhaps a touch more oak than ideal. Orville and Bob Magoon, descendants of a Scottish sea captain who settled in Hawaii, traded acreage in downtown Honolulu for the Guenoc Ranch in a tax deal. The Guenoc winery building is the largest structure of any kind in rural Lake County.

DATE TASTED:

WINERY ADDRESS: 21000 Butts Canyon Road
Middletown, CA 95461   (707) 987-2385

WINERY VISITS: Thurs.–Sun. 10 AM–4:30 PM. Appt. not req. Credit cards.

PERSONAL NOTES:

Guenoc

1983
North Coast
Chardonnay

Produced and Bottled by Guenoc Winery
Middletown, California Alcohol 13.6% by Volume

WINERY:	Gundlach-Bundschu Winery
WINE NAME:	**Chardonnay, Special Selection**
ORIGIN:	Sonoma Valley, Sangiacomo Ranch
VINTAGE: 1982	**RATING:** 17
ALCOHOL: 14.4 percent	
TASTING NOTES:	Pale straw color. Smoky, fruity nose, concentrated, with creamy accents. Chewy, textured, big. Full, round, smoky, creamy, toasty flavor. A stylish, big Chardonnay from an old-line Sonoma producer. Jim Bundschu, the winemaker, names his special bottlings after the vineyards that yielded the grapes—a good practice. The winery dates back to 1858 and lies in the area known as Vineburg.
DATE TASTED:	
WINERY ADDRESS:	3775 Thornsberry Road Sonoma, CA 95487 (707) 938-5277
WINERY VISITS:	11 AM–4:30 PM. Appt. not req. No credit cards.
PERSONAL NOTES:	

WINERY:	Hacienda Wine Cellars
WINE NAME:	**Chardonnay, Clair de Lune**
ORIGIN:	Sonoma Valley
VINTAGE: 1982	**RATING:** 15
ALCOHOL: 12.9 percent	
TASTING NOTES:	Pale straw color. Smoky nose with vanilla accents. Subtle, austere flavor, with hints of oak and cream, but not assertive. Basically bashful, in the style of Mâcon-Blanc, though with slightly more body. What some would call a proper "food wine." Hacienda is in a historic vineyard planted with European vine cuttings in the 1850s by Count Agoston Haraszthy.
DATE TASTED:	
WINERY ADDRESS:	1000 Vineyard Lane Sonoma, CA 95476 (707) 938-3220
WINERY VISITS:	10 AM–5 PM. Appt. not req. Credit cards.
PERSONAL NOTES:	

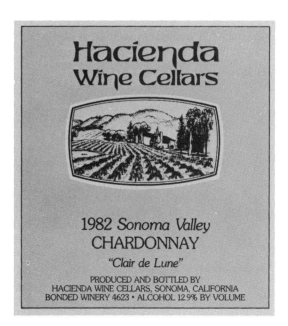

CHARDONNAY

WINERY:	Hagafen Cellars
WINE NAME:	**Chardonnay**
ORIGIN:	Napa Valley, Winery Lake Vineyard
VINTAGE: 1983/5744	**RATING:** 16
ALCOHOL:	13.0 percent
TASTING NOTES:	Straw color. Creamy, fruity nose. Full, firm, textured. Citric flavor accents. Very crisp finish. Slightly tannic, oaky nuances. Somewhere between austere and rich. Hagafen is Hebrew for "the vine." This wine is kosher, produced under the supervision of Rabbi Jacob Traub, and 5744 is the vintage on the Hebrew calendar. There is no such thing as a kosher flavor, and the Hagafen is competitive with other California Chardonnays.
DATE TASTED:	
WINERY ADDRESS:	4195 Silverado Trail Napa, CA 94558 (707) 252-0781
WINERY VISITS:	Appt. req. Credit cards.
PERSONAL NOTES:	

HAGAFEN

הגפן

1983 NAPA VALLEY 5744

CHARDONNAY

WINERY LAKE VINEYARD

PRODUCED & BOTTLED BY HAGAFEN CELLARS, NAPA, CA   ALC. 13.0% BY VOL.

WINERY:	Inglenook Vineyards
WINE NAME:	**Chardonnay**
ORIGIN:	Napa Valley, Estate Bottled
VINTAGE: 1983	**RATING:** 15
ALCOHOL:	12.5 percent
TASTING NOTES:	Light to medium gold color. Buttery, hazelnut nose with vanilla accents. Full-bodied, round, lightly citric flavor, with the same vanilla element carrying through, although lacking texture. Virtually no acid bite in the finish, with little aftertaste. A bit too soft, though quite drinkable, from a winery owned by Heublein and better known for its big, majestic Cabernets.
DATE TASTED:	
WINERY ADDRESS:	1991 St. Helena Highway Rutherford, CA 94573 (707) 963-2616
WINERY VISITS:	10 AM–5 PM. Appt. not req. Credit cards.
PERSONAL NOTES:	

ESTATE   1983   BOTTLED

Inglenook.
V I N E Y A R D S
Chardonnay
NAPA VALLEY

WINERY:	Inglenook Vineyards
WINE NAME:	**Chardonnay, Limited Reserve Selection**
ORIGIN:	Napa Valley, Estate Bottled
VINTAGE: 1983	RATING: 17
ALCOHOL:	12.5 percent

TASTING NOTES:	Pale straw color. Citric/apple nose, very concentrated fruit. Elegant, austere flavor of grapefruit, with oak subdued. Nicely textured. Mâconnais style—it grows on you and becomes more complex as you savor it. Inglenook, along with nearby Beaulieu Vineyard, is part of the Heublein wine empire. Much Heublein capital has gone into Inglenook in recent years, and the wines are on their way up.
DATE TASTED:	
WINERY ADDRESS:	1991 St. Helena Highway Rutherford, CA 94573 (707) 963-2616
WINERY VISITS:	10 AM–5 PM. Appt. not req. Credit cards.
PERSONAL NOTES:	

WINERY:	Iron Horse Vineyards
WINE NAME:	**Chardonnay**
ORIGIN:	Sonoma County, Green Valley, Estate Bottled
VINTAGE: 1983	RATING: 16
ALCOHOL:	12.2 percent

TASTING NOTES:	Straw color. Elegant, lightly oaked vanilla-extract nose. Medium body, fruity, elegant flavor with hints of apples and vanilla nuances. Complex, charming, though flavor could be more concentrated. Basically a bashful Chardonnay, best consumed with lightly flavored seafood.
DATE TASTED:	
WINERY ADDRESS:	9786 Ross Station Road Sebastopol, CA 95472 (707) 887-1507
WINERY VISITS:	Mon.–Fri. 8 AM–5 PM. Appt. req. No credit cards.
PERSONAL NOTES:	

CHARDONNAY

WINERY:	Jekel Vineyard
WINE NAME:	**Chardonnay, Private Reserve**
ORIGIN:	Arroyo Seco, Home Vineyad, Estate Bottled
VINTAGE: 1982	**RATING:** 18
ALCOHOL:	13.0 percent
TASTING NOTES:	Pale gold color. Aromatic nose of fruit with vanilla accents. Big, chewy, sinewy, mouth-filling texture, with restrained cream of oak and citric flavor notes. Butter and concentrated fruit intensify after 15 to 20 minutes of breathing. The bearded Jekel twins, Gus and Bill, are proving that fine wines can be made in the Salinas Valley of Monterey County.
DATE TASTED:	
WINERY ADDRESS:	40155 Walnut Avenue Greenfield, CA 93927 (408) 674-5522
WINERY VISITS:	Thurs.–Mon. 10 AM–5 PM. Appt. not req. Credit cards.
PERSONAL NOTES:	

WINERY:	Robert Keenan Winery
WINE NAME:	**Chardonnay**
ORIGIN:	Napa Valley, Estate Bottled
VINTAGE: 1982	**RATING:** 17
ALCOHOL:	12.9 percent
TASTING NOTES:	Pale straw color. Restrained, lightly fruited nose, with hints of honeydew melon. Creamy, even buttery flavor, but elegant finish. Refined and stylish Chardonnay from one of the wineries on the slopes of Spring Mountain.
DATE TASTED:	
WINERY ADDRESS:	3660 Spring Mountain Road St. Helena, CA 94574 (707) 963-9177
WINERY VISITS:	Mon.–Fri. 8 AM–4 PM. Appt. req. No credit cards.
PERSONAL NOTES:	

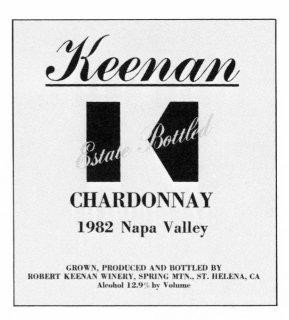

WINERY:	Robert Keenan Winery
WINE NAME:	**Chardonnay**
ORIGIN:	Napa Valley
VINTAGE:	1983 RATING: 14
ALCOHOL:	13.0 percent
TASTING NOTES:	Pale gold color. Light citric nose, with vanilla nuances. Medium body, elegant apple flavor, only a hint of wood evident. Very restrained Chardonnay, lacking the dimension and complexity of a first-rate wine. Keenan has done better.
DATE TASTED:	
WINERY ADDRESS:	3660 Spring Mountain Road St. Helena, CA 94574 (707) 963-9177
WINERY VISITS:	Mon.–Fri. 8 AM–4 PM. Appt. req. No credit cards.
PERSONAL NOTES:	

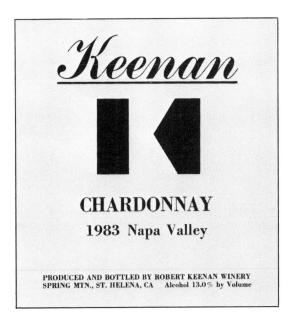

WINERY:	Robert Keenan Winery
WINE NAME:	**Chardonnay**
ORIGIN:	Napa Valley, Estate Bottled
VINTAGE:	1983 RATING: 15
ALCOHOL:	13.0 percent
TASTING NOTES:	Pale gold color. Subtle citric nose with a hint of toast. Elegant, medium-bodied, textured, with oaky overtones. Vanilla emerges after 10 minutes of breathing, but style is basically austere and, like the Keenan non-Estate bottling, there is a certain elusive, diffuse quality that makes the wine less than generous and difficult to get to know.
DATE TASTED:	
WINERY ADDRESS:	3660 Spring Mountain Road St. Helena, CA 94574 (707) 963-9177
WINERY VISITS:	Mon.–Fri. 8 AM–4 PM. Appt. req. No credit cards.
PERSONAL NOTES:	

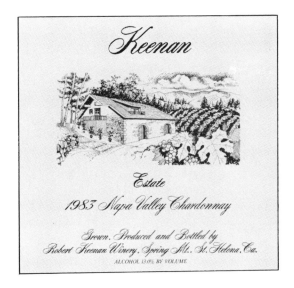

CHARDONNAY

WINERY:	Kendall-Jackson Vineyards and Winery
WINE NAME:	**Chardonnay**
ORIGIN:	California
VINTAGE: 1983	**RATING:** 15
ALCOHOL:	12.6 percent
TASTING NOTES:	Pale straw color. Subtle, austere nose. Appley flavor, but subtle and elegant. Citric nuances. Basically austere Chablis style. Best with shellfish. Clean, but lacking drama. This winery has done better.
DATE TASTED:	
WINERY ADDRESS:	600 Mathews Road Lakeport, CA 95453 (707) 263-9333
WINERY VISITS:	10:30 AM–5:30 PM. Appt. req. Credit cards.
PERSONAL NOTES:	

1983
CALIFORNIA
CHARDONNAY

WINERY:	Kendall-Jackson Vineyards and Winery
WINE NAME:	**Chardonnay, Proprietor's Reserve**
ORIGIN:	60% Napa, 25% Anderson Valley of Mendocino County, 15% Sonoma-Cutrer
VINTAGE: 1983	**RATING:** 16
ALCOHOL:	12.6 percent
TASTING NOTES:	Medium straw color. Subtle nose of almonds with oaky nuances. Intensely fruity flavor—apples and lemons. Creamy overtone. Austere in its youth, but should mature nicely. Proprietor's Reserve designation would indicate more dimension and drama than this wine shows.
DATE TASTED:	
WINERY ADDRESS:	600 Mathews Road Lakeport, CA 95453 (707) 263-9333
WINERY VISITS:	10:30 AM–5:30 PM. Appt. req. Credit cards.
PERSONAL NOTES:	

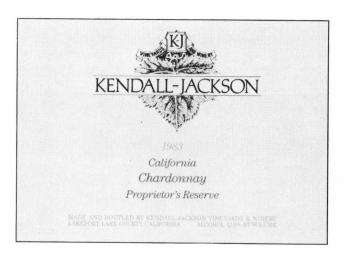

1983
California
Chardonnay
Proprietor's Reserve

WINERY:	Lambert Bridge
WINE NAME:	**Chardonnay**
ORIGIN:	Sonoma County
VINTAGE: 1982	RATING: 17
ALCOHOL: 13.4 percent	

TASTING NOTES:	Light straw color. Very highly perfumed nose with vanilla-bean nuances. Elegant, round, lightly oaky, moderate vanilla-extract flavor. Elegant and stylish, with hints of cream. Nice, stylish Chardonnay from Gerry Lambert, heir to a pharmaceuticals fortune.
DATE TASTED:	
WINERY ADDRESS:	4085 West Dry Creek Road Healdsburg, CA 95448 (707) 433-5855
WINERY VISITS:	Appt. req. No credit cards.
PERSONAL NOTES:	

WINERY:	Laurent-Perrier
WINE NAME:	**Chardonnay Blanc de Blancs**
ORIGIN:	California
VINTAGE: 1982	RATING: 16
ALCOHOL: 12.0 percent	

TASTING NOTES:	Pale straw color. Smoky, slightly citric nose, a Mâconnais scent. Crisp, dry, austere citric flavor. Medium body, elegant, with good acid balance. Reminiscent of the Coteaux Champenois style, which is logical because Laurent-Perrier is a major Champagne producer in France. This wine results from a joint venture between Almadén and Laurent-Perrier. The label says Caves Laurent-Perrier, but the address is Almadén's.
DATE TASTED:	
WINERY ADDRESS:	1530 Blossom Hill Road San Jose, CA 95118 (408) 269-1312
WINERY VISITS:	9 AM–4 PM. Appt. not req. Credit cards.
PERSONAL NOTES:	

CHARDONNAY

WINERY:	Charles Lefranc Cellars
WINE NAME:	**Chardonnay**
ORIGIN:	San Benito County
VINTAGE: 1983	**RATING:** 14
ALCOHOL:	12.0 percent

TASTING NOTES: Medium straw color. Fruity, citric nose. Full-bodied, melony flavor with moderate oak. Would be more interesting with the vanilla and toast associated with new French oak barrels, but fairly stylish anyway. (Lefranc is the name of Almadén's premium line.) Extensive visitor facilities.

DATE TASTED:

WINERY ADDRESS: 1530 Blossom Hill Road San Jose, CA 95118 (408) 269-1312

WINERY VISITS: 9 AM–4 PM. Appt. not req. Credit cards.

PERSONAL NOTES:

WINERY:	Paul Masson Vineyards
WINE NAME:	**Chardonnay**
ORIGIN:	Monterey County, Estate Bottled
VINTAGE: 1983	**RATING:** 15
ALCOHOL:	11.8 percent

TASTING NOTES: Very pale parchment color. Subtly fruity, but restrained, even austere nose. Round, fruity, elegant and flavorful, though not a wine of big character. Oak is very subdued, and creamy elements are lacking. This is the subtle style, but a nicely made wine for consumers who do not want blockbuster Chardonnays.

DATE TASTED:

WINERY ADDRESS: 13150 Saratoga Avenue Saratoga, CA 95070 (408) 257-7800

WINERY VISITS: Fri.–Sun. 10 AM–4 PM. Appt. not req. Credit cards.

PERSONAL NOTES:

WINERY:	Matanzas Creek Winery
WINE NAME:	**Chardonnay**
ORIGIN:	Sonoma County
VINTAGE:	1982 RATING: 15
ALCOHOL:	13.6 percent
TASTING NOTES:	Medium straw color. Oaky nose with smoky accents. Intense oaky flavor with citrus fruit nuances, but oak seems to dominate. Fruit is very subtle and secondary to the wood. A big wine, but unbalanced, although it will please devotees of blockbuster Chardonnays.
DATE TASTED:	
WINERY ADDRESS:	6097 Bennett Valley Road Santa Rosa, CA 95404 (707) 528-6464
WINERY VISITS:	Mon.–Fri. 9 AM–5 PM. Appt. req. No credit cards.
PERSONAL NOTES:	

matanzas CREEK WINERY

1982

SONOMA COUNTY

CHARDONNAY

A TABLE WINE PRODUCED AND BOTTLED BY
MATANZAS CREEK WINERY, SANTA ROSA, CALIF., BW-CA-4848.

WINERY:	Matanzas Creek Winery
WINE NAME:	**Chardonnay**
ORIGIN:	Sonoma Valley, Estate Bottled
VINTAGE:	1982 RATING: 17
ALCOHOL:	13.9 percent
TASTING NOTES:	Medium straw color. Subtle nose, though oaky overtone emerges with breathing. Fruity, citric flavor with challenging oaky background. Complex and long in the mouth, finishing on a high note. Winemaker Merry Edwards, now at Merry Vintners, made this splendid, rich Estate Bottled 1982, but her non-Estate 1982 won more awards despite its greater subtlety.
DATE TASTED:	
WINERY ADDRESS:	6097 Bennett Valley Road Santa Rosa, CA 95404 (707) 528-6464
WINERY VISITS:	Mon.–Fri. 9 AM–5 PM. Appt. req. No credit cards.
PERSONAL NOTES:	

matanzas CREEK WINERY

1982

Estate Bottled
SONOMA VALLEY

CHARDONNAY

A TABLE WINE PRODUCED AND BOTTLED BY
MATANZAS CREEK WINERY, SANTA ROSA, CALIF., BW-CA-4848.

CHARDONNAY

WINERY:	McDowell Valley Vineyards
WINE NAME:	**Chardonnay**
ORIGIN:	McDowell Valley, Estate Bottled
VINTAGE: 1981	**RATING:** 16
ALCOHOL: 13.1 percent	

TASTING NOTES: Medium gold color. Restrained, lightly oaked bouquet. Spicy, melony flavor, with vanilla nuances. Chewy texure, with oaky notes in the aftertaste. A pleasing Chardonnay from the nation's first solar-powered winery, built by Karen and Richard Keehn in the verdant McDowell Valley, at the southern tip of Mendocino County. Located north of the better known Napa/Sonoma region, it is well worth a detour.

DATE TASTED:

WINERY ADDRESS: 3811 Highway 175
Hopland, CA 95449   (707) 744-1053

WINERY VISITS: 10 AM–5 PM. Appt. req. Credit cards.

PERSONAL NOTES:

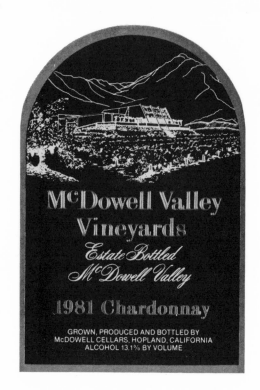

WINERY:	McDowell Valley Vineyards
WINE NAME:	**Chardonnay**
ORIGIN:	McDowell Valley, Estate Bottled
VINTAGE: 1983	**RATING:** 17
ALCOHOL: 13.0 percent	

TASTING NOTES: Medium straw color. Concentrated vanilla-extract nose, with oaky notes. Firm, crisp texture. Vanilla and cream flavor with toasty elements. Superb extract, chewy fruit, strong oak. Perhaps too much oak as the wine evolves over time, but complex and beguiling in its youth. A serious Chardonnay from the first solar-powered winery, a pleasant drive north from the Napa/Sonoma region into Mendocino County.

DATE TASTED:

WINERY ADDRESS: 3811 Highway 175
Hopland, CA 95449   (707) 744-1053

WINERY VISITS: 10 AM–5 PM. Appt. req. Credit cards.

PERSONAL NOTES:

WINERY:	Michtom Vineyards
WINE NAME:	**Chardonnay**
ORIGIN:	Alexander Valley, Sonoma County
VINTAGE: 1983	RATING: 16
ALCOHOL:	12.0 percent
TASTING NOTES:	Medium straw color, gold highlights. Full, rich, vanilla-bean nose, laden with fruit. Ripe, full, textured yet lean citric flavor. Elusive. Much charm up front, but finishes short. Perhaps better with a little more bottle age. Not in the same category as the Michtom Cabernet, an extraordinary wine. Michtom Vineyards is a brand name for wines produced by Jimark Winery, named after partners Jim Wolner and Mark Michtom.
DATE TASTED:	
WINERY ADDRESS:	Jimark Winery, 602 Limerick Lane Healdsburg, CA 95448 (707) 433-3118
WINERY VISITS:	Wed.–Sun. 10 AM–4 PM. Appt. not req. No credit cards.
PERSONAL NOTES:	

WINERY:	Robert Mondavi Winery
WINE NAME:	**Chardonnay**
ORIGIN:	Napa Valley
VINTAGE: 1983	RATING: 17
ALCOHOL:	13.5 percent
TASTING NOTES:	Straw color, with greenish glints. Restrained, lightly toasty nose with fruity underlay. Crisp, firm texture. Flavor of citrus fruit and apples. Full-bodied yet not big. Basically elegant, though the texture is chewy, adding to the impression of character. Less rich, less creamy than some past Mondavi efforts, but a good, clean wine from one of California's foremost producers. Extensive visitor facilities and tours.
DATE TASTED:	
WINERY ADDRESS:	7801 St. Helena Highway St. Helena, CA 94562 (707) 963-9611
WINERY VISITS:	9 AM–5 PM. Appt. not req. Credit cards.
PERSONAL NOTES:	

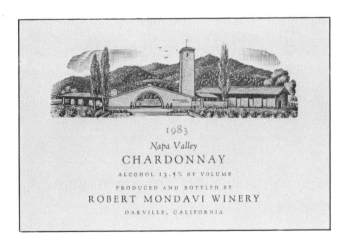

CHARDONNAY

WINERY:	R. Montali Winery
WINE NAME:	**Chardonnay**
ORIGIN:	Santa Maria Valley
VINTAGE: 1982	**RATING:** 16
ALCOHOL:	13.3 percent
TASTING NOTES:	Medium gold color. Melony nose with banana undertone. Fruity, citric flavor of grapefruit accented by the prickle of acidity and oaky notes. Tight, crisp finish. Structure of a Chablis, with the personality of a Mâcon-Blanc. Pleasant, but lacking complexity.
DATE TASTED:	
WINERY ADDRESS:	600 Addison Street Berkeley, CA 94710 (415) 540-5551
WINERY VISITS:	Noon–6 PM. Appt. not req. Credit cards.
PERSONAL NOTES:	

Montali

Chardonnay

Santa Maria Valley

1982

Produced and Bottled by R. Montali Winery
Berkeley, California BW4562
Alcohol 13.3% By Volume

WINERY:	Monticello Cellars
WINE NAME:	**Chardonnay**
ORIGIN:	Napa Valley, Jefferson Ranch, Estate Bottled
VINTAGE: 1983	**RATING:** 17
ALCOHOL:	12.5 percent
TASTING NOTES:	Medium straw color. Muted, subtle nose with a hint of oak. Full in body yet sleek at the same time. Crisp, ripe, lightly buttery, with a nuance of toast. Subtle without being austere. A stylish Chardonnay.
DATE TASTED:	
WINERY ADDRESS:	4242 Big Ranch Road Napa, CA 94558 (707) 253-2802
WINERY VISITS:	10 AM–4 PM. Appt. not req. Credit cards.
PERSONAL NOTES:	

Estate 1983 Bottled

Monticello
CELLARS

JEFFERSON RANCH
1983
NAPA VALLEY
Chardonnay

Grown, produced and bottled by
MONTICELLO CELLARS, NAPA, CALIFORNIA, USA
B.W. 5102   Alcohol 12.5% by volume   Contents 750 ml.

WINERY:	J.W. Morris Winery
WINE NAME:	**Chardonnay**
ORIGIN:	Sonoma County, Alexander Valley
VINTAGE:	1983 RATING: 16
ALCOHOL:	13.1 percent

TASTING NOTES: Pale straw color. Subtle nose, with a hint of apples. Very fruity and concentrated flavor, with oak suppressed and subtle. Firm, clean, nicely balanced and elegant Chardonnay from a winery that initially made its reputation on California Port. But Port is out of fashion, and Morris now is almost entirely in table wines.

DATE TASTED:

WINERY ADDRESS: 101 Grant Avenue
Healdsburg, CA 95448 (707) 431-7015

WINERY VISITS: 8 AM–5 PM. Appt. req. No credit cards.

PERSONAL NOTES:

WINERY:	J.W. Morris Winery
WINE NAME:	**Chardonnay, Black Mountain Vineyard**
ORIGIN:	Sonoma County, Alexander Valley
VINTAGE:	1983 RATING: 17
ALCOHOL:	13.0 percent

TASTING NOTES: Pale straw color. Subtly fruity nose with hint of apple. Concentrated citric flavor with creamy notes and great structure. Oaky accents provide hints of toast. A single-vineyard bottling from Morris, once known mostly for its California Ports. This bottling signals a shift to a new name by Morris, although J.W. Morris remains the winery's name for business purposes.

DATE TASTED:

WINERY ADDRESS: 101 Grant Avenue
Healdsburg, CA 95448 (707) 431-7015

WINERY VISITS: 8 AM–5 PM. Appt. req. No credit cards.

PERSONAL NOTES:

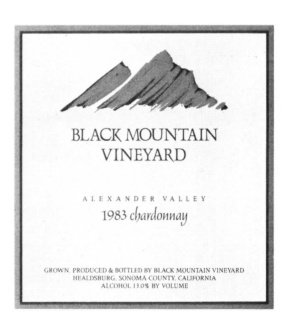

CHARDONNAY

WINERY:	J. Pedroncelli Winery
WINE NAME:	**Chardonnay**
ORIGIN:	Sonoma County
VINTAGE: 1983	**RATING:** 15
ALCOHOL:	12.5 percent

TASTING NOTES: Medium straw color. Subtly smoky, restrained nose with toasty accents. Medium body, crisp, very firm yet austere fruit. Nuances of lemon, but basically short on fruit and structure. Very dry and pleasant, if lacking in concentration and complexity. Oak dominates aftertaste.

DATE TASTED:

WINERY ADDRESS: 1220 Canyon Road
Geyserville, CA 95441   (707) 857-3531

WINERY VISITS: 10 AM–5 PM. Appt. not req. Credit cards.

PERSONAL NOTES:

J. PEDRONCELLI
SONOMA COUNTY
CHARDONNAY
1983

12½% ALC./VOL.
PRODUCED AND BOTTLED BY J. PEDRONCELLI WINERY
GEYSERVILLE, SONOMA COUNTY, CALIFORNIA, U.S.A.

WINERY:	Quail Ridge
WINE NAME:	**Chardonnay**
ORIGIN:	Napa Valley
VINTAGE: 1982	**RATING:** 16
ALCOHOL:	13.1 percent

TASTING NOTES: Very pale straw color. Subtly smoky nose. Elegantly fruity flavor, with only hints of oak—complex but lean. Not strongly fruity. A Chardonnay of austere, even bashful personality from Quail Ridge. Breaks with Quail Ridge tradition, confusing to Quail Ridge devotees who expect big, buttery wines of character and complexity. No flaws in the winemaking with this one, but the stylistic change is abrupt.

DATE TASTED:

WINERY ADDRESS: 1055 Atlas Peak Road
Napa, CA 94558   (707) 226-2728

WINERY VISITS: Mon.–Fri. 9 AM–4 PM; weekends from 11 AM. Appt. req. No credit cards.

PERSONAL NOTES:

Quail Ridge
1982
Napa Valley
CHARDONNAY

Cellared and Bottled by Quail Ridge
Napa, California 94558
ALCOHOL 13.1 % BY VOLUME

WINERY:	Raymond Vineyard and Cellar
WINE NAME:	**Chardonnay**
ORIGIN:	California
VINTAGE: 1983	**RATING:** 15
ALCOHOL:	13.1 percent

TASTING NOTES: Brassy color. Smoky, oaky nose. Round, chewy, crisp, but lower level of fruit than expected. The Raymond California appellation is not up to its Napa appellation. Roy Raymond Sr. broke off from Beringer Vineyards when Nestlé acquired it. He established the Raymond Vineyard on Zinfandel Lane in 1974; now brothers Roy Jr. and Walter are in charge.

DATE TASTED:

WINERY ADDRESS: 849 Zinfandel Lane
St. Helena, CA 94574   (707) 963-3141

WINERY VISITS: 10 AM–4 PM. Appt. not req. No credit cards.

PERSONAL NOTES:

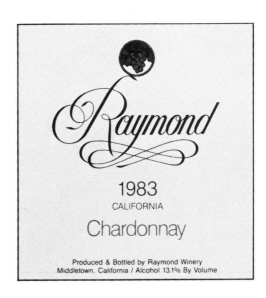

1983
CALIFORNIA
Chardonnay

Produced & Bottled by Raymond Winery
Middletown, California / Alcohol 13.1% By Volume

WINERY:	Raymond Vineyard and Cellar
WINE NAME:	**Chardonnay**
ORIGIN:	Napa Valley
VINTAGE: 1983	**RATING:** 16
ALCOHOL:	13.4 percent

TASTING NOTES: Pale gold color. Toasty nose, hint of honey. Rich, round, toasty flavor with vanilla nuances. Somewhat flabby texture, suggesting relatively low acidity; the oak from the barrels has not yet melded with the fruit and is thus a bit obvious. A good wine from a winery demonstrably capable of making great wines.

DATE TASTED:

WINERY ADDRESS: 849 Zinfandel Lane
St. Helena, CA 94574   (707) 963-3141

WINERY VISITS: 10 AM–4 PM. Appt. not req. No credit cards.

PERSONAL NOTES:

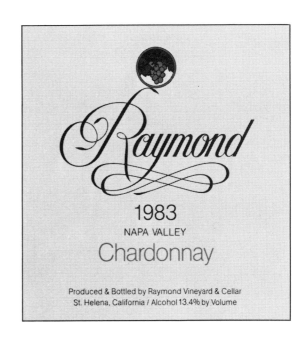

1983
NAPA VALLEY
Chardonnay

Produced & Bottled by Raymond Vineyard & Cellar
St. Helena, California / Alcohol 13.4% by Volume

CHARDONNAY

WINERY:	Rombauer Vineyards
WINE NAME:	**Chardonnay**
ORIGIN:	California
VINTAGE: 1983	**RATING:** 17
ALCOHOL:	13.4 percent

TASTING NOTES: Medium gold color. Buttery, oaky, perfumed nose with honeysuckle nuances. Round yet firm texture. Citric, lemony flavor accented by oak and hints of cream. More elegant and austere than the nose implies. Very fine effort by Koerner Rombauer, an airline pilot who has established a custom-crush winery. Early customers included Christian Moueix of Château Pétrus, who made his early vintages of Dominus there.

DATE TASTED:

WINERY ADDRESS: 3522 Silverado Trail
St. Helena, CA 94574 (707) 963-5170

WINERY VISITS: Mon.–Fri. 8:30 AM–5 PM. Appt. req. No credit cards.

PERSONAL NOTES:

WINERY:	Rutherford Hill Winery
WINE NAME:	**Chardonnay**
ORIGIN:	Napa Valley, Jaeger Vineyards
VINTAGE: 1983	**RATING:** 17
ALCOHOL:	13.8 percent

TASTING NOTES: Medium straw color, glints of gold. Subtly smoky nose. Crisp, chewy texture, full body. Subtly citric flavor with complex vanilla accents. Stylish wine from a facility owned by some of the same people behind Freemark Abbey.

DATE TASTED:

WINERY ADDRESS: 200 Rutherford Hill Road
St. Helena, CA 94574 (707) 963-9694

WINERY VISITS: 10:30 AM–4:30 PM. Appt. not req. Credit cards.

PERSONAL NOTES:

WINERY:	Sanford Winery
WINE NAME:	**Chardonnay**
ORIGIN:	Central Coast
VINTAGE: 1984	RATING: 18
ALCOHOL:	12.8 percent

TASTING NOTES: Medium straw color. Ripe vanilla-bean nose. Rich, buttery flavor. Big and fleshy but complex. Extremely concentrated vanilla-extract and toasty taste keeps challenging the palate. Long, beguiling finish. Much high-quality oak in this wine, but ample fruit to carry it, which creates an overall impression of drama and complexity. Splendid effort by Richard Sanford.

DATE TASTED:

WINERY ADDRESS: 7250 Santa Rosa Road
Buellton, CA 93427   (805) 688-3300

WINERY VISITS: Mon.–Fri. 10 AM–4 PM. Appt. req. No credit cards.

PERSONAL NOTES:

WINERY:	Sebastiani Vineyards
WINE NAME:	**Chardonnay**
ORIGIN:	Sonoma Valley
VINTAGE: 1983	RATING: 15
ALCOHOL:	13.3 percent

TASTING NOTES: Medium straw color, glints of gold. Subtle, smoky nose, with buttery nuances. Crisp, firm texture. Moderately oaky flavor with subtle, fruity, lemony undertone. Basically elegant. Long finish and creamy accents, though lacking breadth and richness. A sleek effort by Sam Sebastiani, who began focusing greater attention on premium varietals after his father, August, died in 1980. The winery is a major Sonoma tourist stop.

DATE TASTED:

WINERY ADDRESS: 389 Fourth Street East
Sonoma, CA 95476   (707) 938-5532

WINERY VISITS: 10 AM–5 PM. Appt. not req. Credit cards.

PERSONAL NOTES:

CHARDONNAY

WINERY:	Shafer Vineyards
WINE NAME:	**Chardonnay**
ORIGIN:	Napa Valley
VINTAGE: 1982	**RATING:** 17
ALCOHOL:	13.0 percent
TASTING NOTES:	Medium gold color. Buttery/vanilla-extract nose. Rich, full, round, creamy flavor with oaky overtones. Very crisp finish. Clean and racy, with citric elements beneath the woody veneer. Excellent white from John Shafer, who is better known for his Cabernets made in the Stag's Leap area of the Napa Valley.
DATE TASTED:	
WINERY ADDRESS:	6154 Silverado Trail Napa, CA 94558 (707) 944-2877
WINERY VISITS:	8 AM–5 PM. Appt. req. No credit cards.
PERSONAL NOTES:	

WINERY:	Shafer Vineyards
WINE NAME:	**Chardonnay**
ORIGIN:	Napa Valley
VINTAGE: 1983	**RATING:** 18
ALCOHOL:	13.5 percent
TASTING NOTES:	Medium straw color, brassy glints. Elegant, light vanilla-extract nose—very concentrated. Buttery flavor filled with fruit extract, almost like butterscotch though not sweet. Oak seems well integrated into fruit. Flavor grows and develops with breathing, as the wine becomes more complex. Long, clean, crisp finish. A very stylish Chardonnay from an emerging producer in the Stag's Leap area of the Napa Valley.
DATE TASTED:	
WINERY ADDRESS:	6154 Silverado Trail Napa, CA 94558 (707) 944-2877
WINERY VISITS:	8 AM–5 PM. Appt. req. No credit cards.
PERSONAL NOTES:	

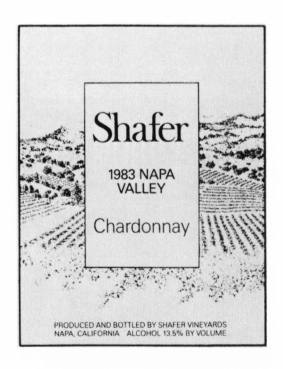

WINERY:	Simi Winery
WINE NAME:	**Chardonnay**
ORIGIN:	Sonoma County
VINTAGE:	1982 RATING: 17
ALCOHOL:	13.3 percent
TASTING NOTES:	Golden hue. Concentrated vanilla-extract nose with an oaky overtone. Rich, full, complex, buttery flavor. Toasty, smoky accents, with an alcoholic finish. A big, ripe Chardonnay. The woody nuances add drama and dimension, but the fruit is less concentrated than some earlier efforts of Zelma Long, the Simi winemaker, from Mendocino grapes.
DATE TASTED:	
WINERY ADDRESS:	16275 Healdsburg Avenue Healdsburg, CA 95448 (707) 433-6981
WINERY VISITS:	10 AM–4:30 PM. Appt. not req. Credit cards.
PERSONAL NOTES:	

WINERY:	Sonoma Vineyards
WINE NAME:	**Chardonnay, Rodney Strong**
ORIGIN:	Russian River Valley, River West Vineyard
VINTAGE:	1981 RATING: 16
ALCOHOL:	13.9 percent
TASTING NOTES:	Medium straw color with gold glints. Buttery, vanilla nose with citric accents. Firm, oaky flavor with toasty background. Citric flavor emerges with breathing, though oak is strong. Rod Strong, winemaker, is now emphasizing his own name on labels. Strong is a former Broadway dancer and choreographer who went west to make wine.
DATE TASTED:	
WINERY ADDRESS:	11455 Old Redwood Highway Healdsburg, CA 95448 (707) 433-6511
WINERY VISITS:	10 AM–5 PM. Appt. not req. Credit cards.
PERSONAL NOTES:	

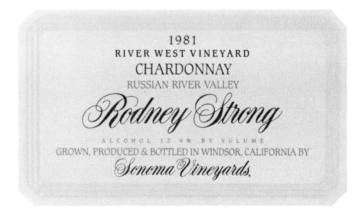

CHARDONNAY

WINERY:	Sonoma-Cutrer Vineyards
WINE NAME:	**Chardonnay**
ORIGIN:	Sonoma County, Russian River Valley, Cutrer Vineyard, Estate Bottled
VINTAGE: 1982	**RATING:** 18
ALCOHOL:	13.2 percent
TASTING NOTES:	Pale gold color. Concentrated vanilla-bean nose. Very intensely flavored, full, rich, oaky, yet with ample fruit to carry the oak. Chewy texture. A big, opulent Chardonnay with great character and abundant fruit. Splendid effort from Bill Bonetti at a winery that dates only from 1981.
DATE TASTED:	
WINERY ADDRESS:	4401 Slusser Road Windsor, CA 95492 (707) 528-1181
WINERY VISITS:	Appt. req. No credit cards.
PERSONAL NOTES:	

CUTRER VINEYARD

SONOMA-CUTRER

1982

RUSSIAN RIVER VALLEY
CHARDONNAY

ESTATE GROWN & BOTTLED BY SONOMA-CUTRER VINEYARDS, WINDSOR, CA. TABLE WINE.

WINERY:	Sterling Vineyards
WINE NAME:	**Chardonnay**
ORIGIN:	Napa Valley, Estate Bottled
VINTAGE: 1982	**RATING:** 17
ALCOHOL:	13.0 percent
TASTING NOTES:	Pale gold color. Subtly smoky nose with vanilla traces. Textured, Mâconnais style. Austere yet stylish. Citric accents, creamy notes. Crisp finish. An elegantly balanced wine from one of the more spectacular Napa Valley wineries. An aerial tramway carries visitors up to the white stucco winery, which offers a commanding view of the northern Napa. Extensive tourist facilities.
DATE TASTED:	
WINERY ADDRESS:	1111 Dunaweal Lane Calistoga, CA 94515 (707) 942-5151
WINERY VISITS:	10:30 AM–4:30 PM. Appt. not req. Credit cards.
PERSONAL NOTES:	

STERLING VINEYARDS

ESTATE BOTTLED

1982

Chardonnay

NAPA VALLEY

GROWN, PRODUCED AND BOTTLED BY
STERLING VINEYARDS
CALISTOGA, NAPA VALLEY, CA • ALC. 13% BY VOL.

WINERY:	Stonegate Winery
WINE NAME:	**Chardonnay**
ORIGIN:	Napa Valley
VINTAGE:	1982 RATING: 16
ALCOHOL:	12.3 percent
TASTING NOTES:	Medium gold color, greenish glints. Subtly smoky, fruity nose. Firm, crisp texture. Very dry with citric, even lemony, undertone and creamy accents, though basically a subtle, restrained Chardonnay that would be perfect with shellfish.
DATE TASTED:	
WINERY ADDRESS:	1183 Dunaweal Lane Calistoga, CA 94515 (707) 942-6500
WINERY VISITS:	10:30 AM–4 PM. Appt. not req. Credit cards.
PERSONAL NOTES:	

STONEGATE

1982
NAPA VALLEY
CHARDONNAY

PRODUCED AND BOTTLED BY STONEGATE WINERY
CALISTOGA, NAPA VALLEY, CALIFORNIA, B.W. 4640
ALCOHOL 12.3 % BY VOLUME

WINERY:	Stonegate Winery
WINE NAME:	**Chardonnay**
ORIGIN:	Napa Valley, Spaulding Vineyard
VINTAGE:	1982 RATING: 17
ALCOHOL:	13.5 percent
TASTING NOTES:	Golden straw color. Ripe, citric nose with vanilla accents. Round, firm, full texture. Oaky overtone in the flavor, with citric undertone. Very stylish, though fruit is submerged. Buttery elements come out with breathing. A firm, tight, Mâconnais-style Chardonnay as the premium bottling from Stonegate, founded in 1973 by Jim and Barbara Spaulding.
DATE TASTED:	
WINERY ADDRESS:	1183 Dunaweal Lane Calistoga, CA 94515 (707) 942-6500
WINERY VISITS:	10:30 AM–4 PM. Appt. not req. Credit cards.
PERSONAL NOTES:	

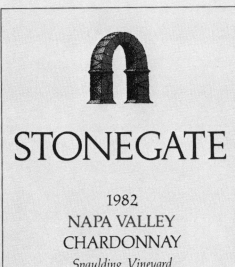

STONEGATE

1982
NAPA VALLEY
CHARDONNAY
Spaulding Vineyard

PRODUCED AND BOTTLED BY STONEGATE WINERY
CALISTOGA, NAPA VALLEY, CALIFORNIA, B.W. 4640
ALCOHOL 13.5 % BY VOLUME

CHARDONNAY

WINERY:	Trefethen Vineyards
WINE NAME:	**Chardonnay**
ORIGIN:	Napa Valley
VINTAGE: 1983	**RATING:** 16
ALCOHOL:	13.0 percent

TASTING NOTES: Very pale straw color. Smoky, fruity nose with vanilla-bean nuances. Very crisp, almost tart. Hints of creamy flavor, but basic impression is of high-acid crispness in the austere style of Chablis. Good backbone for aging, but somewhat sharp and elusive in youth. John and Janet Trefethen, proprietors of this landmark winery, won world acclaim for their 1976 Chardonnay. Subsequent vintages have been less rich and dramatic.

DATE TASTED:

WINERY ADDRESS: 1160 Oak Knoll Avenue
Napa, CA 94558   (707) 255-7700

WINERY VISITS: 10 AM–4 PM. Appt. req. No credit cards.

PERSONAL NOTES:

Trefethen
VINEYARDS

NAPA VALLEY 1983
CHARDONNAY

GROWN, PRODUCED & BOTTLED BY
TREFETHEN VINEYARDS
NAPA, CALIFORNIA, U.S.A.

ALCOHOL 13.0% BY VOLUME

WINERY:	Mark West Vineyards
WINE NAME:	**Chardonnay**
ORIGIN:	Sonoma County, Russian River Valley, Estate Bottled
VINTAGE: 1982	**RATING:** 16
ALCOHOL:	13.2 percent

TASTING NOTES: Light golden hue. Lightly oaked, smoky nose, with apple notes. Rich, full, ripe, appley flavor with citric nuances. Textured and crisp, slightly diffuse. This wine was half barrel-fermented and half steel tank–fermented, and then it was aged in small French oak barrels for six months.

DATE TASTED:

WINERY ADDRESS: 7000 Trenton Healdsburg Road
Forestville, CA 95436   (707) 544-4813

WINERY VISITS: 10 AM–5 PM. Appt. not req. Credit cards.

PERSONAL NOTES:

Mark West Vineyards

Estate Bottled

1982
Russian River Valley
CHARDONNAY
GROWN, PRODUCED & BOTTLED BY MARK WEST
VINEYARDS, FORESTVILLE, SONOMA COUNTY, CA
ALCOHOL 13.2% BY VOLUME

Marcus West was a Sonoma County pioneer. The Mark West Creek, which was named after him, provides our vineyards with water for frost protection.

Harvested between 9/27 and 9/29/82, at 23.0° Brix and 1.043 g/100 ml acid. This wine was 50% barrel, and 50% stainless steel tank fermented, and then all aged 6 months in French oak barrels.

WINERY:	William Wheeler Vineyards
WINE NAME:	**Chardonnay**
ORIGIN:	Sonoma County
VINTAGE: 1983	RATING: 17
ALCOHOL: 13.0 percent	

TASTING NOTES: Medium straw color. Concentrated nose of vanilla extract and grapefruit. Citric flavor with oaky accents and a crisp finish. Big, chewy texture. Clean finish. A well-made Chardonnay with a charming personality. Stylish.

DATE TASTED:

WINERY ADDRESS: 130 Plaza Street
Healdsburg, CA 95448   (707) 433-8786

WINERY VISITS: Appt. req. No credit cards.

PERSONAL NOTES:

1983

Wm. Wheeler

Sonoma County
CHARDONNAY

WINERY:	Stephen Zellerbach Vineyard
WINE NAME:	**Chardonnay**
ORIGIN:	Alexander Valley
VINTAGE: 1983	RATING: 17
ALCOHOL: 13.2 percent	

TASTING NOTES: Medium straw color. Concentrated, melony nose with toasty nuances. Big, structured, powerful Chardonnay filled with fruit and oak. Chewy texture, crisp finish. Much character, though the oak will begin to dominate the fruit in 1986. Stephen Zellerbach is the nephew of the late ambassador to Italy James D. Zellerbach, who founded Hanzell Vineyards, another small Sonoma Valley winery.

DATE TASTED:

WINERY ADDRESS: 4611 Thomas Road
Healdsburg, CA 95448
(707) 433-WINE

WINERY VISITS: 10 AM–5 PM. Appt. not req. Credit cards.

PERSONAL NOTES:

Stephen Zellerbach Vineyard

ALEXANDER VALLEY
CHARDONNAY
1983

PRODUCED AND BOTTLED BY STEPHEN ZELLERBACH VINEYARD
HEALDSBURG, SONOMA COUNTY, CALIFORNIA · ALC. 13.2% BY VOL.

CHENIN BLANC

One of the principal grapes of the Loire Valley of France is the Chenin Blanc, which is responsible for the wines of Vouvray and Saumur, among others. It is also called Pineau de la Loire.

In California the Chenin Blanc has been cultivated increasingly as an alternative to Chardonnay, although no one would suggest that it can compete with the Chardonnay in terms of grace, finesse and elegance. The Chenin Blanc tends to be earthier and often displays a grassy or herbaceous character. It is also used to produce California sparkling wines bearing the champagne name.

WINERY:	Alexander Valley Vineyards
WINE NAME:	**Dry Chenin Blanc**
ORIGIN:	Alexander Valley, Estate Bottled
VINTAGE: 1984	RATING: 15
ALCOHOL: 12.7 percent	

TASTING NOTES: Pale straw color. Subtle, restrained nose, barely a hint of fruit. Round, full, elegant Chenin, lacking aggressive herbaceous elements of some others. Pleasant but simple, and actually dry, as opposed to some so-called "dry" Chenins that are actually somewhat sweet.

DATE TASTED:

WINERY ADDRESS: 8644 Highway 128
Healdsburg, CA 95448   (707) 433-7209

WINERY VISITS: 10 AM–5 PM. Appt. not req. Credit cards.

PERSONAL NOTES:

Alexander Valley

Estate   Bottled

Vineyards ®

1984

ALEXANDER VALLEY

Dry Chenin Blanc

PRODUCED AND BOTTLED BY
ALEXANDER VALLEY WINERY CO.
ALEXANDER VALLEY, HEALDSBURG, CALIFORNIA
ALCOHOL 12.7% BY VOLUME
RESIDUAL SUGAR 0.10% BY WEIGHT

WINERY:	Bandiera Winery
WINE NAME:	**Chenin Blanc**
ORIGIN:	Napa County
VINTAGE: 1984	RATING: 15
ALCOHOL: 11.8 percent	

TASTING NOTES: Very pale straw color. Light, smoky nose, with a hint of vegetation. Firm, chewy texture. Pleasant, herbaceous flavor, but not aggressive. Finishes slightly sweet at 0.85% residual sugar, but could be used with most seafood meals. Simple but charming.

DATE TASTED:

WINERY ADDRESS: 555 South Cloverdale Boulevard
Cloverdale, CA 95425   (707) 894-4298

WINERY VISITS: 10 AM–5 PM. Appt. not req. Credit cards.

PERSONAL NOTES:

Bandiera
Chenin Blanc 1984
Napa County

Produced & Bottled by Bandiera Winery, Cloverdale, CA
BW3998. ALC. 11.8% VOL.

CHENIN BLANC

WINERY:	Callaway Vineyard and Winery
WINE NAME:	**Chenin Blanc-Dry**
ORIGIN:	Temecula
VINTAGE: 1984	**RATING:** 14
ALCOHOL: 12.4 percent	
TASTING NOTES:	Pale straw color. Lightly fruity nose, smoky nuances. Fruity flavor with crisp texture and a hint of sweetness, indicating the wine is not quite bone-dry. No hint of oak. Simple but pleasant white from southern California.
DATE TASTED:	
WINERY ADDRESS:	32720 Rancho California Road Temecula, CA 92390 (714) 676-4001
WINERY VISITS:	10 AM–5 PM. Appt. not req. Credit cards.
PERSONAL NOTES:	

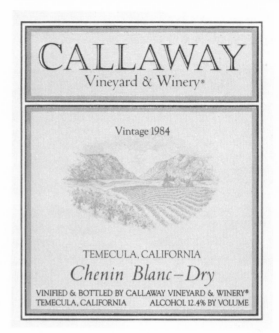

WINERY:	Dry Creek Vineyard
WINE NAME:	**Dry Chenin Blanc**
ORIGIN:	Sonoma County
VINTAGE: 1984	**RATING:** 15
ALCOHOL: 12.5 percent	
TASTING NOTES:	Straw color. Fruity, subtle, mildly smoky nose. Fruity, firm, almost elegant flavor, with slight sweetness masked by clean finish. Pleasant semi-dry white, lacking complexity but typical of the varietal. Slightly vegetal notes. The winemaker, David Stare, knows what he's doing.
DATE TASTED:	
WINERY ADDRESS:	3770 Lambert Bridge Road Healdsburg, CA 95448 (707) 443-1000
WINERY VISITS:	10:30 AM–4:30 PM. Appt. not req. Credit cards.
PERSONAL NOTES:	

WINERY:	Guenoc Winery
WINE NAME:	**Chenin Blanc**
ORIGIN:	Guenoc Valley
VINTAGE:	1984 RATING: 14
ALCOHOL:	12.2 percent
TASTING NOTES:	Very pale straw hue. Concentrated fruity nose. Slightly sweet, fruity flavor, simple. A bit boring, though not much more to be expected from Chenin Blanc. Guenoc's more serious varietals are Chardonnay, Sauvignon Blanc and Cabernet Sauvignon. The Guenoc Valley lies in the southern part of Lake County and spills partly into Napa County on the south.
DATE TASTED:	
WINERY ADDRESS:	21000 Butts Canyon Road Middletown, CA 95461 (707) 987-2385
WINERY VISITS:	Thurs.–Sun. 10 AM–4:30 PM. Appt. not req. Credit cards.
PERSONAL NOTES:	

Guenoc

1984
Guenoc Valley
Chenin Blanc

Produced and Bottled by Guenoc Winery
Middletown, California Alcohol 12.2% by Volume

WINERY:	Hacienda Wine Cellars
WINE NAME:	**Dry Chenin Blanc**
ORIGIN:	California
VINTAGE:	1983 RATING: 15
ALCOHOL:	10.9 percent
TASTING NOTES:	Very pale straw color, almost white. Austere, slightly herbal nose. Lightly herbaceous flavor. Firm, clean, but simple. Lacking strong definition, though fairly typical of the varietal. A bland wine for consumers who prefer that style.
DATE TASTED:	
WINERY ADDRESS:	1000 Vineyard Lane Sonoma, CA 95476 (707) 938-3220
WINERY VISITS:	10 AM–5 PM. Appt. not req. Credit cards.
PERSONAL NOTES:	

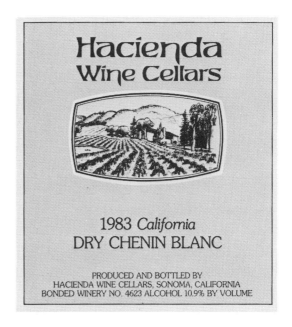

Hacienda Wine Cellars

1983 *California*
DRY CHENIN BLANC

PRODUCED AND BOTTLED BY
HACIENDA WINE CELLARS, SONOMA, CALIFORNIA
BONDED WINERY NO. 4623 ALCOHOL 10.9% BY VOLUME

CHENIN BLANC

WINERY:	J. Lohr Winery
WINE NAME:	**Chenin Blanc**
ORIGIN:	Clarksburg, Pheasant's Call Vineyards
VINTAGE: 1984	**RATING:** 16
ALCOHOL:	11.0 percent

TASTING NOTES: Pale straw color. Smoky, restrained nose. Chewy texture. Nutty, almond flavor—unusual and interesting for a varietal that normally is somewhat dull. Crisp finish. A charming Chenin Blanc that finishes slightly sweet at 1.3% residual sugar.

DATE TASTED:

WINERY ADDRESS: 1000 Lenzen Avenue
San Jose, CA 95126   (408) 288-5057

WINERY VISITS: 10 AM–5 PM. Appt. not req. Credit cards.

PERSONAL NOTES:

CHENIN BLANC
Clarksburg
Pheasant's Call Vineyards

PRODUCED & BOTTLED BY J. LOHR WINERY
SAN JOSE, CALIFORNIA ALCOHOL 11% BY VOLUME

WINERY:	Monterey Vineyard
WINE NAME:	**Chenin Blanc**
ORIGIN:	Monterey County
VINTAGE: 1984	**RATING:** 16
ALCOHOL:	12.3 percent

TASTING NOTES: Very pale straw color. Subtle nose, hinting of freshly mowed grass. Full, rich, round, grassy flavor. Slightly sweet, but fruit is high quality and palate impression is not cloying. Stylish wine from a grape variety not noted for complexity. The winery, once owned by Coca-Cola, is now owned by the House of Seagram.

DATE TASTED:

WINERY ADDRESS: 800 South Alta Street
Gonzales, CA 93926   (408) 675-2481

WINERY VISITS: 10 AM–5 PM. Appt. not req. Credit cards.

PERSONAL NOTES:

THE
MONTEREY VINEYARD®
1984
CHENIN BLANC
MONTEREY COUNTY

PRODUCED AND BOTTLED BY THE MONTEREY VINEYARD B.W. 4674
GONZALES, MONTEREY COUNTY, CA., U.S.A. • ALCOHOL 12.3% BY VOL.

WINERY:	Parducci Wine Cellars
WINE NAME:	**Chenin Blanc**
ORIGIN:	Mendocino County
VINTAGE: 1983	**RATING:** 15
ALCOHOL:	11.5 percent
TASTING NOTES:	Pale straw color. Restrained nose, showing only hints of fruit. Fruity, slightly sweet, charming but simple. A typical Chenin Blanc from one of the leading producers in picturesque Mendocino County.
DATE TASTED:	
WINERY ADDRESS:	501 Parducci Road Ukiah, CA 95482 (707) 462-3828
WINERY VISITS:	9 AM–6 PM. Appt. not req. Credit cards.
PERSONAL NOTES:	

WINERY:	Preston Vineyards and Winery
WINE NAME:	**Dry Chenin Blanc**
ORIGIN:	Sonoma County, Dry Creek Valley, Estate Bottled
VINTAGE: 1984	**RATING:** 17
ALCOHOL:	12.8 percent
TASTING NOTES:	Very pale straw color. Lightly grassy and fragrant bouquet. Medium body, herbaceous flavor, with a hint of licorice and spicy accents. Not complex, but utterly charming in its straightforward, fruity manner. One of the more beguiling Chenin Blancs, reminiscent of some Vouvrays made from the same grape variety in France.
DATE TASTED:	
WINERY ADDRESS:	9282 West Dry Creek Road Healdsburg, CA 95448 (707) 433-3372
WINERY VISITS:	Appt. req. No credit cards.
PERSONAL NOTES:	

GEWÜRZTRAMINER

The Gewürztraminer is probably the most unusual variety of white wine made in California, for its name means "spicy Traminer," describing the intense spiciness of its flavor. It is not a subtle wine, but its devotees adore its distinctiveness, its special quality that sets it apart from all others. It is a basic varietal of the Alsatian region of France, on the German border, and as such is a member of the European *Vitis vinifera* family.

Some oenophiles contend that the Gewürztraminer has a musky or earthy flavor. Others suggest that the flavor is herbaceous, grassy, even tasting of asparagus. It certainly is one of the few wines that can be drunk when asparagus is being eaten.

The Gewürztraminer grapes are relatively small and reddish in color, although they make strictly white wine. At one time, in Alsace, there were both Gewürztraminers and Traminers cultivated, with the Traminers being the less spicy versions. Nowadays there is only the Gewürztraminer, due to selective breeding over the years. In favorable vintages, when the weather is hot, the alcohol levels can rise above 13 percent and the wine tastes slightly sweet.

In California the Gewürztraminer is highly successful—full of spices and complex. Sometimes it contracts the *Botrytis cinerea* fungus disease, also called noble rot, that creates a honeylike quality in the wine by concentrating the juice. These are among the most treasured of California wines and are very expensive.

WINERY:	Alexander Valley Vineyards
WINE NAME:	**Gewürztraminer**
ORIGIN:	Alexander Valley, Estate Bottled
VINTAGE: 1984	RATING: 16
ALCOHOL:	12.0 percent
TASTING NOTES:	Very pale straw color. Muted smoky nose. Spritzy texture. Slightly sweet, but crisp and firm, good balance. Spicy but not vegetal. Very tight and sleek Gewürztraminer with a subdued personality. Pleasant as an aperitif or with oriental cuisine. Residual sugar of 1.3% is balanced by backbone of acid.
DATE TASTED:	
WINERY ADDRESS:	8644 Highway 128 Healdsburg, CA 95448 (707) 433-7209
WINERY VISITS:	10 AM–5 PM. Appt. not req. Credit cards.
PERSONAL NOTES:	

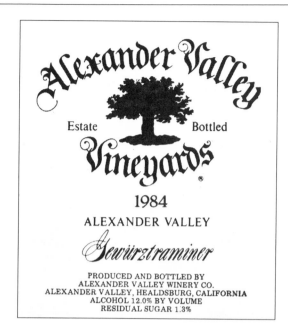

WINERY:	Belvedere Winery
WINE NAME:	**Gewürztraminer, Winery Lake**
ORIGIN:	Napa Valley, Los Carneros
VINTAGE: 1984	RATING: 17
ALCOHOL:	12.5 percent
TASTING NOTES:	Very pale color. Spicy, fruity nose. Slightly spritzy with tiny bubbles. Crisp, clean, classic spicy asparagus flavor with hint of cloves. Superb Gewürztraminer from Peter Friedman, who makes wines from grapes grown in some of California's most celebrated vineyards that do not have their own wineries. The Winery Lake Vineyard, for example, sells to a number of wineries and has developed a reputation for excellence.
DATE TASTED:	
WINERY ADDRESS:	4035 Westside Road Healdsburg, CA 95448 (707) 433-8236
WINERY VISITS:	Mon.–Fri. 8 AM–5 PM. Appt. req. No credit cards.
PERSONAL NOTES:	

GEWÜRZTRAMINER

WINERY:	Callaway Vineyard and Winery
WINE NAME:	**Gewürztraminer**
ORIGIN:	California
VINTAGE: 1984	**RATING:** 16
ALCOHOL:	11.9 percent

TASTING NOTES: Very pale hue. Muted, subtle nose with only a hint of spice. Crisp, clean texture with slight *pétillance*. Concentrated spicy flavor, classic herbaceousness, very stylish, though the overall palate impression is subtle. Sweetness blends well with the spices. A nice aperitif wine from the winery founded by Ely Callaway, former president of Burlington Industries, and now owned by the liquor company Hiram Walker & Sons.

DATE TASTED:

WINERY ADDRESS: 32720 Rancho California Road
Temecula, CA 92390　(714) 676-4001

WINERY VISITS: 10 AM–5 PM. Appt. not req. Credit cards.

PERSONAL NOTES:

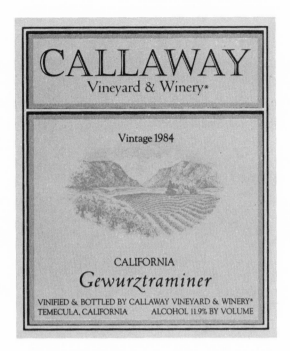

WINERY:	De Loach Vineyards
WINE NAME:	**Gewürztraminer, Early Harvest**
ORIGIN:	Sonoma County, Russian River Valley, Estate Bottled
VINTAGE: 1984	**RATING:** 17
ALCOHOL:	12.5 percent

TASTING NOTES: Pale straw color. Smoky, spicy, asparagus nose. Fruity, spicy flavor with a touch of sweetness (1.0% residual sugar). Light, elegant, not aggressively spicy, though the Gewürztraminer is readily identifiable both in the nose and mouth. Stylish, spicy white from Cecil De Loach. Best as an aperitif or with spicy oriental cuisine or curry.

DATE TASTED:

WINERY ADDRESS: 1791 Olivet Road
Santa Rosa, CA 95401　(707) 526-9111

WINERY VISITS: 10 AM–4:30 PM. Appt. not req. Credit cards.

PERSONAL NOTES:

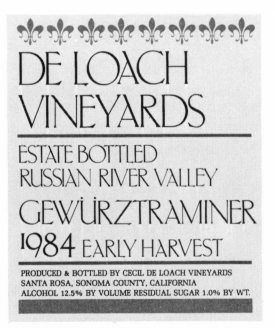

WINERY:	Felton-Empire Vineyards
WINE NAME:	**Gewürztraminer, Select Late Harvest**
ORIGIN:	Sonoma County, Russian River Valley
VINTAGE: 1981	**RATING:** 17
ALCOHOL: 9.5 percent	

TASTING NOTES: Polished brass color. Honeyed nose with earthy elements. Fresh, clean, fruity flavor with honey accents. Crisp, clean finish, showing excellent acid balance. Very sweet (15% residual sugar), but seems less sweet than it really is because of acid balance. Very stylish, but less spicy than expected for a Gewürztraminer. This is the kind of wine that winemaker Leo McCloskey seems to revel in.

DATE TASTED:

WINERY ADDRESS: 379 Felton-Empire Road
Felton, CA 95018 (408) 335-3939

WINERY VISITS: Weekends 11 AM–4:30 PM. Appt. not req. Credit cards.

PERSONAL NOTES:

WINERY:	Hacienda Wine Cellars
WINE NAME:	**Gewürztraminer**
ORIGIN:	Sonoma County
VINTAGE: 1983	**RATING:** 16
ALCOHOL: 12.2 percent	

TASTING NOTES: Pale straw color, with glints of green. Subtly herbaceous, spicy nose. Firm, clean, lightly spiced Gewürztraminer flavor, with very crisp, clean finish showing nice acid balance. Only subtle asparagus flavor, so would be pleasant with shellfish and other seafoods. Charming effort by Steve MacRostie, the winemaker at Hacienda.

DATE TASTED:

WINERY ADDRESS: 1000 Vineyard Lane
Sonoma, CA 95476 (707) 938-3220

WINERY VISITS: 10 AM–5 PM. Appt. not req. Credit cards.

PERSONAL NOTES:

GEWÜRZTRAMINER

WINERY:	Charles Lefranc Cellars
WINE NAME:	**Gewürztraminer, Late Harvest**
ORIGIN:	San Benito County
VINTAGE: 1982	**RATING:** 17
ALCOHOL:	9.3 percent

TASTING NOTES: Light brassy hue. Spicy, rich nose. Full, rich texture, crisp and clean. Sweet, with a hint of spritz. Moderately herbaceous, without the asparagus elements typical of some Gewürztraminers. A superb dessert wine. Late-harvested wines seem to be one of the strengths of Klaus Mathes, Almadén's winemaker, who is from Germany. (The Lefranc bottlings are Almadén's premium line.)

DATE TASTED:

WINERY ADDRESS: 1530 Blossom Hill Road
San Jose, CA 95118   (408) 269-1312

WINERY VISITS: 9 AM–4 PM. Appt. not req. Credit cards.

PERSONAL NOTES:

WINERY:	Monterey Vineyard
WINE NAME:	**Gewürztraminer**
ORIGIN:	Monterey County
VINTAGE: 1984	**RATING:** 16
ALCOHOL:	9.7 percent

TASTING NOTES: Pale straw color. Spicy, herbal, slightly vegetal nose. Textured, elegant, charming herbaceous, spicy flavor. Classic Gewürztraminer, though more subtle and stylish than some. Fairly sweet, with 1.6% residual sugar, but Gewürztraminers are best with a little sweetness. The winery was owned by Coca-Cola, now by the House of Seagram.

DATE TASTED:

WINERY ADDRESS: 800 South Alta Street
Gonzales, CA 93926   (408) 675-2481

WINERY VISITS: 10 AM–5 PM. Appt. not req. Credit cards.

PERSONAL NOTES:

JOHANNISBERG RIESLING (WHITE RIESLING)

The most celebrated grape of Germany is the Riesling, which is responsible for the best white wines of the Mosel and Rhine valleys. At one time the most renowned vineyard of the Rheingau was Schloss Johannisberger, and the Johannisberg name was added to the Riesling name for this grape varietal when cultivated in California.

The most dramatic Johannisberg Rieslings, also called White Rieslings, are vinified sweet. These are similar to the extraordinary Beerenauslesen and Trockenbeerenauslesen produced in minute quantities from very late harvested grapes in the best German vineyards. They are intensely sweet and are best drunk with dessert or with fresh foie gras.

The majority of Johannisberg Rieslings from California are vinified fairly dry. They have what is often described as a "peachy" quality, and sometimes the flavor of nectarines, even oranges and lemons, can be detected. Their bouquet often is flowery and aromatic. The best versions are very slightly sweet, containing perhaps 1 or 2 percent residual sugar at most. Often they are very pleasant as aperitif wines, but they can also be drunk throughout a meal.

JOHANNISBERG RIESLING (WHITE RIESLING)

WINERY:	Alexander Valley Vineyards
WINE NAME:	**Johannisberg Riesling**
ORIGIN:	Alexander Valley, Estate Bottled
VINTAGE: 1984	**RATING:** 16
ALCOHOL: 12.0 percent	

TASTING NOTES: Straw color. Very ripe, peachy nose with a hint of honey, indicating some *Botrytis* noble rot in the grapes. Ripe, firm, richly fruity flavor with superb concentration. Soft, elegant and sweet (1.5% residual sugar). Stylish effort from the Wetzel family, proprietors, who are to be commended for noting residual sugar on the label, which should be standard practice at all wineries when significant residual sugar is present.

DATE TASTED:

WINERY ADDRESS: 8644 Highway 128
Healdsburg, CA 95448   (707) 433-7209

WINERY VISITS: 10 AM–5 PM. Appt. not req. Credit cards.

PERSONAL NOTES:

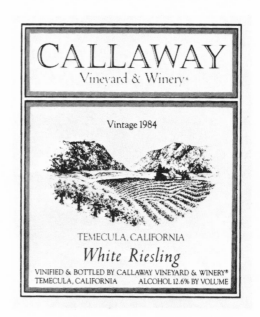

Alexander Valley Vineyards
Estate   Bottled
1984
ALEXANDER VALLEY
Johannisberg Riesling
PRODUCED AND BOTTLED BY
ALEXANDER VALLEY WINERY CO.
ALEXANDER VALLEY, HEALDSBURG, CALIFORNIA
ALCOHOL 12.0% BY VOLUME
RESIDUAL SUGAR 1.5%

WINERY:	Callaway Vineyard and Winery
WINE NAME:	**White Riesling**
ORIGIN:	Temecula
VINTAGE: 1984	**RATING:** 16
ALCOHOL: 12.6 percent	

TASTING NOTES: Very pale straw color. Muted, restrained nose—undeveloped, elusive. Firm texture, with a superb acid balance adding complexity to a peachy, Mosel-style flavor. Far more evolved in flavor than bouquet, showing excellent fruit and moderate sweetness typical of Rieslings in general. Reedy aftertaste. Extensive facilities for visitors at this southern California facility.

DATE TASTED:

WINERY ADDRESS: 32720 Rancho California Road
Temecula, CA 92390   (714) 676-4001

WINERY VISITS: 10 AM–5 PM. Appt. not req. Credit cards.

PERSONAL NOTES:

CALLAWAY
Vineyard & Winery

Vintage 1984

TEMECULA, CALIFORNIA
White Riesling
VINIFIED & BOTTLED BY CALLAWAY VINEYARD & WINERY
TEMECULA, CALIFORNIA   ALCOHOL 12.6% BY VOLUME

WINERY:	Felton-Empire Vineyards

WINE NAME: **White Riesling, Maritime Series**

ORIGIN: California

VINTAGE: 1982   **RATING:** 16

ALCOHOL: 10.5 percent

TASTING NOTES: Very pale gold hue. Peachy nose. Round, firm, peachy flavor, with pleasant natural sweetness typical of Riesling, balanced by a crisp finish indicating good acid backbone. This is the style of wine that this winery is known for. Charming aperitif, not sweet enough to be a dessert wine. Leo McCloskey, president and winemaker, spent several years at Ridge Vineyards before starting Felton-Empire in 1976.

DATE TASTED:

WINERY ADDRESS: 379 Felton-Empire Road
Felton, CA 95018   (408) 335-3939

WINERY VISITS: Weekends 11 AM–4:30 PM. Appt. not req. Credit cards.

PERSONAL NOTES:

FELTON-EMPIRE 1982 California White Riesling Maritime Series©

Produced and bottled by Felton-Empire Vineyards, Felton, **Santa Cruz Mountains**, California. Alcohol 10.5% by volume.

WINERY:	Geyser Peak Winery

WINE NAME: **Soft Johannisberg Riesling**

ORIGIN: Sonoma County, Carneros District

VINTAGE: 1984   **RATING:** 14

ALCOHOL: 9.5 percent

TASTING NOTES: Medium straw color. Peachy nose with tangerine nuances. Just as soft as the name indicates, which means low acidity, bringing out the sweetness of 2.9% residual sugar. Pleasant but simple. The winery, which dates to 1880, has picnic grounds and panoramic views.

DATE TASTED:

WINERY ADDRESS: 22281 Chianti Road
Geyserville, CA 95441   (707) 433-6585

WINERY VISITS: 10 AM–5 PM. Appt. not req. No credit cards.

PERSONAL NOTES:

GEYSER PEAK

1984

CARNEROS – SONOMA COUNTY

SOFT JOHANNISBERG RIESLING

A soft, delicate White Riesling
in the German Style

PRODUCED AND BOTTLED BY
GEYSER PEAK WINERY
GEYSERVILLE, CALIFORNIA BW29   ALC. 9.5% BY VOL.

JOHANNISBERG RIESLING (WHITE RIESLING)

WINERY:	Kendall-Jackson Vineyards and Winery
WINE NAME:	**Johannisberg Riesling**
ORIGIN:	Lake County
VINTAGE: 1983	**RATING:** 16
ALCOHOL:	10.0 percent
TASTING NOTES:	Very pale straw color. Smoky, citric nose. Firm, peachy flavor, with crisp, balanced finish. Stylish. The pungence in the nose, no doubt due to sulphur in the processing, should abate steadily and be gone by 1987. Winemaker Jed Steele, one of the characters of Lake County, used to be at Edmeades. This is the California lake country, a scenic place to visit, very rural and quietly beautiful.
DATE TASTED:	
WINERY ADDRESS:	600 Mathews Road Lakeport, CA 95453 (707) 263-9333
WINERY VISITS:	10:30 AM–5:30 PM. Appt. req. Credit cards.
PERSONAL NOTES:	

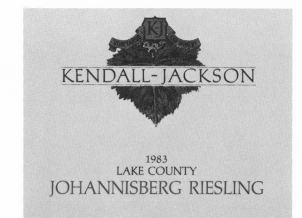

WINERY:	Kendall-Jackson Vineyards and Winery
WINE NAME:	**Johannisberg Riesling, Select Late Harvest**
ORIGIN:	Mendocino County, Anderson Valley
VINTAGE: 1983	**RATING:** 19
ALCOHOL:	8.0 percent
TASTING NOTES:	Pale straw color. Deeply honeyed nose with tangerine nuances and flowery with the aroma of honeysuckle. Very, very honeyed flavor. Superb acid balance for crisp finish, despite extraordinary 20.6% residual sugar, which means one-fifth of every mouthful is sugar! Classic young Riesling capable of rivaling a great Trockenbeerenauslese from Germany. A wine of drama and complexity.
DATE TASTED:	
WINERY ADDRESS:	600 Mathews Road Lakeport, CA 95453 (707) 263-9333
WINERY VISITS:	10:30 AM–5:30 PM. Appt. req. Credit cards.
PERSONAL NOTES:	

WINERY:	Kendall-Jackson Vineyards and Winery
WINE NAME:	**Johannisberg Riesling**
ORIGIN:	Monterey County
VINTAGE: 1984	**RATING:** 16
ALCOHOL:	9.0 percent

TASTING NOTES: Pale straw color. Fruity, slightly grassy nose. Very fruity peach flavor in the Mosel style, with moderate effervescence for a spritzy accent that is not atypical of Rieslings. Bubbles are even visible in the glass. Charming, simple Riesling for a summer picnic, made in Lake County from grapes grown in Monterey County.

DATE TASTED:

WINERY ADDRESS: 600 Mathews Road
Lakeport, CA 95453   (707) 263-9333

WINERY VISITS: 10:30 AM–5:30 PM. Appt. req. Credit cards.

PERSONAL NOTES:

KENDALL-JACKSON

1984
MONTEREY COUNTY
JOHANNISBERG RIESLING

PRODUCED AND BOTTLED BY KENDALL-JACKSON VINEYARDS & WINERY
LAKEPORT, LAKE COUNTY, CALIFORNIA   ALCOHOL 9.0% BY VOLUME

WINERY:	J. Lohr Winery
WINE NAME:	**Johannisberg Riesling**
ORIGIN:	Monterey County, Greenfield Vineyards
VINTAGE: 1984	**RATING:** 18
ALCOHOL:	11.0 percent

TASTING NOTES: Medium straw color. Ripe, peachy nose. Round, rich, firm, clean, slightly sweet and fruity. Clipped finish, with long peachy aftertaste. Stylish and very well made Riesling from a leading Monterey County winery.

DATE TASTED:

WINERY ADDRESS: 1000 Lenzen Avenue
San Jose, CA 95126   (408) 288-5057

WINERY VISITS: 10 AM–5 PM. Appt. not req. Credit cards.

PERSONAL NOTES:

1 9 8 4

J. Lohr

JOHANNISBERG RIESLING
Monterey County
Greenfield Vineyards

PRODUCED & BOTTLED BY J. LOHR WINERY
SAN JOSE, CALIFORNIA ALCOHOL 11% BY VOLUME

JOHANNISBERG RIESLING (WHITE RIESLING)

WINERY:	Robert Mondavi Winery
WINE NAME:	**Johannisberg Riesling**
ORIGIN:	Napa Valley
VINTAGE: 1984	**RATING:** 16
ALCOHOL: 11.5 percent	

TASTING NOTES: Pale straw color. Subtly peachy nose, in the Mosel style. Full, firm texture. Fresh citric flavor with sweetness balanced by acidity. An odd, chemical note in the finish, but basically a stylish Riesling from California's best-known wine personality. This bottling is less concentrated and drier than the Mondavi Special Selection from the same vintage.

DATE TASTED:

WINERY ADDRESS: 7801 St. Helena Highway
St. Helena, CA 94562   (707) 963-9611

WINERY VISITS: 9 AM–5 PM. Appt. not req. Credit cards.

PERSONAL NOTES:

1984
Napa Valley
JOHANNISBERG RIESLING
ALCOHOL 11.5% BY VOLUME
PRODUCED AND BOTTLED BY
ROBERT MONDAVI WINERY
OAKVILLE, CALIFORNIA

WINERY:	Robert Mondavi Winery
WINE NAME:	**Johannisberg Riesling, Special Selection**
ORIGIN:	Napa Valley
VINTAGE: 1984	**RATING:** 16
ALCOHOL: 9.0 percent	

TASTING NOTES: Pale straw color. Fruity, citric nose, with a hint of apricot. Textured and firm. Rich, full, peachy flavor, though texture dominates fruit, no doubt due to strong acid balance. This is a fairly robust wine for a Riesling. Stylish, but "Special Selection" designation is confusing because it usually indicates concentrated sweetness in a Riesling, and this one is only semi-sweet.

DATE TASTED:

WINERY ADDRESS: 7801 St. Helena Highway
St. Helena, CA 94562   (707) 963-9611

WINERY VISITS: 9 AM–5 PM. Appt. not req. Credit cards.

PERSONAL NOTES:

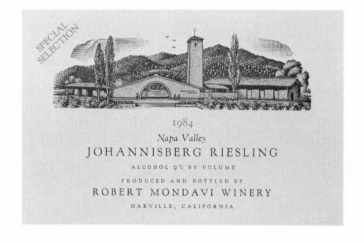

SPECIAL SELECTION
1984
Napa Valley
JOHANNISBERG RIESLING
ALCOHOL 9% BY VOLUME
PRODUCED AND BOTTLED BY
ROBERT MONDAVI WINERY
OAKVILLE, CALIFORNIA

WINERY:	Raymond Vineyard and Cellar
WINE NAME:	**Johannisberg Riesling, Late Harvest**
ORIGIN:	Napa Valley, Estate Bottled
VINTAGE: 1982	**RATING:** 18
ALCOHOL:	11.1 percent

TASTING NOTES: Pale gold color. Ripe, smoky nose. Very sweet and rich and ripe flavor. Opulent fruit, tangerines and peaches. Utterly charming and special, demonstrating what a sweet Riesling can achieve in the Napa Valley. The grapes contained 26.5% residual sugar at harvest, and the wine has 7.5% residual sugar—splendid for dessert of ripe fruit or cheesecake.

DATE TASTED:

WINERY ADDRESS: 849 Zinfandel Lane
St. Helena, CA 94574   (707) 963-3141

WINERY VISITS: 10 AM–4 PM. Appt. not req. No credit cards.

PERSONAL NOTES:

1982
NAPA VALLEY · ESTATE BOTTLED
Johannisberg Riesling
LATE HARVEST
Sugar at Harvest 26.5% by wt.   Sugar at Bottling 7.5% by wt.
Grown, Produced & Bottled by Raymond Vineyard & Cellar
St. Helena, California / Alcohol 11.1% by Volume

WINERY:	Raymond Vineyard and Cellar
WINE NAME:	**Johannisberg Riesling**
ORIGIN:	Napa Valley
VINTAGE: 1983	**RATING:** 17
ALCOHOL:	11.9 percent

TASTING NOTES: Pale straw color. Subtly peachy nose, with a whisp of smoke, probably due to sulphur treatment—standard procedure and due to resolve itself before age three. Firm, full, peachy fruit flavor, with clean, crisp finish balancing a hint of sweetness. Stylish.

DATE TASTED:

WINERY ADDRESS: 849 Zinfandel Lane
St. Helena, CA 94574   (707) 963-3141

WINERY VISITS: 10 AM–4 PM. Appt. not req. No credit cards.

PERSONAL NOTES:

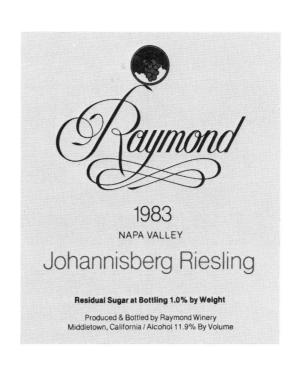

1983
NAPA VALLEY
Johannisberg Riesling
Residual Sugar at Bottling 1.0% by Weight
Produced & Bottled by Raymond Winery
Middletown, California / Alcohol 11.9% By Volume

SAUVIGNON BLANC (FUME BLANC)

The Sauvignon Blanc grape is widely cultivated in France and now in California. It is the grape of Pouilly-Fumé in the Loire Valley and it is one of the two grapes responsible for the best white Bordeaux (the other being Sémillon). The great Château d'Yquem of Sauternes is vinified mostly from Sauvignon Blanc, and the best dry white Bordeaux also are made from this grape.

In California the Sauvignon Blanc achieved great popularity in the late 1970s as an alternative to Chardonnay. At one time it was vinified to yield heavy, awkward, herbaceous wines that lacked charm and finesse. Now it is widely vinified to produce crisp, dry, more elegant wines, although its herbaceous, grassy character often is evident. Frequently it is labeled Fumé Blanc, suggesting the smoky or earthy character of Pouilly-Fumé. Whether it is actually smoky is up to the individual taster to decide.

The Sauvignon Blanc is rarely a match for the Chardonnay in terms of elegance and sheer charm. But it is a viable alternative of sharply rising popularity. Sometimes it is vinified sweet to yield dessert-style wines derivative of the Sauternes character. But at its best it is crisp and dry, with an assertive personality.

WINERY:	Bandiera Winery
WINE NAME:	**Sauvignon Blanc**
ORIGIN:	Mendocino County
VINTAGE: 1982	**RATING:** 16
ALCOHOL:	12.8 percent
TASTING NOTES:	Straw color. Herbaceous nose. Grassy. Classic Sauvignon. Full, crisp, grassy flavor of pronounced character. Stylish white if you like aggressive Sauvignons.
DATE TASTED:	
WINERY ADDRESS:	555 South Cloverdale Boulevard Cloverdale, CA 95425 (707) 894-4298
WINERY VISITS:	10 AM–5 PM. Appt. not req. Credit cards.
PERSONAL NOTES:	

Black Mustard

Bandiera
Vintage 1982
Sauvignon Blanc
Mendocino

Produced & Bottled by Bandiera Winery; Cloverdale, Ca.
BW 3998; ALC. 12.8% by VOL.

WINERY:	Bandiera Winery
WINE NAME:	**Fumé Blanc**
ORIGIN:	Mendocino County
VINTAGE: 1983	**RATING:** 14
ALCOHOL:	11.0 percent
TASTING NOTES:	Pale straw color. Vegetal, herbaceous nose—aggressive. Vegetal flavor, smoky accents. Crisp finish, though the aftertaste is vegetal. Slight sweetness pervades due to 1.5% residual sugar. The overall impression is diffuse. Bandiera is obviously covering all the bases; it's one of the few wineries to produce both a Sauvignon Blanc and a Fumé Blanc in the same vintage.
DATE TASTED:	
WINERY ADDRESS:	555 South Cloverdale Boulevard Cloverdale, CA 95425 (707) 894-4298
WINERY VISITS:	10 AM–5 PM. Appt. not req. Credit cards.
PERSONAL NOTES:	

Calypso

Bandiera
Fumé Blanc 1983
Sauvignon Blanc
Mendocino County

Produced & Bottled by Bandiera Winery; Cloverdale, CA
BW3998; ALC. 11% VOL.

SAUVIGNON BLANC (FUMÉ BLANC)

WINERY:	Bandiera Winery
WINE NAME:	**Sauvignon Blanc**
ORIGIN:	Mendocino County
VINTAGE: 1983	**RATING:** 15
ALCOHOL:	11.0 percent

TASTING NOTES: Very pale straw color. Grassy, herbaceous, fruity nose. Medium body. Aggressive, characterful, smoky/grassy flavor. Perhaps lacking finesse, but stylish for people who like aggressive Sauvignon Blancs. This wine is not bashful.

DATE TASTED:

WINERY ADDRESS: 555 South Cloverdale Boulevard
Cloverdale, CA 95425   (707) 894-4298

WINERY VISITS: 10 AM–5 PM. Appt. not req. Credit cards.

PERSONAL NOTES:

Black Mustard

Bandiera
Sauvignon Blanc 1983
Mendocino County

Produced & Bottled by Bandiera Winery; Cloverdale, CA
BW3998; ALC. 11% VOL.

WINERY:	Beringer Vineyards
WINE NAME:	**Fumé Blanc, Private Reserve**
ORIGIN:	Sonoma County, Alexander Valley
VINTAGE: 1982	**RATING:** 18
ALCOHOL:	13.5 percent

TASTING NOTES: Medium straw color. Herbaceous nose, fairly intense, even aromatic. Grassy flavor, fairly aggressive, balanced by intense fruit. Long, firm, dramatic finish. A big, rich, complex Sauvignon Blanc. Splendid effort from one of the more picturesque wineries of the Napa Valley. The Rhine House, built in 1876, is one of the most popular tourist spots of the valley.

DATE TASTED:

WINERY ADDRESS: 2000 Main Street
St. Helena, CA 94574   (707) 963-7115

WINERY VISITS: 9:30 AM–4:30 PM. Appt. not req. Full tours. Credit cards.

PERSONAL NOTES:

Beringer

1982

Sonoma County

Fumé Blanc
Dry Sauvignon Blanc

This private reserve Fumé Blanc was produced exclusively from Sauvignon Blanc grapes grown in Alexander Valley. The wine is finished dry with a total acidity of .72 gm/100ml. The wine was aged for nine months in French Nevers oak barrels. Produced and bottled by Beringer Vineyards, St. Helena, Napa Valley, California.
Alcohol is 13.5% by volume

WINERY:	Boeger Winery
WINE NAME:	**Sauvignon Blanc**
ORIGIN:	El Dorado County
VINTAGE:	1984 RATING: 15
ALCOHOL:	12.5 percent
TASTING NOTES:	Very pale straw color, brassy accents. Lightly smoky nose with subtle fruit undertone. Fruity, elegant flavor, with virtually no grassy or vegetal overtones that are typical of so many Sauvignons. Slightly sweet, pleasant and simple. Boeger, located in the gold rush country, does better with reds.
DATE TASTED:	
WINERY ADDRESS:	1709 Carson Road Placerville, CA 95667 (916) 622-8094
WINERY VISITS:	Wed.–Sun. 10 AM–5 PM. Appt. not req. Credit cards.
PERSONAL NOTES:	

WINERY:	Callaway Vineyard and Winery
WINE NAME:	**Sauvignon Blanc**
ORIGIN:	Temecula
VINTAGE:	1983 RATING: 15
ALCOHOL:	12.8 percent
TASTING NOTES:	Pale straw color. Subtle nose with fruity nuances. Very restrained, crisp, slightly sweet, almost rich flavor, with sweetness a dominant part of the personality. Smoky nuances beneath the fruit. Pleasant, but lacking complexity. What some would call a "food wine," because it will conflict with no food flavors.
DATE TASTED:	
WINERY ADDRESS:	32720 Rancho California Road Temecula, CA 92390 (714) 676-4001
WINERY VISITS:	10 AM–5 PM. Appt. not req. Credit cards.
PERSONAL NOTES:	

SAUVIGNON BLANC (FUME BLANC)

WINERY:	Chateau Lefranc
WINE NAME:	**Sauvignon Blanc, Late Harvest**
ORIGIN:	Monterey County
VINTAGE: 1982	**RATING:** 17
ALCOHOL: 9.9 percent	

TASTING NOTES: Gold color with lemony glints. Ripe, melony nose with honeyed nuances. Very rich, ripe, full flavor—concentrated sweetness and lingering mouth presence. Still young in 1985, probably best in 1986–87 when it will take on toasty elements. Opulently fruity. Comes in half-bottles, as every sweet wine should. Not noted on the label is the fact that this wine is from Almadén—another clandestine bottling under the premium Lefranc label.

DATE TASTED:

WINERY ADDRESS: 1530 Blossom Hill Road
San Jose, CA 95118   (408) 269-1312

WINERY VISITS: 9 AM–4 PM. Appt. not req. Credit cards.

PERSONAL NOTES:

WINERY:	Concannon Vineyard
WINE NAME:	**Sauvignon Blanc**
ORIGIN:	Livermore Valley
VINTAGE: 1983	**RATING:** 17
ALCOHOL: 12.5 percent	

TASTING NOTES: Pale straw color. Creamy nose with grassy accents. Firm, full-bodied, textured. Moderate herbaceous flavor typical of Sauvignon Blanc, with strong underlying fruit and hints of vanilla. Crisp, clean finish. Sergio Traverso, the winemaker, has been improving the quality at Concannon since moving there from Sterling Vineyards.

DATE TASTED:

WINERY ADDRESS: 4590 Tesla Road
Livermore, CA 94550   (415) 447-3760

WINERY VISITS: Mon.–Sat. 9 AM–4:30 PM; Sun. noon–4:30 PM. Appt. not req. Credit cards.

PERSONAL NOTES:

WINERY:	Corbett Canyon Vineyards
WINE NAME:	**Sauvignon Blanc**
ORIGIN:	San Luis Obispo County
VINTAGE: 1983	**RATING:** 14
ALCOHOL:	12.0 percent

TASTING NOTES: Medium straw color. Spicy, herbaceous nose, subtle. Medium body, slightly vegetal, crisp, clean, but lacking character. Fruit almost too suppressed to taste. Another innocuous "food wine" from what used to be called the Lawrence Winery before ownership changed.

DATE TASTED:

WINERY ADDRESS: 2195 Corbett Canyon Road
San Luis Obispo, CA 93403
(805) 544-5800

WINERY VISITS: 8 AM–5 PM. (Thurs. from 9:30 AM). Appt. not req. Credit cards.

PERSONAL NOTES:

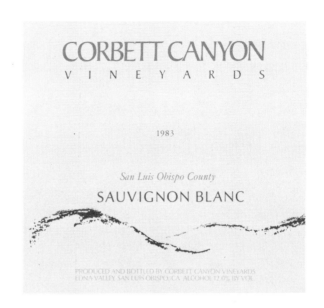

WINERY:	De Loach Vineyards
WINE NAME:	**Fumé Blanc**
ORIGIN:	Sonoma County, Russian River Valley
VINTAGE: 1983	**RATING:** 17
ALCOHOL:	12.5 percent

TASTING NOTES: Brassy gold color. Herbaceous, spicy nose with undertone of vanilla. Fully flavored, grassy taste, very typical of Sauvignon Blanc, but with subdued herbaceousness and hints of oak for balance and complexity. A Fumé Blanc that will please Chardonnay fanatics. Cecil De Loach, owner and winemaker, is a master at both varietals.

DATE TASTED:

WINERY ADDRESS: 1791 Olivet Road
Santa Rosa, CA 95401   (707) 526-9111

WINERY VISITS: 10 AM–4:30 PM. Appt. not req. Credit cards.

PERSONAL NOTES:

SAUVIGNON BLANC (FUME BLANC)

WINERY:	Franciscan Vineyards
WINE NAME:	**Sauvignon Blanc, Reserve**
ORIGIN:	Sonoma County, Alexander Valley
VINTAGE: 1982	**RATING:** 17
ALCOHOL:	13.0 percent
TASTING NOTES:	Straw color. Smoky, lightly fruity nose, with hints of vegetation. Concentrated oak and vanilla-bean flavors, with fruity undertone. Oak is strong, but spicy accents emerge after breathing. Complex, with a sleek and long finish and just enough underlying fruit.
DATE TASTED:	
WINERY ADDRESS:	1178 Galleron Road Rutherford, CA 94573 (707) 963-7111
WINERY VISITS:	10 AM–5 PM. Appt. not req. Credit cards.
PERSONAL NOTES:	

WINERY:	Inglenook Vineyards
WINE NAME:	**Sauvignon Blanc, Limited Reserve Selection**
ORIGIN:	Napa Valley, Estate Bottled
VINTAGE: 1983	**RATING:** 17
ALCOHOL:	12.5 percent
TASTING NOTES:	Pale straw color. Lightly herbaceous, almost flowery nose, but not aggressive. Firm, textured, crisp. Subtle hints of grass and smoke. A nicely made Sauvignon Blanc with plenty of character and good balance. Excellent with fully flavored seafood, including bluefish, turbot and any fish with a Mornay Sauce.
DATE TASTED:	
WINERY ADDRESS:	1991 St. Helena Highway Rutherford, CA 94573 (707) 963-2616
WINERY VISITS:	10 AM–5 PM. Appt. not req. Credit cards.
PERSONAL NOTES:	

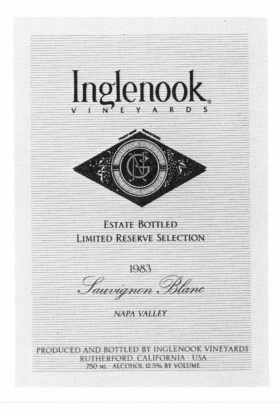

WINERY:	Iron Horse Vineyards
WINE NAME:	**Fumé Blanc**
ORIGIN:	Alexander Valley
VINTAGE: 1983	**RATING:** 17
ALCOHOL: 12.5 percent	

TASTING NOTES: Medium straw color. Fruity, spicy, herbal nose. Spicy, almost minty flavor, with only a hint of the herbaceousness typical of many Sauvignon Blancs. Creamy overtones from oak barrels. Not aggressive, but very stylish Fumé that some tasters might mistake for a Chardonnay due to the creamy element.

DATE TASTED:

WINERY ADDRESS: 9786 Ross Station Road
Sebastopol, CA 95472   (707) 887-1507

WINERY VISITS: Mon.–Fri. 8 AM–5 PM. Appt. req. No credit cards.

PERSONAL NOTES:

WINERY:	Iron Horse Vineyards
WINE NAME:	**Fumé Blanc**
ORIGIN:	Alexander Valley
VINTAGE: 1984	**RATING:** 16
ALCOHOL: 13.3 percent	

TASTING NOTES: Very pale straw color. Lightly fruited bouquet, with hints of smoke and vegetation. Firm, crisp texture. Subtly fruity flavor, without the aggressive vegetal character typical of some Sauvignons. Elegantly rich and charming, though not complex.

DATE TASTED:

WINERY ADDRESS: 9786 Ross Station Road
Sebastopol, CA 95472   (707) 887-1507

WINERY VISITS: Mon.–Fri. 8 AM–5 PM. Appt. req. No credit cards.

PERSONAL NOTES:

SAUVIGNON BLANC (FUME BLANC)

WINERY:	Kendall-Jackson Vineyards and Winery
WINE NAME:	**Chevriot du Lac**
ORIGIN:	Lake County
VINTAGE: 1983	**RATING:** 16
ALCOHOL:	12.6 percent
TASTING NOTES:	Pale straw color. Intensely grassy nose with herbal accents. Crisp, clean, dry and chewy. Assertive, not bashful. Much character. Best with strongly flavored seafood and poultry. Could be called Sauvignon or Fumé Blanc, because the wine is 89% Sauvignon Blanc and 11% Sémillon, but Kendall-Jackson wanted to try to promote a brand name. A stylish effort from a major Lake County winery.
DATE TASTED:	
WINERY ADDRESS:	600 Mathews Road Lakeport, CA 95453 (707) 263-9333
WINERY VISITS:	10:30 AM–5:30 PM. Appt. req. Credit cards.
PERSONAL NOTES:	

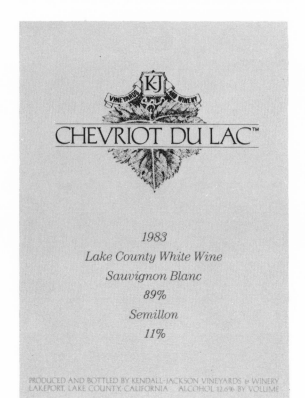

WINERY:	Kendall-Jackson Vineyards and Winery
WINE NAME:	**Essence of Sauvignon, Select Late Harvest**
ORIGIN:	California
VINTAGE: 1983	**RATING:** 18
ALCOHOL:	13.0 percent
TASTING NOTES:	Medium brass color. Rich, roasted, honeyed nose. Concentrated, sweet honey flavor with tangerine accents. *Botrytis* noble rot shows beautifully. A very full, rich dessert wine with superb acid balance for a crisp finish, though the palate impression is basically very sweet. Composition is 42% Sauvignon Blanc, 38% White Riesling, 12% Muscat Blanc, 8% Grey Riesling.
DATE TASTED:	
WINERY ADDRESS:	600 Mathews Road Lakeport, CA 95453 (707) 263-9333
WINERY VISITS:	10:30 AM–5:30 PM. Appt. req. Credit cards.
PERSONAL NOTES:	

SAUVIGNON BLANC (FUME BLANC)

WINERY:	Charles Lefranc Cellars
WINE NAME:	**Fumé Blanc**
ORIGIN:	California
VINTAGE: 1983	**RATING:** 17
ALCOHOL: 12.5 percent	

TASTING NOTES: Very pale straw color. Lightly smoky nose, grassy accents. Full, rich, round and stylish, with long fruit. Not aggressively herbaceous, but with enough grassiness to let you know it is Sauvignon Blanc. Elegant. A nice effort by Klaus Mathes, the winemaker at Almadén Vineyards. (The Charles Lefranc bottlings are Almadén's premium line, far superior to the jug wines that have made Almadén a familiar name to generations of American consumers.)

DATE TASTED:

WINERY ADDRESS: 1530 Blossom Hill Road
San Jose, CA 95118   (408) 269-1312

WINERY VISITS: 9 AM–4 PM. Appt. not req. Credit cards.

PERSONAL NOTES:

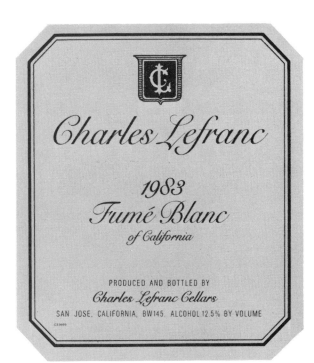

WINERY:	Matanzas Creek Winery
WINE NAME:	**Sauvignon Blanc**
ORIGIN:	Sonoma County
VINTAGE: 1983	**RATING:** 17
ALCOHOL: 13.5 percent	

TASTING NOTES: Medium straw color. Restrained herbal nose, grassy notes, fruity background. Subtly smoky flavor with elegant style. Round, moderately textured, with only hints of oak. Nicely balanced. A very restrained Sauvignon Blanc with a gentle personality from a winery much better known for its buttery, rich Chardonnays. Merry Edwards, the winemaker, has since left to set up her own operation at Merry Vintners.

DATE TASTED:

WINERY ADDRESS: 6097 Bennett Valley Road
Santa Rosa, CA 95404   (707) 528-6464

WINERY VISITS: Mon.–Fri. 9 AM–5 PM. Appt. req. No credit cards.

PERSONAL NOTES:

SAUVIGNON BLANC (FUME BLANC)

WINERY:	McDowell Valley Vineyards
WINE NAME:	**Fumé Blanc**
ORIGIN:	McDowell Valley
VINTAGE: 1983	**RATING:** 17
ALCOHOL:	12.6 percent
TASTING NOTES:	Pale straw color. Herbaceous, spicy nose. Chewy, crisp texture. Firm, full, smoky flavor. Very stylish Fumé from a winery with its own sub-appellation in Mendocino County, north of the Napa Valley. Tasting room with beautiful view of McDowell Valley.
DATE TASTED:	
WINERY ADDRESS:	3811 Highway 175 Hopland, CA 95449 (707) 744-1053
WINERY VISITS:	10 AM–5 PM. Appt. req. Credit cards.
PERSONAL NOTES:	

WINERY:	Robert Mondavi Winery
WINE NAME:	**Fumé Blanc**
ORIGIN:	Napa Valley
VINTAGE: 1983	**RATING:** 17
ALCOHOL:	13.0 percent
TASTING NOTES:	Medium straw color. Fragrant, elegantly herbal nose. Full, firm texture with a lightly grassy, smoky flavor. Not overly aggressive. In fact, fairly subtle as Fumés go. Mondavi is the standard-bearer for Sauvignon Blanc in California and popularized calling it Fumé Blanc because of its often smoky nose and flavor. It is one of his many major accomplishments.
DATE TASTED:	
WINERY ADDRESS:	7801 St. Helena Highway St. Helena, CA 94562 (707) 963-9611
WINERY VISITS:	9 AM–5 PM. Appt. not req. Credit cards.
PERSONAL NOTES:	

SAUVIGNON BLANC (FUME BLANC)

WINERY:	Monterey Vineyard
WINE NAME:	**Fumé Blanc**
ORIGIN:	Monterey County
VINTAGE: 1983	**RATING:** 17
ALCOHOL: 13.3 percent	

TASTING NOTES: Pale straw color. Fruity, melony nose. Round, richly fruity flavor, with a hint of smoke and citric accents, but no aggressively vegetal components as in many other Sauvignons. Chewy texture, with nice equilibrium. Very stylish, approaching some Chardonnays in complexity. Unusually high alcohol for a Sauvignon is not obvious and seems to be nicely melded with the fruit. Another well-made wine from Dick Peterson.

DATE TASTED:

WINERY ADDRESS: 800 South Alta Street
Gonzales, CA 93926   (408) 675-2481

WINERY VISITS: 10 AM–5 PM. Appt. not req. Credit cards.

PERSONAL NOTES:

THE
MONTEREY VINEYARD®
1983
FUMÉ BLANC
MONTEREY COUNTY

PRODUCED AND BOTTLED BY THE MONTEREY VINEYARD B.W. 4674
GONZALES, MONTEREY COUNTY, CA., U.S.A. • ALCOHOL 13.3% BY VOL.

WINERY:	J.W. Morris Winery
WINE NAME:	**Sauvignon Blanc**
ORIGIN:	Sonoma County, Alexander Valley
VINTAGE: 1984	**RATING:** 16
ALCOHOL: 12.5 percent	

TASTING NOTES: Very pale straw color. Fruity, smoky, herbaceous nose, but not overly grassy. Round, full, with grassy nuances and spicy notes appearing with the breathing. An elegant white from a winery once known mostly for its California Ports.

DATE TASTED:

WINERY ADDRESS: 101 Grant Avenue
Healdsburg, CA 95448   (707) 431-7015

WINERY VISITS: 8 AM–5 PM. Appt. req. No credit cards.

PERSONAL NOTES:

Cliff House & Seal Rocks – San Francisco – 1863

J.W. MORRIS
SAUVIGNON BLANC
1984   SONOMA COUNTY
ALEXANDER VALLEY

TABLE WINE PRODUCED AND BOTTLED BY
J. W. MORRIS WINERY, HEALDSBURG, CALIFORNIA

SAUVIGNON BLANC (FUME BLANC)

WINERY:	Parducci Wine Cellars
WINE NAME:	**Sauvignon Blanc**
ORIGIN:	North Coast
VINTAGE: 1983	**RATING:** 16
ALCOHOL:	12.5 percent
TASTING NOTES:	Very pale straw color, almost white. Smoky, vegetal, herbal nose. Chewy, firm texture. Medium grassy/smoky flavor, with fruity accents. A Sauvignon Blanc full of character from one of the leading Mendocino County producers.
DATE TASTED:	
WINERY ADDRESS:	501 Parducci Road Ukiah, CA 95482 (707) 462-3828
WINERY VISITS:	9 AM–6 PM. Appt. not req. Credit cards.
PERSONAL NOTES:	

WINERY:	J. Pedroncelli Winery
WINE NAME:	**Sauvignon Blanc**
ORIGIN:	Sonoma County
VINTAGE: 1983	**RATING:** 16
ALCOHOL:	12.5 percent
TASTING NOTES:	Straw color. Concentrated fruity nose, with strong herbaceous undertone. Full, chewy, very firm and crisp texture. Charming grassy fruit flavor, just short of weedy. A stylish Sauvignon from a family winery that predates 90 percent of those now in business.
DATE TASTED:	
WINERY ADDRESS:	1220 Canyon Road Geyserville, CA 95441 (707) 857-3531
WINERY VISITS:	10 AM–5 PM. Appt. not req. Credit cards.
PERSONAL NOTES:	

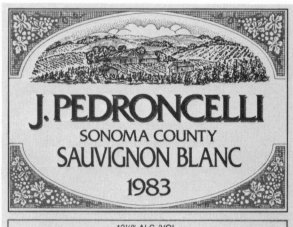

WINERY:	Preston Vineyards and Winery
WINE NAME:	**Dry Sauvignon Blanc, Cuvée de Fumé**
ORIGIN:	Sonoma County, Dry Creek Valley, Estate Bottled
VINTAGE: 1984	RATING: 15
ALCOHOL:	13.0 percent
TASTING NOTES:	Very pale straw hue, almost colorless. Smoky, lightly frutied scent, with a hint of melon. Medium body, soft, restrained fruit flavor. Pleasant, but elusive and lacking strength, structure and complexity. Will be charming for consumers who prefer mild, smooth wines.
DATE TASTED:	
WINERY ADDRESS:	9282 West Dry Creek Road Healdsburg, CA 95448 (707) 433-3372
WINERY VISITS:	Appt. req. No credit cards.
PERSONAL NOTES:	

WINERY:	Preston Vineyards and Winery
WINE NAME:	**Sauvignon Blanc, Reserve**
ORIGIN:	Sonoma County, Dry Creek Valley, Estate Bottled
VINTAGE: 1984	RATING: 17
ALCOHOL:	12.6 percent
TASTING NOTES:	Pale straw color. Restrained, elegant, lightly smoky nose. Very full, round, elegant and complex. Nicely developed fruit and a sleek finish with smoky accents. Good example of an unaggressive Sauvignon Blanc, showing that this varietal need not be vegetal.
DATE TASTED:	
WINERY ADDRESS:	9282 West Dry Creek Road Healdsburg, CA 95448 (707) 433-3372
WINERY VISITS:	Appt. req. No credit cards.
PERSONAL NOTES:	

SAUVIGNON BLANC (FUME BLANC)

WINERY:	Rutherford Hill Winery
WINE NAME:	**Sauvignon Blanc**
ORIGIN:	Napa Valley
VINTAGE: 1983	**RATING:** 17
ALCOHOL: 13.3 percent	

TASTING NOTES: Pale straw color. Grassy, smoky nose. Firm, crisp texture, full body. Herbaceous, fruity flavor. Much character, though perhaps too aggressive for oenophiles who like their Sauvignons subdued.

DATE TASTED:

WINERY ADDRESS: 200 Rutherford Hill Road St. Helena, CA 94574   (707) 963-9694

WINERY VISITS: 10:30 AM–4:30 PM. Appt. not req. Credit cards.

PERSONAL NOTES:

RUTHERFORD HILL

1983
Napa Valley
SAUVIGNON BLANC

PRODUCED AND BOTTLED BY RUTHERFORD HILL WINERY
RUTHERFORD, CALIF., USA · ALCOHOL 13.3% BY VOLUME

WINERY:	Simi Winery
WINE NAME:	**Sauvignon Blanc**
ORIGIN:	Sonoma County
VINTAGE: 1982	**RATING:** 18
ALCOHOL: 12.9 percent	

TASTING NOTES: Pale straw color. Fruity, herbal nose. Round, full texture. Grassy flavor, but not aggressively herbaceous, with very stylish fruity elements indicating very high quality grapes. A classic Sauvignon Blanc with a firm finish, from Zelma Long, a leading woman winemaker. Winery owned by Moët & Chandon, the world's largest Champagne producer.

DATE TASTED:

WINERY ADDRESS: 16275 Healdsburg Avenue Healdsburg, CA 95448   (707) 433-6981

WINERY VISITS: 10 AM–4:30 PM. Appt. not req. No credit cards.

PERSONAL NOTES:

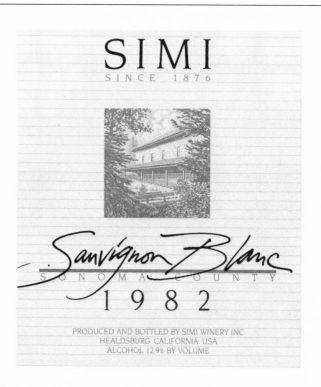

SIMI
SINCE 1876

Sauvignon Blanc
SONOMA COUNTY
1982

PRODUCED AND BOTTLED BY SIMI WINERY INC
HEALDSBURG, CALIFORNIA, USA
ALCOHOL 12.9% BY VOLUME

WINERY:	Stonegate Winery
WINE NAME:	**Sauvignon Blanc**
ORIGIN:	Napa Valley
VINTAGE:	1983 RATING: 17
ALCOHOL:	12.4 percent
TASTING NOTES:	Pale straw color. Smoky, fruity nose. Full, firm, textured. Very crisp and dry, yet with abundant fruit. Herbaceous, but not aggressively so, and thus nicely balanced. Clean and charming. A nice effort by David Spaulding.
DATE TASTED:	
WINERY ADDRESS:	1183 Dunaweal Lane Calistoga, CA 94515 (707) 942-6500
WINERY VISITS:	10:30 AM–4 PM. Appt. not req. Credit cards.
PERSONAL NOTES:	

STONEGATE

1983
NAPA VALLEY
SAUVIGNON BLANC

PRODUCED AND BOTTLED BY STONEGATE WINERY
CALISTOGA, NAPA VALLEY, CALIFORNIA, B.W. 4640
ALCOHOL 12.4% BY VOLUME

WINERY:	William Wheeler Vineyards
WINE NAME:	**Sauvignon Blanc**
ORIGIN:	Sonoma County
VINTAGE:	1983 RATING: 16
ALCOHOL:	12.8 percent
TASTING NOTES:	Straw color. Herbaceous nose with melony nuances—attractive and concentrated. Very crisp and dry. Herbaceous but not aggressive, though fruit is long and full. The overall style is sleek and tightly knit. Charming.
DATE TASTED:	
WINERY ADDRESS:	130 Plaza Street Healdsburg, CA 95448 (707) 433-8786
WINERY VISITS:	Appt. req. No credit cards.
PERSONAL NOTES:	

1983

Wm. Wheeler

Sonoma County
SAUVIGNON BLANC

PRODUCED AND BOTTLED BY WHEELER VINEYARDS
HEALDSBURG, CA. B.W. 5010. ALCOHOL 12.8% BY VOL.

SPARKLING WINES

The only true Champagne comes from the Champagne district of France, for the name is geographical and applies to that particular region some 90 miles northeast of Paris around the city of Reims and the village of Epernay. But the champagne name is widely borrowed and is applied to most of the sparkling white wines produced in California. One exception is Domaine Chandon in Napa, which is owned by the French Champagne house of Moët & Chandon. Its California sparkling wine does not bear the champagne name and is simply called Napa Valley Brut or Cuvée de Pinot Noir.

The best California champagnes are made by the process called the *méthode champenoise*. The key to this method is to permit a second fermentation to occur after the wine has been bottled. This captures the carbon dioxide gas that is a normal by-product of fermentation and gives Champagne its special character. Sparkling wines are also made by the bulk, or closed-container, process, whereby the bubbles are captured inside large fermenting tanks, from which the wine is bottled.

In recent years, the quality of California champagne has risen dramatically. Some devotees contend that no winery in this country has achieved the quality heights of the best Champagne of France, but certainly a number of California versions come close. They are made from a number of grape varieties, including the Chardonnay, Pinot Blanc, Chenin Blanc and Pinot Noir.

WINERY:	Almadén Vineyards
WINE NAME:	**Golden Champagne**
ORIGIN:	California
VINTAGE:	N.V. RATING: 14
ALCOHOL:	12.5 percent

TASTING NOTES: Pale gold color. Ripe, fruity nose, yeasty, hints of candy apple. Round, fruity, sweet apple flavor. Simple but pleasant, almost like an Asti Spumante. Second in the "golden" series following Almadén's highly successful Golden Chablis. The Golden Champagne, pushed with a $4 million ad campaign, is destined to be a big seller at under $4 a bottle.

DATE TASTED:

WINERY ADDRESS: 1530 Blossom Hill Road
San Jose, CA 95118   (408) 269-1312

WINERY VISITS: 9 AM–4 PM. Appt. not req. Credit cards.

PERSONAL NOTES:

WINERY:	Chateau St. Jean
WINE NAME:	**Brut Sparkling Wine**
ORIGIN:	Sonoma County
VINTAGE:	1981 RATING: 16
ALCOHOL:	12.0 percent

TASTING NOTES: Pale straw color. Tiny bubbles. Creamy nose, yeasty nuances, quite fragrant. Ripe apple flavor, fairly assertive. Crisp and dry, yet flavorful, with more pronounced character than most other premium California sparkling wines. High fruit level. Should be interesting to watch this age. St. Jean is owned by Suntory of Japan.

DATE TASTED:

WINERY ADDRESS: 8555 Sonoma Highway
Kenwood, CA 95452   (707) 833-4134

WINERY VISITS: 10:30 AM–4:30 PM. Appt. not req. Credit cards.

PERSONAL NOTES:

SPARKLING WINES

WINERY:	Domaine Chandon
WINE NAME:	**Chandon Napa Valley Brut Sparkling Wine**
ORIGIN:	Napa Valley
VINTAGE:	N.V. **RATING:** 17
ALCOHOL:	12.0 percent
TASTING NOTES:	Pale gold color—more golden than normal because this wine is mostly the 1981 vintage, which was deeply colored. Restrained nose with toasty accents. Sleek, fruity, dry flavor. Very elegant sparkler from one of the American subsidiaries of Moët & Chandon. Extensive visitor facilities and a very fine restaurant.
DATE TASTED:	
WINERY ADDRESS:	California Drive Yountville, CA 94599 (707) 944-2280
WINERY VISITS:	11 AM–6 PM. Appt. not req. Credit cards.
PERSONAL NOTES:	

WINERY:	Domaine Chandon
WINE NAME:	**Chandon Reserve Sparkling Wine**
ORIGIN:	Napa Valley
VINTAGE:	N.V. **RATING:** 18
ALCOHOL:	12.0 percent
TASTING NOTES:	Pale straw color. Toasty nose. Full, rich, round but elegant sparkler, with tiny bubbles. Long finish, with toasty accents. Elegant. A fine American sparkling wine. Initially released in 1985, this wine is 50% Pinot Noir, 35% Chardonnay and 15% Pinot Blanc. The winery has extensive facilities for visitors and the restaurant is one of the best in the Napa Valley.
DATE TASTED:	
WINERY ADDRESS:	California Drive Yountville, CA 94599 (707) 944-2280
WINERY VISITS:	11 AM–6 PM. Appt. not req. Credit cards.
PERSONAL NOTES:	

WINERY:	Gloria Ferrer
WINE NAME:	**Brut Natural Champagne, Cuvée Emerald**
ORIGIN:	Sonoma County
VINTAGE: N.V.	**RATING:** 15
ALCOHOL:	12.0 percent
TASTING NOTES:	Very pale straw color. Smoky, yeasty nose. Frothy, citric, with some unresolved odd notes. This is the first California wine from Freixenet, the huge, Spanish sparkling wine producer that is establishing a foothold in California. The winery is named after the wife of Jose Ferrer, chairman of Freixenet.
DATE TASTED:	
WINERY ADDRESS:	Winery under construction. 23555 Highway 121 Sonoma, CA 95476 (707) 996-7256
WINERY VISITS:	Commencing late fall 1986; call to check exact date. 10:30 AM–5:30 PM. No appt. req. Credit cards.
PERSONAL NOTES:	

WINERY:	Iron Horse Vineyards
WINE NAME:	**Brut Sparkling Wine**
ORIGIN:	Sonoma County, Green Valley, Estate Bottled
VINTAGE: 1981	**RATING:** 17
ALCOHOL:	12.0 percent
TASTING NOTES:	Pale straw color. Very elegant yeasty nose, with fruity nuances. Very lightly toasty flavor, with a fruity overtone and crisp finish. Stylish, elegant sparkling wine from Forrest Tancer, the winemaker.
DATE TASTED:	
WINERY ADDRESS:	9786 Ross Station Road Sebastopol, CA 95472 (707) 887-1507
WINERY VISITS:	Mon.–Fri. 8 AM–5 PM. Appt. req. No credit cards.
PERSONAL NOTES:	

SPARKLING WINES

WINERY:	Iron Horse Vineyards
WINE NAME:	**Blanc de Noirs Sparkling Wine, Wedding Cuvée**
ORIGIN:	Sonoma County, Green Valley
VINTAGE: 1981	**RATING:** 18
ALCOHOL:	12.0 percent

1981
BLANC DE NOIRS
SONOMA COUNTY GREEN VALLEY
IRON HORSE™
SPARKLING WINE SONOMA COUNTY-GREEN VALLEY • GROWN, PRODUCED & BOTTLED BY IRON HORSE VINEYARDS
SEBASTOPOL, CA, USA ALCOHOL 12% BY VOL. NET CONTENTS 750ML

TASTING NOTES: Pale gold/brass color. Very toasty aroma, with hints of cream. Crisp and dry, yet assertive, though retaining elegance. More characterful than the Iron Horse Brut. Very stylish. Made from black grapes.

DATE TASTED:

WINERY ADDRESS: 9786 Ross Station Road
Sebastopol, CA 95472   (707) 887-1597

WINERY VISITS: Mon.–Fri. 8 AM–5 PM. Appt. req. No credit cards.

PERSONAL NOTES:

WINERY:	F. Korbel and Bros.
WINE NAME:	**Brut Champagne**
ORIGIN:	California
VINTAGE: N.V.	**RATING:** 16
ALCOHOL:	12.0 percent

INDIVIDUALLY FERMENTED IN THIS BOTTLE
MÉTHODE CHAMPENOISE
KORBEL®
Brut
California Champagne
EST 1882
ALCOHOL 12% BY VOLUME

TASTING NOTES: Pale straw color. Elegant apple fruit nose wells up with tiny bubbles. Very elegant, clean, light body. Hints of apples and yeast in the flavor, but very drinkable. Easy to understand why this is the largest-selling premium American sparkling wine. Perhaps lacking a bit in complexity, but utterly charming.

DATE TASTED:

WINERY ADDRESS: 13250 River Road
Guerneville, CA 95446   (707) 887-2294

WINERY VISITS: 9 AM–5 PM. Appt. not req. Credit cards.

PERSONAL NOTES:

WINERY:	Papagni Vineyards
WINE NAME:	**Sparkling White Zinfandel**
ORIGIN:	California
VINTAGE: 1984	RATING: 15
ALCOHOL:	11.5 percent

TASTING NOTES: Coral blush. Moderate effervescence, with tiny bubbles. Fruity, spicy nose. Spicy flavor, somewhat sweet. Like an Asti Spumante, though more elegant and lighter. Hints of candy apple and melon. Soft, mellow finish. Pleasant aperitif, though simple.

DATE TASTED:

WINERY ADDRESS: 31754 Avenue 9
Madera, CA 93638   (209) 485-2760

WINERY VISITS: Mon.–Fri. 8:30 AM–4 PM. Appt. not req. No credit cards.

PERSONAL NOTES:

PAPAGNI VINEYARDS

CALIFORNIA

SPARKLING WHITE ZINFANDEL

SPARKLING WHITE WINE

PRODUCED AND BOTTLED BY PAPAGNI VINEYARDS
MADERA, CALIFORNIA, USA • ALC. 11.5% BY VOLUME

WINERY:	Piper Sonoma Cellars
WINE NAME:	**Blanc de Noirs Sparkling Wine**
ORIGIN:	Sonoma County
VINTAGE: 1981	RATING: 17
ALCOHOL:	12.0 percent

TASTING NOTES: Medium straw color. Tiny bubbles. Yeasty nose, toasty accents. Light but toasty flavor. Very elegant and beguiling. Crisp and firm, with a long, toasty finish under a creamy overlay. Very stylish sparkler, a joint venture of Piper-Heidsieck, the French Champagne firm, and Sonoma Vineyards.

DATE TASTED:

WINERY ADDRESS: 11447 Old Redwood Highway
Healdsburg, CA 95448   (707) 433-8843

WINERY VISITS: 10 AM–5 PM. Appt. not req. Credit cards.

PERSONAL NOTES:

Vintage 1981   ALCOHOL 12% BY VOL.
750 ml

Piper Sonoma

SONOMA COUNTY
BLANC DE NOIRS

SONOMA COUNTY SPARKLING WINE

PRODUCED AND BOTTLED BY PIPER SONOMA, WINDSOR, CA. IN THE METHODE CHAMPENOISE
UNDER THE DIRECT SUPERVISION OF CHAMPAGNE PIPER HEIDSIECK, REIMS, FRANCE.

SPARKLING WINES

WINERY:	Schramsberg Vineyards
WINE NAME:	**Blanc de Blancs Champagne**
ORIGIN:	Napa Valley
VINTAGE: 1982	**RATING:** 18
ALCOHOL: 12.5 percent	

TASTING NOTES: Pale straw color. Small bubbles. Fruity, lightly toasty, yeasty nose, elegant. Toasty, round, full flavor with accents of vanilla, yet very crisp and dry. Surprisingly full for a Blanc de Blancs, yet elegant at the same time. Very stylish California sparkling wine. Schramsberg is one of the very top producers of sparkling wines in the U.S.

DATE TASTED:

WINERY ADDRESS: Schramsberg Road
Calistoga, CA 94515   (707) 942-4558

WINERY VISITS: Mon.–Sat. 11 AM–4 PM. Appt. req. No credit cards.

PERSONAL NOTES:

BLANC DE BLANCS

NAPA VALLEY CHAMPAGNE

VINTAGE 1982

PRODUCED AND BOTTLED BY SCHRAMSBERG VINEYARDS CALISTOGA, CALIFORNIA

ALCOHOL 12.5% BY VOLUME CONTENTS 750 MLS